Folklore: In All of Us, In All We Do

Folklore: In All of Us, In All We Do

Edited by
Kenneth L. Untiedt

Publications of the Texas Folklore Society LXIII

UNT PRESS

University of North Texas Press
Denton, Texas

10 9 8 7 6 5 4 3 2 1

Permissions:
University of North Texas Press
P.O. Box 311336
Denton, TX 76203-1336

The paper used in this book meets the minimum requirements of the American National Standard for Permanence of Paper for Printed Library Materials, z39.48.1984. Binding materials have been chosen for durability.

Library of Congress Cataloging-in-Publication Data

Folklore : in all of us, in all we do/edited by Kenneth L. Untiedt.
p. cm. — (Publications of the Texas Folklore Society ; 63)
Includes bibliographical references and index.
ISBN-13: 978-1-57441-223-9 (cloth : alk. paper)
ISBN-10: 1-57441-223-X (cloth : alk. paper)
1. Folklore—Texas. 2. Occupations—Texas—Folklore. 3. Texas—Folklore. 4. Texas—Social life and customs. I. Untiedt, Kenneth L., 1966- II. Texas Folklore Society.
GR110.T5F65 2006
398'.09764—dc22

2006024644

Folklore: In All of Us, In All We Do is Number LXIII in the Publications of the Texas Folklore Society

CONTENTS

PREFACE

History and folklore go hand in hand, and people frequently confuse the two in light conversation. There may be good reason, for in many ways the subjects are closely related. The study of folklore is often historical in its focus. Folklore is the *traditional* knowledge of a culture, and the word "traditional" carries with it the idea of things that are established, time-honored. We recognize things folkloric as those things that are passed down from one generation to another. We look at what came before us and try to keep alive the "old ways," usually by word of mouth, a method of instruction which in itself seems old-fashioned or even antiquated. Also, to fully appreciate folklore one needs to have an understanding of the history behind it. When does folklore become historical fact? When ceremonies or customs are documented, do they not become historical accounts of the people who practice them? Folklore provides unique views of the events, beliefs, customs, ceremonies, materials, and skills of a particular group. History provides the factual circumstances that may have influenced each of those things, or more specifically, the members of the group. In history, you get the ingredients; in folklore, you get the flavor. The two can complement one another and give us a finished product. However, you must be prepared to decipher both and understand the difference.

Why is this important? History might tell us that a person was a doctor or a politician or an oilfield worker, but folklore provides insight into those individuals' professions that might otherwise be lost. The same is true for every person whose knowledge we learn, for folklore can come from anyone. Indeed, it comes from all of us. This sixty-third volume of the Publications of the Texas Folklore Society is a traditional miscellany, and it contains articles on many diverse topics and individuals, including articles on topics not frequently discussed, and ones by people who have never published anything with us before. However, even a miscellany must have some structure. Therefore, I have arranged the articles in five chapters. The first tackles this issue of folklore and its relationship to history, with some of the articles trying to provide some of that folkloric filler to historical facts. Another chapter focuses on women; one features various types of occupational lore; and another is a tongue-in-cheek look at "shady characters" such as police officers, politicians, and horsetraders. A final chapter has no theme; it is a catch-all, containing a few interesting articles you may remember from some of our most recent meetings.

I have included another "throwback article." J. Frank Dobie's article in the first chapter tells a little about our history as an organization and why he settled on the roadrunner as our symbol. "The Roadrunner in Fact and Fiction" first appeared in the 1939 PTFS *In the Shadow of History.* I doubt that many of our current members have a complete collection of our publications, and even if they do they probably have not read all the articles in them. Therefore, my goal in reprinting older articles is twofold. First, I want to share select articles with readers who have never read them, thereby presenting them with something new even when it is quite old. Second, I want to expose readers (and perhaps researchers) to the original source for those articles, perhaps to encourage readers to obtain the past issues from which they came. This way, they may discover other articles they might enjoy, from contributors they never had a chance to meet in person, thereby maintaining a link to our folklore ancestors.

Early in the process of selecting which papers to include in this book, I decided on Mary Margaret Dougherty Campbell's paper about Bill Phillips, who routinely hosts a gathering where friends swap stories and keep alive the lore of their local area. This article verifies that the "spit and whittle club" is not dead. In today's world of isolation through global communication, it is important to realize that some people still honor the oral tradition. As we were communicating regarding the article, Mary Margaret sent me what she called her follow-up to the article, and although it is unusual to feature two articles by one author, I decided to include both. This second article is a good way to transition into the chapter on women. "The Cooking Extravaganza" shows men and women doing something together in a setting traditionally viewed as a woman's place. It also shows how folklore can be found somewhere as simple as a kitchen. This group of lay cooks is challenging the past, experimenting with the future, and rediscovering uses for skills long-forgotten. Their language, the tools they use, and the rules to which they adhere are all distinct to a particular group. All of these activities blend, much like their recipes, and their time together as a group is time spent sharing with and learning from each other.

The chapter on women covers a lot of ground, both socially and historically. It examines brave women of the early frontier days, a mystic, and La Llorona, that centuries-old symbol of a woman who suffers eternally for her mistakes. However, I also wanted to include contemporary women and their connection to folklore. I found Kelly Mosel-Talavera's paper on the ceremonies and rituals associated with beauty pageants interesting and unique, even if I had a bit of a hard time finding Kelly. The detective work was worth it, though, as it was on a couple of other articles whose authors I had to track down (because they were out of the country, hard to reach after having moved, or were deceased and only next-of-kin could be located). I extended my goal of finding more recent examples of folklore to the chapter on occupational lore, a topic which certainly deserves more study. Especially now when modern technology allows instant access to people and places practically anywhere anytime—all of which is generally taken for granted—it is good to look back at the beginnings of that technology and learn about those who created it. Hopefully, these articles will help us have a better appreciation for those who came before us, whose experience and knowledge not only established policies that others could follow, but also set standards for their occupations.

Many of these articles focus on oral history; several feature excerpts from diaries or personal accounts that show the less glamorous sides of professions such as medicine and politics, in the own words of the people who worked in those fields. Some things would never be written today, in our ever increasingly politically correct world. We see how one mail carrier not only provided a service for a community throughout his career, but how he also kept alive traditions and history of that community over a few generations. We get to meet some rather famous—if not seedy—characters who have ties to Texas. We learn not just the lore of various trades such as water engineers and nurserymen, but also legends of the area where the work is done, as well as folk remedies, customs, and superstitions. The sources for this information come from some unusual places, including back yards, garages, laboratories, and retirement homes.

These articles are from members who are alive and still active at the annual meetings, as well as from members who are no longer with us. They cover diverse topics: at home and at work, about serious business and things just for fun, related to the mystical and the factual, in the distant past and in our contemporary lives, by and about the professional and the layperson, women, men, politicians, doctors, legendary figures, housewives, cooks, preachers, inventors, beauty pageant contestants, teachers, and the elderly. These people have shared their knowledge, and that knowledge becomes a part of us, for what they have to say is important to all of us, in all that we do.

I give thanks to several people, including all of the contributors, the administrators and my colleagues at Stephen F. Austin State University, Karen DeVinney and the staff at the UNT Press, and especially to Janet Simonds, our new office secretary. She came in at the early part of this publication, and she has been a tremendous asset. She eagerly took part in the 2006 meeting, and she has made many changes to our office procedures and recordkeeping, dramatically improving how efficiently we do things. Her ideas are innovative and yet simple, and they are very much appreciated.

This publication is dedicated to Kenneth W. Davis, a teacher, a mentor, and a friend. He has enriched my life more than any other person I know. Kenneth is the one who first introduced me to Elmer Kelton and Clay Reynolds, Robert Earl Keen and the Gillette Brothers, and Shiner Bock beer and Whistlin Dixie BBQ. In many ways, he is himself a miscellany. He once told me he knew everything there was to know about English. Surely this was in jest, but still, it took me a considerable time before I discovered something he did not know—and know thoroughly. I'm sure there were courses he did not teach during his thirty-nine years at Texas Tech University, but they probably were not introduced until after he was "no longer bucking for tenure or promotion." A master of many areas, he is very much responsible for my association with this organization, for it was he who first encouraged me to submit a paper. That was only eleven years ago, and I thank him for all he did to expedite my rise through the ranks. I am not the only active member he introduced to this organization, and we all should be grateful for his role as a faithful contributor, Board member, and all-around advocate of the Texas Folklore Society.

Kenneth L. Untiedt
Stephen F. Austin State University
Nacogdoches, Texas
July 5, 2006

FIRST COUSINS:

FOLKLORE AND HISTORY

Tom Crum in his library of history and folklore books

1

IS IT FOLKLORE OR HISTORY? THE ANSWER MAY BE IMPORTANT

by Tom Crum

There is a great deal of history in folklore, and that's good. There also is a great deal of folklore in history, and that's not good. I suspect that many of you are either historians or folklorists. I am neither one. I am a lawyer, although I do have some friends in both camps. If you look around, you will be able to tell which people at this meeting are historians and which are folklorists. The folklorists are the ones who look smug and content. That is because they know that unless they are foolish enough to write about the *history* of folklore it's impossible for them to make a mistake. They know that no one will ever accuse them of getting their facts wrong or of writing politically correct folklore and, of course, there is no such thing as revisionist folklore. If someone ever said that a folklorist got it wrong, all the folklorist has to say is, "that's the way I heard it" and immediately he or she is off the hook and waiting for an apology. Sadly, it is not the same for historians; they are seldom off the hook and never receive apologies. It's enough to make even folklorists sympathetic toward historians, and I am sure the more charitable ones are. I personally have never witnessed any concern on their part, but that may say more about the company I keep than folklorists as a group.

Although they would be hesitant to admit it, historians are much like trial lawyers, in that both historians and trial lawyers look at the world from a perspective a little different from most people—and certainly from folklorists. They have acquired the habit of skepticism, which W. J. Cash claimed, in *The Mind of the*

South, is essential to any generally realistic attitude.[1] They seek proof, for they understand, like Thoreau, that no way of thinking can be trusted without proof.[2]

In contrast, it's not that folklorists are naïve or don't care about the truth, it's just that by the very nature of folklore the folklorist does not need proof or skepticism. In fact, in an article in the Texas Folklore Society's publication *In the Shadow of History,* Radoslav Tsanoff tells us that folklore "falls to pieces under the stern touch of factual research."[3] Folklorists may search for folklore, but they never research for it. Their attitude is that if you have to research it, it ain't folklore. Folklorists are so laid-back that if indeed Jimmy crack corn, they don't care. They just blame it all on the blue tail fly.

If historians and folklorists have such different perspectives, how would their worlds collide? It is not the folklorist who has difficulty in navigation. Wilson Hudson writes in his preface to *In the Shadow of History,* "Every folklorist is aware of the interaction between historical events and popular imagination."[4] In his 1949 article "American Folklore," B. A. Botkin tells us that "the relation of history to legend is close in America—and that the mixture of the two has given rise to a large body of unhistorical 'historical' traditions—or apocryphal traditions of doubtful exploits of historical characters and untrustworthy traditions of doubtful events."[5]

Francis Abernethy has defined folklore as the traditional knowledge of a culture.[6] J. Frank Dobie claimed that an anecdote of doubtful historicity might reveal more about a man or a people than a bookful of facts.[7] Joyce Roach states that folklore exists on two levels, one of which is historical myth. She describes these myths as "those stories which often explain a culture's conception and birth and of the heroes and heroines who accomplished the deeds to bring it about. . . ."[8]

These and other folklorists point out that to understand a culture you need to know not only the facts of its history but also its perception of that history. In her article in *Texas Myths,* Louise Cowan states, "One discerns a society's vision of the nature and destiny of humanity through its legendary material, its folklore, its fairytales."[9]

Since there are many different cultures in any society, there are often many different stories or accounts passed on as traditional knowledge of any one historical event. As folklore, all of these stories or accounts are of equal value. However, although each of them may have some nodding acquaintance with the actual facts of the event, none of them may be factually true. The southern whites' traditional knowledge of slavery and the antebellum South as passed on to them by their cultural ancestors may be very different from the traditional knowledge of the same subjects that was passed on to the descendants of slaves. The same could be said of the folklore of hundreds of different cultures regarding any historical event or period. There is likely some truth in each of the culture's folklore, but to ascertain which is closer to reality you need the historical facts. As folklore, one culture's traditional knowledge of its conception, birth, heroes and heroines is as valid as that of any other culture. Knowing this, a folklorist does not intend his or her work to be taken as historically accurate.

A people's perception of their history is often formed not so much from knowledge of facts as from the traditional knowledge passed on to them through folklore. A great many people are much more familiar with folklore's rendition of an historical event than they are with the actual facts of the event, and this forms their opinion of and sets the standard for "truth" as to the event. Yet, if these people were asked if they ever read folklore, they would probably answer in the negative.

Where do these people get the folkloric rendition of these events? Unfortunately, from articles or books passed off as historical accounts. Persons who have read Wilbarger, DeShields, a great many of the reminiscences of the Texas Rangers and other pioneers, some of the articles in *Frontier Times* and the former *Texana Quarterly,* many of the earlier accounts of reconstruction and the fall of the Alamo, or any of the books that cite these publications, has read a great deal of folklore, possibly without being aware of it. The folklore contained in these writings, which of course is perpetuated each time it is cited in another work, are excellent examples of Botkin's unhistorical "historical" traditions or apocryphal traditions of doubtful exploits of historical characters and untrustworthy traditions of doubtful events.

Some historical writings are not meant to inform but rather to persuade. By controlling the evidence, the writer supports his or her evaluations and interpretations. A writer might present only evidence that supports his or her position or only contrary evidence that the writer believes he or she can effectively argue against, ignoring all other evidence that refutes the writer's position. We seldom read historical accounts in which the facts do not support the writer's evaluation and interpretation. This is so because the writer is the only person presenting the facts. In other words, he or she controls the facts and if a writer can't come to a logical conclusion using controlled facts, well, he or she is not much of a writer.

Historians are not the authors of all of the books in the history section of your library. The writing of an historical account does not make the writer an historian. He or she may be an excellent writer but still not an historian. However, there should be no criticism of a history writer's evaluation and interpretation of accurate facts because after all, history is nothing more than an accumulation of facts about past events and an evaluation and interpretation of those facts. It is the historian's primary objective to make a thorough search for the facts.

Other than having some agenda, what would cause writers of historical accounts to "folklorize" their accounts? As much as I dislike being the bearer of bad news, I must advise you that some of these writers are just plain lazy. These writers are easy to identify because they show a remarkable distaste for primary sources. Most of their research depends upon that of other historians. In other words they rely principally on secondary sources, which often are themselves the product of other secondary sources. If you trace them back you may never come to a primary source. This summer I read a recently published book concerning atrocities committed during the American-Indian War. The author, who by the way was a lawyer, used nothing but secondary sources. This writer also labeled historical revisionism as false history.[10] Of course, since he relied entirely on secondary sources he could never be accused of revising history, only of quoting or editing it.

Besides telling us that we ought to demand proof, Thoreau also gives us some good advice about travelers, which could apply also to writers who rely on secondary sources. Thoreau states, "He who is only a traveler learns things at second-hand and by the halves, and is poor authority."[11] The same would apply to those writers who rely on secondary sources.

The traditional knowledge of a culture serves some need or other useful purpose of the culture. It may be economic, defensive, or political, but no matter what purpose is served it may be harmed if such knowledge is questioned. If an historical article deviates from this traditional knowledge it is often labeled as "revisionist history." That label is not meant to be complimentary. The folk don't want anyone messing with their history, the emphasis being on *their.*

If someone writes something that really upsets the folk, they may not only call the writer a revisionist but also accuse him or her of writing "politically correct" history. They do not intend that to be a compliment, either. Of course, to them, politically correct history is any history that even implies that any historical accomplishment was the product of anyone other than a white (preferably Anglo-Saxon), Protestant, male (preferably southern); or, that casts any white (especially if he is Anglo-Saxon), Protestant, male (most assuredly if he is southern) in an unfavorable light. Usually, the history they complain about contains what they consider to be both flaws—that is, revisionist and politically correct.

We want Crockett to have fought to the last, dying only when overpowered by overwhelming numbers. We want Travis to have made his grand speech and to have drawn the line in the dirt, across which every Alamo defender except one crossed.

How Crockett died or whether or not Travis actually made his speech or drew a line at the Alamo is of no great consequence. Believing that Crockett fought to the end or surrendered thinking he could talk his way out of death, or that Travis did or did not make his speech or draw the line will not substantially affect the actions of anyone, except perhaps in their writing hate mail to anyone questioning their belief. However, it is of great consequence when a writer of historical events intentionally or carelessly states something that advises his readers that a people are in some way either superior or inferior to another group of people. Since actions often follow beliefs, believing such statements can lead to serious consequences.

When the competent and respected historian Walter Prescott Webb tells us that there is a cruel streak in the nature of the Mexican that may be of Spanish heritage (and doubtless should be attributed partly to Indian blood),[12] was he correct or factual? Was he politically correct? That was undoubtedly his scholarly interpretation of the facts as he saw them in 1935. Perhaps what he meant is that there is a cruel streak in human nature and that the Mexican, being a member of humanity, shares that streak with the rest of us. If that is what he meant, with my knowledge of the Sand Creek Massacre, the Mountain Meadows Massacre and the Porvenir Massacre; the labor trouble in Ludlow, Colorado; slavery and the countless lynchings, whether by rope or fire, of black Americans; the atrocities by the Germans against the Jews as described and pictured in the book, *The Good Old Days;*[13] not to mention all of the court cases I have heard, I might agree with his interpretation of the facts. Was he politically correct in what he actually did say? I would say for his 1935, white, male, Protestant readers his political correctness was right on target. Many of them would readily accept his interpretation because it reinforced their feelings of superiority, and it is always good politics to tell the people what they want to hear, regardless of its truthfulness.

However, if some later historian were to interpret the facts that he or she had gleaned from a study of the past concerning the nature of Mexicans differently, he or she would certainly be accused by some of being politically correct and perhaps even a revisionist. As Jose Enrique de la Pena, who fought for the Mexicans at the Alamo, wrote, "Be very careful because it is very difficult to be a historian."[14]

Many historical writings are politically correct for their time. All writers want acceptance from their readers. One of the most effective ways to do this is to tell them something that they will agree with or to reinforce some opinion or prejudice that they have. If that's not politics I don't know what is! In the political arena, practitioners of this are usually successful in getting elected.

In a fifth and sixth grade textbook, *Workers and Wealth of Texas,* Texas school children were taught in the 1930s that "there is something about a cotton patch that seems to appeal to most Negroes. They look upon cotton picking as play, as a kind of game, rather than work. . . . But all people like to pick cotton after they are used it."[15] Are these statements of historical truths, or are they closer to folklore, and if folklore, whose culture? I suspect that like Dobie told us, they might reveal more about a people (in this case the school boards) than a bookful of facts. I believe it was Mark Twain who was first credited with saying, "In the first place God made idiots. This was for practice. Then He made school boards."[16]

There may be some of you that have never had the good fortune to play in a cotton patch. For you, I will quote from a book by those revisionist and politically correct historians Thad Sitton and Dan Utley. They quoted an old cotton picker who told them, "You'd pick standing up until your back hurt so bad you could hardly stand it, and you'd get down on your knees and go along until your knees got to hurting so bad you couldn't stand it, and you'd get back up and bend over again. Something was always hurting."[17] Which statements concerning picking cotton are closer to the historical truth, and which are closer to folklore?

Historian James Crisp has told us, "We should never allow even the most revered of our society's 'sacred narratives' to be accepted as simple truths, nor to be mistaken for legitimate history. Myths offer the false comfort of simplicity. . . ."[18] I suspect he was not just warning us about picking cotton but also about the folklorization of history. It is a warning we all should heed. Of course, when someone says that history has been folklorized, such a statement is really just a politically correct way to say that we have been lied to and that a revision is necessary in order to set the record straight.

[Portions of this article were taken from the author's Presidential Address for the 2003 West Texas Historical Association Meeting, also published as "A Lawyer Looks at Historical Research" in the *WTHA Year Book*, Volume LXXIX, Ed. Monte L. Monroe, 2003, 170–178.]

Endnotes

1. W.J. Cash. *The Mind of the South.* 1941. New York: Vintage Books, 1991. 45.
2. Henry David Thoreau. *Walden; or, Life in the Woods.* 1854. Mount Vernon: Peter Pauper Press, 1966. 12.
3. Radoslav Tsanoff. "Folk-Lore and Tradition in a Growing Society." *In the Shadow of History.* 1939. Ed. J. Frank Dobie. Dallas: SMU Press, 1980. 2.
4. Wilson Hudson. "Preface to the Reprint Edition." *In the Shadow of History.* i.
5. B.A. Botkin. "American Folklore (1949)." *Folk Nation, Folklore in the Creation of American Tradition.* Ed. Simon J. Bronner. Wilmington: Scholarly Resources, Inc., 2002. 136.
6. F.E. Abernethy. "Classroom Definition of Folklore." *Between the Cracks of History: Essays on Teaching and Illustrating Folklore.* Ed. Francis E. Abernethy. Denton: University of North Texas Press, 1997. 4.
7. Hudson, i.
8. Joyce Roach. "Defining Folklore for My Students." *Between the Cracks of History: Essays on Teaching and Illustrating Folklore.* 12.
9. Louise Cowan. "Myth in the Modern World." *Texas Myths.* Ed. Robert F. O'Conner. College Station: Texas A & M University Press, 1986. 10.
10. William M. Osborn. *The Wild Frontier: Atrocities During the American-Indian War from Jamestown Colony to Wounded Knee.* New York: Random House, 2000. 271–272.
11. Thoreau. 204.
12. Walter Prescott Webb. 1935. *The Texas Rangers: A Century of Frontier Defense.* Austin: University of Texas Press, 1987. 14.
13. Ernst Klee, Willi Dressen, and Wolker Riess, Eds. *The Good Old Days, the Holocaust as Seen by its Perpetrators and Bystanders.* Old Saybrook: Koneck & Koneck, 1988.
14. James E. Crisp. *Sleuthing the Alamo, Davy Crockett's Last Stand and Other Mysteries of the Texas Revolution.* New York: Oxford University Press, 2005. 117.

15. W.A. Stigler and William T. Tardy. *Workers and Wealth of Texas.* Dallas: Banks Upshaw and Co., 1935. 23–24.
16. Mark Twain. *Following the Equator, A Journey Around the World,* Vol. II. New York: Harpers & Brokers Publishers, 1899. 295.
17. Thad Sitton and Dan K. Utley. *From Can See to Can't, Texas Cotton Farmers on the Southern Prairies.* Austin: University of Texas Press, 1997. 208.
18. Crisp. 178.

A collection of paisanos (including a Mody Boatright paisano, bottom center) recently donated to the Texas Folklore Society Archive by Joyce Roach, TFS Fellow

2

THE ROADRUNNER IN FACT AND FOLK-LORE

by J. Frank Dobie

Born and reared in Southwest Texas, I was grown before I knew that the bird had any other name than paisano (pronounced pie-sah'-no), by which Mexicans of Texas and northern Mexico know it. The word means *fellow-countryman, compatriot, native.* It is sometimes said to be a corruption of *faisán* (pheasant), a word changed in some Mexican localities to *faisano.* Yet the bird belongs to the cuckoo, and not to the pheasant, family. Its scientific name, *Geococcyx californianus,* signifies "ground cuckoo," the type specimen having been collected in California. It is known to Mexicans also as *corre camino* (runs the road), *churella, churrea,* and other names.

The names in English are just as numerous, varying according to locality. Roadrunner, chaparral cock, chaparral bird, and chaparral are the more common names, exclusive of paisano—which name I intend to keep on using, because it expresses a quality that is to me fundamental. The bird and I are fellow natives of the country. Lizard bird, war bird, snake-eater, medicine bird, cock of the desert, and ground cuckoo are names met with in print, though not used to any extent, I think, by people belonging to the land. I have never met "bird-of-paradise" as a name except in the well-worn anecdote of the West Texas real estate agent—this was before the "realtors" arrived—who in answer to his prospective client's question, "What's that bird?" replied, "Bird-of-paradise, some folks call it," whereupon the stranger commented, "He's a hell of a long ways from home, ain't he?"

In 1932 the Texas Folk-Lore Society adopted the paisano as its emblem. It is the State bird of New Mexico. Perhaps no other native bird of North America, excepting the eagle and the turkey, which the Aztecs had domesticated long before Columbus sailed, has been so closely associated with the native races of this continent. It appears in the mythology, songs and legends of more than one tribe of Indians. English-speaking men living over the paisano's range—Texas, New Mexico, Arizona, California, most of Mexico, and into Colorado, Oklahoma, and Kansas—have generated an interest in it that not even unjust persecution has diminished. Descriptions of the bird, with emphasis always on its long legs, a tail that serves as a brake, running ability, brilliantly colored head, comical antics and insectivorous appetite, are to be found in many books. But the best description I know is Eve Ganson's in her delightful and delightfully illustrated *Desert Mavericks:*

> The Road-Runner runs in the road,
> His coat is speckled, á la mode.
> His wings are short, his tail is long,
> He jerks it as he runs along.
> His bill is sharp, his eyes are keen,
> He has a brain tucked in his bean.
> But in his gizzard—if you please—
> Are lizards, rats, and bumble bees;
> Also horned toads—on them he feeds—
> And rattlesnakes! and centipedes!

The roadrunner is the most interesting bird of the Southwest.

I. FACTS

"On Them He Feeds"

Now that the urban hunter is envious of every quail that makes the morning cheerful and the evening tranquil with his call, the roadrunner has been charged with eating quail eggs and killing and eating young quail, and is even being killed out in many places on the assumption that this charge is true. It is a pity that authentic evidence is not as easy for the public to digest as superstition and rumor.

During the summer of 1938 Roy Bedichek, who is a good ornithologist, was on a United States Wild Life Refuge in southern Texas in company with a man employed by the government to help "balance nature." This man carried a gun and had, he said, "orders from Washington" to kill roadrunners off the refuge. "Why?" Bedichek asked. "Oh, because they eat other birds." Bedichek proposed to examine the craws of two roadrunners killed. The contents, spread out on white paper, consisted of nothing but legs and wings of grasshoppers—nothing else at all.

In the early spring of 1932 two paisanos killed in the country near San Antonio were brought to the Witte Museum, where Mrs. Ellen Schulz Quillin examined the crops. In the crop of one killed on a cool day were found twenty-one snails, one cutworm, one bee, one spider, three daddy-longlegs, two pods of a nettle, two crickets, seven small beetles, [and] two June bugs. In the crop of the other, killed on a warm day, were found thirty-one cutworms, twelve snails, nine beetles, one cricket, and many moths.

In *Arizona Wild Life*, October, 1932, D.M. Gorsuch of the U.S. Biological Survey printed a very interesting report on the food habits of roadrunners as determined by field observation and the official examination of one hundred roadrunners taken in close proximity to quail at a time when the quail were nesting or were leading their broods afield. Grasshoppers constituted 62 per cent of the stomach contents of the hundred roadrunners examined. Other insects included centipedes, scorpions, and tarantulas. The reptilian contents were mostly lizards, but part of a rattlesnake was found. "No evidence of quail or their eggs was found," although two cactus wrens, an unidentified sparrow, and a nestling meadow lark were found.

"About two years ago," Mr. Gorsuch continues, "I saw a roadrunner following a family of twelve newly hatched Gambel quail and their parents, as they fed through the grass. This appeared to be a splendid opportunity for the roadrunner to secure one of the chicks, for although the adult quail knew of its presence, they gave it little attention. The roadrunner's interest centered upon those grasshoppers that the quail started up and that flew beyond their reach. This continued until the roadrunner darted immediately in front of the cock quail to get a grasshopper, whereupon the cock turned and savagely attacked the roadrunner, who escaped by jumping into a mesquite, from which it sailed into an adjoining wash. On many other occasions a like proceeding has been observed, and it is my conviction that the roadrunner follows such feeding quail for the grasshoppers thus started up."

Just so, roadrunners—like robins and blackbirds—sometimes follow a plow to get the worms exposed. The procedure is common in wild life. I have seen cowbirds hanging around the heads of grazing cattle to catch the insects routed out by the grazers. Gulls, terns, and other shore birds follow boats to catch the mullet dispersed. Coyotes squat around badgers to catch the rats that the badgers chase out of nests they are digging into. During the drouth of 1935 in Southwest Texas, while ranchers around Brady were singeing off spines from prickly pear so that their stock could eat it, two men reported to a friend of mine that roadrunners followed the pear-burner every day searching the singed pear for roasted worms and bugs.

In 1916 the University of California issued a pamphlet on *Habits and Food of the Roadrunner in California,* by Harold C. Bryant. Insects comprised 74.93 per cent of the contents of the stomachs of eighty-four roadrunners examined. No quail were found, but two small birds were found, [and] also lizards, mice, and a tiny cottontail rabbit. The small amount of vegetable matter consumed by the roadrunners appeared to consist of sour berries.

It must be admitted, however, that a few roadrunners do at times destroy a few young quail. Yet there is no evidence to support the common belief that roadrunners in general are persistent and customary predators on young quail; and in all the evidence both oral and written I have examined I have not found one single authentic instance of a roadrunner's having destroyed quail eggs. It may be that occasionally a roadrunner does eat quail eggs. But there are numerous instances of the destruction of mice, large wood rats, and various kinds of snakes by the bird—and snakes and rats are undoubtedly much more destructive of quail eggs and young quail than the roadrunners are themselves.

An old-time Mexican ranchero whom I met at Parral, in the state of Chihuahua, told me that country people in that region sometimes catch the paisano young, tame it, and utilize it to catch mice and rats.

Nature balances itself far better than man can ever balance it. The most roadrunners I have ever seen are in that part of Texas where the blue, or scaled, quail are admittedly more plentiful than anywhere else in the United States. I refer to the brush country of Southwest Texas centering around the counties of Duval, McMullen, La Salle, and Webb. By riding a day in some of the big pastures of this region in late summer of seasonable years a man might count a thousand blue quail, many bob whites, and easily a hundred paisanos. In the sand hills north and east of these counties, still in the brush country, bob whites used to abound by the thousands—are yet plentiful on some protected land—along with many, many paisanos.

You will not find the most colts and the most panthers in the same pasture, or the most lions and the most lambs. You will not find the most shotgun hunters and the most quail in the same pasture.

And what if the paisano is now and then directly responsible for one less quail to shoot at? He is a poor sportsman whose only interest in wild life is something to kill. How much more interesting and delightful is a country where a variety of wild life abounds! If it were necessary to choose between ten quail and no paisanos, or nine quail and one paisano, not many people who have any response towards nature or capacity for being delighted by the countryside would hesitate to choose the latter. The value of the roadrunner to the farmer as an insect destroyer need not be dwelt upon.

A few years ago a rancher named John Henderson who was trying to raise young turkeys on Honey Creek in Kerr County, Texas, began missing several from his bunch. Taking his shotgun, he one day followed a flock to the creek. He saw a huge bullfrog leap out of the water, snap a little turkey up, and dive back into the water. He waited, and before long the bullfrog reappeared. He shot him, dissected him, and found the freshly swallowed turkey inside the frog. One swallow does not make a summer. Bullfrogs in general cannot be considered as destroyers of young turkeys. There are many individual variations among roadrunners just as there are among horses, men, and other kinds of animals.

Once while watching at a dirt tank on a ranch in Webb County, I saw a paisano that came up to drink peck at a frog, which escaped. A Mexican told me that the day preceding he had seen a paisano catch a small frog, beat it to death on the ground, and swallow it. Yet paisanos are characteristic of a country generally devoid of frogs, and certainly they are not generally frog-catchers. At a well not ten miles away from the one just mentioned, I saw half a dozen paisanos running around and around on the rim of a circular water trough, trying to reach down for a drink. The water was too low. Out in the middle of the trough, which was about eight feet in diameter, floated a good-sized board attached to the valve-float; this board was half covered with frogs. Not a paisano had sense enough to jump to the board and drink from it, and no paisano had the least intention of catching a frog.

I placed a dead mesquite limb in the trough so that one end of it went down into the water while the other rested on the rim. Not one had sense enough to walk down the limb to water. Two or three paisanos were at the same time running around on the tin roof of the cistern that fed the trough, trying to get at water. The saying in Southwest Texas, "as crazy as a paisano," seemed here well founded, although in some ways the bird certainly is not "crazy." Paisanos cannot swim at all and they frequently drown in cement troughs and cisterns.

I estimated there were probably a hundred paisanos within a radius of half a mile of the cement trough. On August 9 I discovered near it a nest up about ten feet in a mesquite tree. On my horse I could watch the old bird feeding her young. There were three nestlings, two about ready to leave, and a third less mature. The parent bird fed them exactly in rotation, exclusively on grasshoppers, as long as I watched, which was about an hour, the provider at the end of that time disappearing. She—or he—needed a rest. A youngster would open its mouth wide; the old one would poke grasshopper-laden bill down the orifice and hold it there until the morsel was swallowed. Then she would volplane down to the ground and scoot up into another mesquite or fly directly from the nest into another tree. The ground about was entirely shadowed by mesquites. She was catching most of her grasshoppers in the mesquites among the leaves. From a point of vantage she would cock her head this way and that until she located an insect, fly softly to a spot near it, and thence make a swift dart. Usually she caught, but sometimes the grasshopper escaped. From her position up in a tree she could see grasshoppers flying and lighting. If she located one lighting on the ground, the way she volplaned and nabbed it was a pretty sight. She never missed a grasshopper on the ground as she sometimes missed one among the leaves.

Within a few rods of this paisano nest I saw five or six dove nests on which the doves were peacefully brooding, and I saw a little mocking-bird just out of its nest. The doves and mocking-birds did not seem to regard the paisanos as enemies. I saw a paisano make a pass at a rusty lizard, on a tree trunk, and miss it; the paisano seemed to expect this. I have seen dozens of green lizards in the bills of paisanos but never a rusty lizard. There is a very tall tale about a roadrunner in California that kept a hill full of lizards growing tails for him to eat. This paisano discovered that a lizard would, unlike Little Bo Peep's sheep, leave its tail behind it if the tail was snapped up, and would then grow a new tail just as good to swallow as the original.

An astounding revelation of the voracity of the bird is given by G. M. Sutton in an account of two pet roadrunners, "Titania and Oberon," in his book *Birds in the Wilderness.* He tells how they manage to swallow horned frogs. The paisano digests rapidly. He will begin swallowing a snake inches long and after he has got a certain portion of it down must wait for the digestive juices to act before he can swallow further. Thus he may have to go about for hours with a part of the snake dangling out of his mouth before he can get it all down. He is truly, to use the phrase out of an old folk rhyme, a "greedy gut."

When Doctor H. A. Pilsbury of Philadelphia came to Texas and Mexico a few years ago hunting snails, I told him he should throw in with the paisanos. He didn't understand what I meant. I explained how in Southwest Texas—and probably elsewhere—the paisano picks up a snail, breaks the shell on a rock, and then eats the meat; how he will bring snail after snail to the rock he has selected as a meat-block, or table, to break it, passing scores of other rocks on his way; how sometimes at one of these rocks, or maybe a hard bit of bare ground, more than a cupful of broken snail shells may be picked up. Doctor Pilsbury replied that, so far as he knew, there was but one other bird in the world that eats snails in this way. That is an English thrush, and the places where the thrushes collect the snails are called "thrush altars." Should the paisano have an altar, a chuck wagon, or a *mesa?*

Eggs and Habits

The average clutch of eggs seems to be from four to six, but two or three often compose the number, and there are records of up to twelve. As soon as the first egg is laid, incubation begins, and the succeeding eggs are laid irregularly. In consequence, the birds hatch off over such a long period of time that the first fledgling will sometimes be ready to leave the nest before the last egg is pipped. After the second or third bird is hatched, the adults—for the cock is said to do a share in setting—spend little daylight time on the nest, the body heat of the young sufficing to keep the eggs warm. According to Mrs. Bruce Reid, the male bird takes care of the first young ones to come off the nest, while the female feeds the last nestlings. Mrs. Reid had a pet male three years old that adopted and took charge of feeding two baby-roadrunners she brought home; he favored in many ways the female of this pair of young ones.

The nest is loosely built in an old log fence, in a Spanish dagger, up in a mesquite, within a clump of brush, etc. Owing to the long neck and longer tail of the bird, one sitting on a nest appears to be cramped, but perhaps isn't.

Little seems to be known about the mating maneuvers of the paisano. Do they pair for life? My brother, Elrich Dobie, who ranches in Webb and LaSalle counties, told me that twice he had seen a male paisano mount a female, and in each instance with a worm in his mouth that he reached around and gave to the female. There are more variations in the calls made by the bird than many people realize, and during mating season the calls are rich.

While not to be classed as migratory, roadrunners do, I believe, shift their grounds to an extent in the winter. In August of 1936 I counted between 75 and 100 in a day on the old Buckley ranch near Cotulla, Texas. I could not be sure of the count, for some of the birds were certainly met twice. The next December on a deer hunt on the same ranch I saw only one bird during the day. Mexicans said the paisanos were down in the thickest thickets, but I was not convinced. A man who has a stock-farm out a short distance from San Marcos says that a particular roadrunner stayed on his place, often appearing about the barn and corrals, for several years. It would disappear during the winter and reappear with early spring.

Paisanos are found far from water and in waterless deserts. Some observers have thought water not essential to them. This may well be in places where they have adapted themselves to desert conditions, especially since they eat animal food containing a high percent of fluid. In Sonora there are deer that almost never drink water, although the same deer in other parts of the word drink more or less regularly. Where water is available, however, roadrunners are thirsty drinkers in the hot summer. In Southwest Texas they are exceedingly methodical and regular in coming to water. One time while I was watching a gasoline engine pumping water for cattle during the dog days of August, a period when the wind habitually fails to blow enough to turn windmills, I noticed how a particular paisano came every day about a quarter of twelve o'clock to drink. He was as regular as the sun.

The bird has a great deal of curiosity and is easily domesticated if taken young. One will hop into the open door of a house and stand there a long time, looking this way and that. Perhaps he has an idea that some shade-loving creature suited to his diet is in the house. He will come up to a camp to investigate in the same way. I never tire of watching one of these birds dart down a trail or road, suddenly throw on the brakes by hoisting his tail, stand for a minute dead still except for panting and cocking his head to one side and then to the other, and then suddenly streak out again. The way he raises and lowers the plumage on his lustrous-feathered head while he goes *crut, crut, crut* with his vocal organs is an endless fascination. He must surely be the most comical bird of America. He will go through more antics and cut up more didos in an hour than a parrot can be taught in a lifetime.

How the idea that he cannot fly at all got started, I cannot imagine. Down a hill or a mountain he can volplane for long distances. Frequently one will fly up into a tree to get a wide view. Of course, however, he is essentially a ground bird. His speed, like nearly everything else connected with him, had been greatly exaggerated. Any good horse can outrun one on a considerable stretch. Walter Fry of the Sequoia National Park, California, is quoted as saying that a roadrunner he was chasing in an automobile attained the speed of 26 miles per hour. Bailey's *Birds of New Mexico* gives his top speed, tested by automobile, as fifteen miles an hour. Running down a path ahead of a buggy or a horseman, the roadrunner often seems to enjoy the exercise as much as a pup enjoys chasing a chicken or calf. While speeding, he stretches out almost flat. Sometimes he falls in behind a traveler and follows down a trail. He enjoys a dust bath. He can stand terrific heat, but on hot days he likes to pause in the shade, even though it be nothing but a shadow of a three-inch mesquite fence post.

Killers of Rattlesnakes

That paisanos, singly and in pairs, kill rattlesnakes is a fact established beyond all doubt, although folk-lore amassed around the subject has made ornithologists slow to admit the fact. One vice of erudition is that it tends to patronize popular knowledge, great-natured men of science like Audubon and W. H. Hudson being exceptions to the general tendency. In the fall of 1928 near Robstown, Texas, some dogs overtook a roadrunner unable to get out of the way because of a rattlesnake in its mouth. They killed the bird before men could stop them. After a photograph was taken of the dead bird with the snake dangling out of its bill, the snake was extracted and measured. It was eighteen inches long and had four or five rattles.

For many years I have hoped to come upon a paisano-rattlesnake combat—just as I have hoped to come upon two buck dear with antlers locked in mortal combat. The witnessing of either phenomenon depends so much upon chance that only a few individuals among many who spend their lives out of doors happen upon the scene at the right time. I have questioned scores of *hombres del campo*—men of range and countryside—about paisano-rattlesnake fights, and I have the testimony of several whose word cannot be doubted.

In October, 1932, Bob Dowe, of Eagle Pass, a strong-bodied and strong-minded man who had had a great deal of experience on ranches on both sides of the Rio Grande, told me that he once saw a paisano kill a rattlesnake about three and a half feet long. The fight was in a cow pen. The bird in its maneuvers raised a great amount of dust. With wings extended and dragging in the dust, it would run at the snake, aiming at its head. The snake struck blindly, several times hitting the paisano's wings, without effect, of course. Finally the bird pecked a hole in the snake's head and punctured the brain. It ate the brain but nothing else. The shrike, or butcher bird, is said to thus eat only the brains of small birds it kills, which may sometimes be seen hanging intact on thorns or the barbs of barbed wire fences—a manner of wasteful selection employed also by plainsmen who shot down giant buffaloes merely for the tongues and by those ancient gourmands who banqueted on nightingale tongues.

I have heard of the paisano's killing little chickens and eating only the brain. I do not know this to be a fact, however. I know that on the ranch of my boyhood and youth in Live Oak County we had many chickens and many paisanos, which often came among the chickens, big and little; the chickens never seemed to pay the paisanos any more attention than they paid the blackbirds, doves and quail. Between the pens at the stables and the branding pens was about a hundred yards of old log fence that had been built as part of a little horse pasture before the advent of barbed wire. In this old fence there were paisano nests every year. Snakes—particularly chicken snakes, but also sometimes coach-whips and bull snakes—ate eggs and little chickens; coyotes were a constant menace; but we never thought of the paisanos as being destructive to the chickens. The snake's most vulnerable part, his head, reminds me of a saying made by Victoriano Huerta while he was president of the southern republic: "*Mexico es come un serpiente; toda la vida es en la cabeza.*" (Mexico is like a serpent; all the life is in its head—the capital city.)

And this brings me to Don Alberto Guajardo, of Piedras Negras, one of the best nature observers I have ever met. "I have never seen a paisano kill a rattlesnake," he said, in February, 1935, "but not long ago a boy on my ranch told me he had seen this thing so often reported by others. I asked him many questions to trap him in falsehood. In the end I was convinced that he was telling the truth. The boy said he first heard the paisano and then, looking about, saw the combat very near. With outstretched wings the paisano was making passes at the snake, evidently with intention of infuriating him. After many violent lunges, the snake subsided. Then with a swift leap the bird lit on the neck of the snake, seeming to hold it in his claws, while he pecked at the head two or three times. The writhing body of the snake made the bird leap away. A drop of blood showed on the head of the snake, and now it tried to hide its head under its body. Again the paisano attacked. This time he killed the snake. He ate only the brains."

Mrs. Bruce Reid, of Port Arthur, who has raised several roadrunners as well as many other birds and who has supplied much information to the Biological Survey, tells of having witnessed two paisano-rattlesnake combats. In each instance, the snake's head was bruised and bloody. One rattler, about three feet long, sought refuge in some cactus, but the paisano, as hot after it as a hound after a wildcat, got to it. In its writhings, the rattler brushed an irregular line of dead cactus leaves about its body—a circumstance that might account for the tradition of a cactus corral.

Sometimes the paisano is described as giving a "war dance" about the rattler to confuse and infuriate him. Wild turkeys are said to make attacks, occasionally, on rattlesnakes in much the same manner.

In the spring of 1932 Ellen Schulz Quillin, botanist, something of a naturalist, and director of the excellent Witte Museum in San Antonio, was quoted in an article appearing in the San Antonio *Express* as saying that while the paisano is an avid destroyer of field pests, there was little foundation for the belief that it kills rattlesnakes. Within a few days she received a letter from Alfred Toepperwein, rancher of Bulverde, Bexar County. Toepperwein wrote that he had shot many of the birds while riding in his pasture but that a single experience had put a stop to all shooting. His letter as quoted in the *Express* on March 17, 1932, reads:

"One day I saw one of the birds, feathers turned forward like an angry deer turns its hair, jumping up and down, back and forth. I paid no attention, but pulled my .45 and fired, missing the bird barely by an inch. The bird, not a bit frightened, kept its feathers up and kept jumping towards the same place. Then the rattlesnake story I had heard several times came to my memory. I went to the place and found a rattlesnake almost dead. I have killed no more chaparral birds since then."

I might adduce further evidence, considered by me unimpeachable, from Nat Gunter, rancher at Balmorhea, Texas, John

Wildenthal, deputy sheriff at Cotolla, Texas, and other men, but I will conclude the testimony by a quotation from *Time* magazine, March 7, 1938, which reproduced also a picture, not fabricated, showing a roadrunner about to leap at a rattler, more than twice as long as the bird, with head and forepart raised to strike. "Last week," the article runs, "a full-length documentary film on Mexican animals, produced by Brothers Stacy and Horace Woodard, made the roadrunner-rattlesnake story a little less tall but no less telling. *The Adventures of Chico* shows ten-year-old Goatherd Chico taking his siesta, guarded by his roadrunner pet. A rattlesnake approaches. Without hesitation the bird attacks, head feathers fanned and wings tensely spread. Like a matador, it lures the snake into striking, easily swings out of reach. Like a matador, it waits and feints till the enemy tires, then kills with swift skill."

The filmers of this scene spent a year in Mexico taking animal pictures. The relation of the boy Chico to the bird may easily have been arranged, but the fight between snake and bird admits of no faking. The story of how a sleeping shepherd awakes to find a rattlesnake threatening him and is saved by the timely intervention of the snake's inveterate enemy is common. Jack H. Lee in his book of verse, *West of Powder River* (New York, 1933), has a ballad relating the incident.

An old Mexican in northern Coahuila told me that one time he found four paisano eggs in a nest and put them under a hen and hatched them out. They grew up to be pets around his lone *jacal* (cabin) out in the chaparral. One time after dinner, he said, he went to take a siesta under a runty mesquite tree not far from the *jacal*. He was sleeping soundly when the noise made by the paisanos awoke him. Impatiently, he gave them a scare; then he discovered that they had three medium-sized rattlesnakes cornered. He was convinced that the birds had saved his life. He did not explain why there were not four rattlesnakes instead of just three.

Leaving man out of the picture entirely, the truth is being proven, and there is no reason why ornithologists should henceforth use the words "seems," "perhaps," or "it is generally said" in modifying remarks about lethal combats between paisanos and rattlesnakes.

II. FOLKLORE

The Corral of Thorns

If I were writing an article strictly scientific, I should at this point drop the rattlesnake; but any animal is interesting to man not only for the facts about him but for what human beings associated with the animal have taken to be facts. "No man," Mary Austin says, "has ever really entered into the heart of any country until he has adopted or made up myths about its familiar objects." Hardly any established fact about the paisano is as familiar to the public as some form of the story about the bird's corralling a rattlesnake with cactus joints and then either killing it or making it kill itself. The bird is certainly more interesting for this commonly believed and more commonly told story. It has appeared various times in print, nowhere so divertingly told as by The Old Cattleman in Alfred Henry Lewis's *Wolfville*, which account I borrowed for *On the Open Range*. Other forms of the story appear in other books for children: to cite two recent ones, *Indians of the Pueblos*, by Therese O. Deming, and *Thinking, Speaking and Writing* (Book Two), by Jameson, Clark and Veit.

Nor am I prepared to deny that paisanos ever corral rattlesnakes. Perhaps they could. The act would be no more of a strain on nature than the building of a web by a spider to entrap a fly. It is claimed that snakes hear through the ground and that a sleeping rattlesnake could not be corralled without his becoming aroused. I do not know. The roadrunner runs lightly. But I make no argument, no denial. The stories are interesting. They are part of the history of the most interesting bird of the Southwest. Some of the narratives are very circumstantial—as all good narratives must be.

In May, 1933, I was introduced to E. V. Anaya, a practicer in international law of Mexico City. He was reared on a hacienda in Sonora, where he was associated with Opata Indians. He is as swart as a desert Indian himself and as decisive as Mussolini. The Indians and Mexicans of Sonora call the paisano *churella*, he said.

"Have you ever seen one kill a rattlesnake?" he asked. "No? Well, I have—once.

"I was out gathering pitayas," he went on. The pitaya, or pitalla, is a cactus fruit. "It was in the month of May—the month of pitayas. I was just a boy, about 1908. I was with an Opata Indian.

"Just as we got to the top of a mesa, the Indian very cautiously beckoned me to come nearer. Then when I was close to him, he whispered, 'See the churella.'

" 'Churella,' I replied. 'What of it?' The bird is so common in that country that little attention is usually paid to it.

" 'This one is killing a rattlesnake,' the Indian spoke softly. 'Let us watch.'

"We crept up silently, until we were within twelve or fifteen yards of the churella. A rattlesnake lay coiled on the ground, out in a little open space, apparently asleep. The churella had already gathered a great many joints of the cholla cactus and had outlined a corral around the snake. The corral was maybe three feet in diameter.

"The churella was working swiftly. Cholla was growing all around us and the joints were lying everywhere on the ground. The bird would carry a joint in its long beak without getting pricked. He built the little corral up, laying one joint on top of another, until it was maybe four inches high. Then he dropped a joint right on top of the sleeping snake. The snake moved, and when he did, the spines found the openings under his scales. The snake became frantic and went to slashing against the corral. That made it more frantic. Then the churella attacked it on the head and had little trouble in killing it. The spines made it practically defenseless."

If a roadrunner were going to use any kind of cactus to corral or torment a rattlesnake with, cholla joints would surely be best suited to the purpose. Each joint is so spined that if one single thorn takes hold of an object and the object moves the least bit, another and then several other thorns will dig in. Instead of throwing off the cholla joint, movement causes the one thorn in the flesh to act as a lever for giving more thorns entrance. In the bad cholla country of Sonora I have ridden a native horse, wary of the thorns, that, nevertheless, caught several in his pastern. Then the only thing to do was to dismount, get a stick, and with it jerk the cholla joint directly out. I have seen a cave in that same country with enough cholla joints heaped in it to fill a freight car. They had been placed there by rats. The Papago Indians used to dispose of their dead by laying the body on open ground and then heaping cholla over it—a thorough protection against all beasts of prey.

Snakes, rattlesnakes included, eat rats. All kinds of rats in all parts of the Southwest build about their nests a defense of thorns against snakes and other enemies. The rattlesnake may not, as folk theory once held, be sensitive to the tickling of a hair rope; but he can't go like a shadow through an armor of thorns.

Not long after Lawyer Anaya of Mexico City told me his story of the churella, the cholla, and the rattlesnake, I went to see General Roberto Morelos Zaragoza in the city of San Luís Potosí. An ardent hunter and outdoors man, he was issuing monthly a small magazine called *Aire Libre* (Open Air), made up of hunting and fishing chronicles. The general's primary interest in wild life was that of a killer, but he was naturally alert, and had made many observations on the habits of animals.

He called the paisano a *faisán* (pheasant)—the name the bird goes by around San Luís Potosí. "Yes," he said, "with my own eyes I have seen a *faisán* kill a very large rattlesnake. The *faisán* took a tuna (the Indian fig, or apple) from a *cardón* cactus, dropped it on the neck of the snake, and while the snake was maddened by the thorns pecked it to death on top of the head."

An old German mining engineer named Engelbert Brokhurst, widely traveled, learned, observant, and cranky, whom I met in Mazatlan, told me that Indians of the West Coast of Mexico regard the paisano as a sacred bird and will not kill it. They all say that the bird corrals sleeping rattlesnakes and then torments them to death with thorns.

The evidence, however, is by no means all from Indians and Mexicans. *Black Range Tales* (New York, 1936) is a book of reminiscences by an old-time prospector and miner named James A.

McKenna, of New Mexico. "One spring in Lake Valley," he relates, "my partner and I watched a pair of roadrunners. Morning after morning we met them outside the tunnel where we worked. Not far from the mouth of the tunnel a rattlesnake used to climb on a rock to take a sleep in the early morning sun. [They were out-of-the-ordinary outdoors men not to kill it.] It soon became plain to us that the roadrunners had spotted the rattlesnake. One morning we saw them making a corral of cholla joints and thorns around the snake. How quietly they worked until the crude circle was nearly three inches high! Then both birds ran with a strange cry towards the cholla coral, waking up the rattlesnake, which struck instantly. Hundreds of fine sharp thorns were buried in the tender underside of the snake's throat. The more he twisted and turned, the deeper the spines of the cholla worked into his neck. After a half-hour of writhing, he lay still. The roadrunners hung around long enough to make sure he was dead; then they hacked him to pieces, which they carried off to feed their young. Prospectors always keep on the lookout for rattlesnakes if they take note of a pair of roadrunners in the vicinity of the camp."

Yet some critic has spoiled this story by claiming that a paisano does not have enough force in his beak to tear the flesh from a rattlesnake carcass.

Something of a variation in the use of cactus comes in an account written by Hampton McNeill of the Texas Panhandle. Hunting quail one day, McNeill heard "some kind of unfamiliar chuckling" going on just over a small mound. He stepped up on top of the mound, and there a "chaparral and a rattlesnake were fighting for life and death. The snake was completely encircled by cactus leaves. Its head had been pierced so many times by the cactus thorns that a match-head could hardly have been placed anywhere on it without covering a thorn hole." The narrator probably had no magnifying glass to look at the holes. Remember, however, that the prickly pear in the Panhandle grows low and scrawny; the leaves (known to botany as pads) are not strongly jointed.

"The chaparral would run up to a cactus bush, take a good hold on a leaf with its bill, shake the leaf loose, and then return to the scene of battle. Using this thorny leaf as a shield, the chaparral would rile the rattler into striking at him. After the snake had struck several times, the bird would lay the leaf down near the snake.

"The chaparral repeated this action several times. In the course of time, the rattler seemed to become completely exhausted, for he would no longer offer resistance when the chaparral returned with more cactus leaves. Having brought up two or three leaves without arousing the snake to action, he then disappeared in the sage brush. The snake was not dead, but I put him out of his misery."

Philip Ashton Rollins, in his generally excellent treatise, *The Cowboy,* describes still another mode of attack whereby the bird used thorns but does not bother with a pen. "The chaparral-cock," he says, "might stop its hunt for bugs, seize in its bill a group of cactus thorns, spread its wings wide and low, and, running more speedily than could any race horse, dodging as elusively as does heat-lightning, drive those thorns squarely into the snake's open mouth, peck out both the beady eyes, and then resume the hunt for bugs." According to the *gente,* a paisano upon finding a rattlesnake charming a rabbit, slips up and jabs a cactus joint into the waiting jaws of the would-be-killer.

The more usual end, perhaps, of the story of the rattler corralled by cactus spines is that narrated by The Old Cattleman in Alfred Henry Lewis' *Wolfville.* "At last comes the finish, and matters get dealt down to the turn. The rattlesnake suddenly crooks his neck, he's so plumb locoed with rage an' fear, an' socks his fangs into himself. That's the fact; bites himse'f, an' never lets up till he's dead."

I am not sure of final findings but I have been informed by scientific men that rattlesnake venom injected into the blood system of the very creature carrying the venom will be as deadly as in the blood system of any other animal. Such an end is not impossible. According to the tales, then, there are three possible ways for the rattler to die after paisanos have corralled him. (1) He may bite himself to death; (2) he may have his brain punctured by the bird's beak just as it is sometimes punctured without benefit of the corral; (3) he may be brained by thorns themselves.

What would happen if a rattlesnake bit the paisano in a vital spot may be deduced from an account in a book first published in Cincinnati in 1847, by C. Donavan, *Adventures in Mexico.* During his captivity in the Mexican War, Donavan visited an extensive botanical garden near San Luís Potosí, and there became acquainted with *huaco*—the most celebrated herbal cure for snakebite in Mexico and the southern tip of Texas. The discovery of the medicinal qualities of *huaco,* Donovan learned from the natives, was attributed to a bird that "feeds upon snakes and reptiles." Indians in the far past noticed that after a combat with a snake the bird would "search for the herb and eat it." Thus they learned from the bird, which Donavan calls the guayaquil but which is patently the paisano, the "sure remedy" for snakebite.

From the paisano, too—perhaps—certain Indians of the Southwest took the idea of putting long fringes on their moccasins and leggings as a protection against snakebite, the fringes suggesting feathers to the snake. Indeed, the wands used to calm rattlesnakes in the Hopi snake dance are of feathers, though they are of the eagle, which preys on snakes.

Other Lore

The very track of the roadrunner has among some of the Pueblo Indians of New Mexico given the bird significance and protection. This track shows two toes pointed forward and two backward, and Indians duplicate it on the ground all about the tent of one of their dead so as to mislead evil spirits seeking the course taken by the departed soul. Again, an Indian mother will tie the bright feathers of a roadrunner on the cradle-board so as to confuse evil spirits that would trouble her child's mind. Here the feathers signify the track, which not only points two ways but is four-directioned like the Cross.

In his "Report" on New Mexico, printed by the United States Government in 1848 and containing much on the fauna and flora

One of the many paisanos that adorn our office

of the region, Lieutenant J.W. Albert inserts a curious note concerning the bird's toes. Although they are, he quotes an informer as saying, "disposed in opposite pairs, as in other species of the cuckoo family, yet the outer hind toe, being reversible and of great flexibility, is in either position (whether pointed forward or backward) aptly applied in climbing or perching as well as on the ground. Thus he at times pitches along the ground in irregular hops; again, when the outer hind toe is thrown forward, he runs smoothly and with such rapidity as always to be able to elude a dog in the chaparral without taking wings." Did anybody ever see paisano tracks with three toes pointing forward?

Certain of the Plains Indians hung the whole skin of the roadrunner—to them the medicine bird—over a lodge door to keep out henchmen of the Bad God. Before setting out on an expedition, a warrior would attach one or more paisano feathers to his person. At least one tribe of California Indians used the feathers for adorning their headdress—probably with symbolic intent also.

An Austrian mining engineer I met in Mexico City told me that during many years of mule-back travel through mountains all over Mexico he had heard *mozas*—those indispensable muleteer guides and servants—in different parts of the country say that the *corre camino* is a guide for mankind, that if a lost man will find one of the birds and follow it, it will lead him to a trail. The *corre camino* not only fancies trails but follows them for the tumblebugs (beetles) and other insects that come to feed on the droppings of pack animals passing over the trail.

One time while I was crossing the Sierra Madre from the Pacific Ocean to the city of Oaxaca, I saw three Indian men at a stream. Their shirtless torsos revealed them as fine physical specimens, and after I had, with permission, taken a picture of them, I asked which of the three was the *jefe* (chief). The two end men pointed to the center man. I gave him a package of cigarettes and rode on, trotting to catch up with my companions and the pack mules. The *jefe* kept at my heels. He had held this position for perhaps half an hour when I noticed a roadrunner just ahead of me about to cross the trail from right to left. The Indian picked up two or three rocks and chunked at the bird with intense earnestness, missing him, however.

I was surprised, and asked the Indian why he wanted to kill a bird that brought good luck. He said something in reply that I could not understand. He could speak only a few incoherent Spanish words and talked in his own dialect. Arriving in Oaxaca, I had considerable conversation with a savant named Paul Van de Velde. He told me that the Indians of that region claimed the bird brought good luck if it crossed the road from left to right but bad luck if from right to left. I remembered then that the bird my Indian escort tried so earnestly to kill was crossing from right to left. He was trying to prevent bad luck from coming to me.

Yet in many places in Mexico the bird is regarded as benevolent without respect to the direction in which it may be traveling. "Look, *patrón*," I have had a *mozo* say to me in the morning, "Look at that paisano over there. We'll have good traveling today."

A paisano that stays about the house is often cherished by Mexicans as much as the swallow building its nest under the shed roof—the swallow that always betokens good fortune. Among Mexicans on the Texas border the paisano takes the place of the stork in bringing babies into the world.

The bird is a true *cristiano*. One time Mr. Boyles of the Witte Museum in San Antonio, while out hunting specimens, stopped at a shack occupied by some poor white people. The woman here told him that nearly every day they saw one or more paisanos stop at noon and bow their heads to pray. "Is that what the paisanos are doing when they make bows?" Mr. Boyles asked. "Yes," the woman replied, "the Mexicans all believe the paisano stops at noon to pray, no matter where he is." The American woman's expression as she gave this information showed she wanted mighty bad to believe the Mexicans.

As has already been said, the very virtues of the bird may at times prove his death. The Tarahumare Indians of the Sierra Madre, perhaps the most remarkable runners in the world, regard the flesh of the paisano as not only wholesome but conducive to speed and endurance.

The eating of a paisano roasted over the coals is supposed by some Mexicans to cure the itch. This is a local cure based on a legend that centuries and centuries ago a tramp came to an Indian village, the inhabitants of which welcomed and fed him. Before long an epidemic of severe itch broke out among them. The medicine men finally examined the body of the tramp and found it covered with itch. He had brought the curse. They turned him into a paisano, killed, roasted and ate him—and were all cured.

The paisano cure for boils is known all over the Southwest and Mexico. The fifteen-year-old son of the owner of a big ranch in West Texas had been with the cow outfit for two months. Then he became so plagued with Job's worst affliction that he had to be carried to the ranch in a car. One of the *gente* went out and shot two paisanos. The boy ate them fried and got well of the boils almost at once. Boiling, though, is usually better than frying; but any way taken, paisano meat beats sarsaparilla all hollow as a blood purifier.

Mexican women grow flowers no matter if their home is only a box car housing a railroad construction crew; perhaps it is fortunate for the paisano that these cherishers of flowers do not set out many shrubs and trees. If you want such to grow, "kill a paisano, cut out the entrails, and put them at the bottom of the hole, just under the roots."

In northern Mexico I have several times heard of the wonderful fighting cock, high jumping and lightning-quick with his spurs, produced by crossing a paisano with a game chicken. But I have never been able to come upon this bird—just as I have never been able to come upon the marvelous hybrid resulting from a cross between a ram and a sow. A young man named Ramón who traveled with me into the desert of the Bolsón de Mapimí claimed to have once owned a very, very superior fighting cock out of an egg laid by a game hen fertilized by a pet paisano. He kept the origin of this extraordinary *gallo* a secret, he said, and won many bets off him. I might have been more inclined to credit Ramón's account had he not asserted that a paisano when run down will turn over on its back, hiding its head in grass, and stick up its rusty legs so that they appear to be dry weed-stalks or twigs. Yet, after all, why shouldn't a paisano use its legs as camouflage? One scared off a nest has been known to try to toll the intruder away by simulating a broken leg, as some flying birds simulate broken wings.

An even more wonderful bird than the paisano game cock is the *pájaro cu*.[1] Nobody claims to have ever seen the *pájaro cu*. In the beginning of things he was naked, and all the birds held a kind of convention at which the owl proposed that each bird chip in a feather or two and thus make up a decent covering for the poor naked one. The peafowl objected to the proposal, arguing that a suit of so many colors would make the bird impossibly vain. But King Eagle, overruling the objection, ordered the feathers donated, provided two birds would stand as sponsors for the *pájaro cu* and guarantee his decent conduct. The paisano and the owl volunteered as sponsors. The new plumage was brighter and more varied in colors than a rainbow. It went to the *pájaro cu*'s head, and he offended many birds, especially the peafowl, by his vanity. King Eagle called another convention of the birds to consider the case, but the *pájaro cu* was not present.

Then the sponsors, the paisano and the owl, were ordered to produce him. They could not find him. They have been looking for him ever since. The owl at night calls *whu, whu, whu,* the closest he can get to *cu, cu, cu,* and the paisano runs up and down the roads by day, looking this way and that way, and shooting [sic] out like the sounds of a *matrace,* his *cru, cru, cru,* the nearest he can get to *cu, cu, cu.* A good deal of the time, though, he seems to say *crut, crut, crut,* rolling and trilling and twirling the *r* sound with such mastery that you know Spanish is his native tongue.

Although not at all a pheasant, early Spaniards are said on good authority to have called the paisano *faisán real.* And a "royal pheasant" indeed this bird that now runs the roads once considered himself, as Jovita González[2] heard the story among the border people. He had proud ways, as he still has at times, walking in the evening time with crest erected, long tail switching from side to side, lifting one foot deliberately before the other, and often raising himself to a stately height. He would not speak to such humble birds as the sparrows. The dove was too modest for him to notice, and the wren too pert. But all the bright, lofty and noble birds he addressed with cousinly familiarity. It was "Good morning, Paisano Zenzontle, and how is your Lordship," as he noticed a mockingbird singing on a high twig, or "How are you, Paisano?" ruffling his throat feathers to vie with the colors of the cardinal he thus addressed. Even the eagle was *paisano* to him.

One day while this king of the bird world had his lords and nobles together discussing grave matters of state, the vain fellow who considered himself a "royal pheasant" stalked into their presence without announcement, cocked his head over with the same ceremony he would use in looking at an earthworm crawl out of moist ground, and said, "How fares my countryman? And, my *paisanos* all, how are you?"

The eagle was simply furious at such familiarity. He screamed, "Out of my presence, you low-born thing of the ground. Never again presume to be a *faisán.* Henceforth stay on the ground where you belong. Forget to try to fly. Feed on tarantulas, scorpions, and beetles. Go."

The poor bird tried to fly from the courtroom, but could not. His wings had lost their strength. He had to run out of the room like a chicken. He has belonged to the ground ever since. And the name *paisano* that both people and birds call him by now is a mockery of the presumption he so long ago paid for.

Yet people like the paisano. When one man in this bird's wide range meets another that he feels warm sympathy for, he may say, "We speak the same language." But, if there is great gusto in the correspondence of spirits, he will say, "*Nosotros somos paisanos*—we are fellow countrymen—we belong to the same soil." And we true paisanos of mankind include in our kinship the paisanos of birdkind.

Endnotes

1. Riley Aiken tells the story of "El Pájaro Cú" in *Puro Mexicano* (Publication of the Texas Folk-Lore Society, 1935), pp. 19–20; I tell it in my book, *Tongues of the Monte,* pp. 100–103.
2. "Tales and Songs of the Texas-Mexicans," by Jovita González, in *Man, Bird and Beast,* Pub. No. VIII of the Texas Folk-Lore Society, Austin, 1930, pp. 92–93.

[This essay on the roadrunner appeared, somewhat abbreviated, in the *Natural History Magazine,* New York, September, 1939.]

Paisano hand-carved out of ironwood, a treasured souvenir the Secretary-Editor purchased in Mexico during the 2005 meeting in El Paso

Trooper Sancho Mazique of the Tenth Cavalry

3

CAVALRY TRADITIONS ON THE TEXAS FRONTIER

by James T. Matthews

On the late show, John Ford's dog-faced soldiers of the U.S. Cavalry ride forth against the Indians of the Texas frontier. Again and again, they cross the screen on campaigns of heroism and sacrifice in battle. Watching these films, it is easy to forget that duty on the frontier was more often a monotonous routine beginning when the soldiers awoke to the sound of the "morning gun," followed by "the tap of the drum at daylight, the calling of the roll at six, the breakfast at seven, the drill at nine with another at three. . . ."[1] Between drills, those soldiers not on guard assembled to perform various fatigue duties, including the cleaning and repair of equipment and buildings, hauling wood and supplies, and care of the animals. Often the heroism of the cavalryman was demonstrated by his ability to survive the boredom and discomfort of frontier life. Many of the traditions associated with the mounted service developed from efforts to combat the isolation and routine encountered while guarding the vast, unsettled lands.

Cavalry service on the Texas frontier began in 1854, when the First and Second Cavalry were authorized by Congress to patrol boundaries greatly expanded by the war with Mexico. The Second Cavalry, known as "Jeff Davis' Own" after Secretary of War Jefferson Davis, was organized specifically for service in Texas. This was to be an offensive unit, operating from unprotected outposts, to strike out against Indian raiders wherever necessary along the frontier.[2] Under field officers such as Colonel Albert Sidney Johnston, Lieutenant Colonel Robert E. Lee, and Major George H. Thomas, the

Second Cavalry swiftly developed a reputation which set the standard for future cavalry service on the frontier. When the Civil War began in 1861, the Second provided sixteen general officers from members of its staff, eleven to the South and five to the North.[3]

During the war, most of the frontier defense commitment was fulfilled by Texas state troops. Units such as Captain Robert B. Halley's ranger company from Bell County, known as the "Salado Mounted Troop," were organized for service on the Texas frontier. Halley's troop received the surrender of Camp Colorado from Captain Kirby Smith and then proceeded to Fort Chadbourne, where they relieved the U. S. troops providing garrison and patrol duties.[4] Throughout the war, companies of Texas cavalry maintained a frontier defense which allowed other Texan men to leave their families in relative safety while they served in every major theater of operations.

Oftentimes, veterans of the Mexican War or U. S. Army service volunteered for the Confederate frontier cavalry. George A. King had joined the regular U. S. Army as a bugler at age 15 in 1847. He remained on active duty with the army until 1857, when he was discharged at Fort Stanton, New Mexico. When the Civil War began, King was offered a commission by the Union commander at Fort Stanton, which he refused. Instead, he joined Sibley's Confederate column in the invasion of New Mexico. When the Confederate army returned to Texas, King and his family followed. He settled his family in Bell County and later raised a Confederate cavalry company from that area, which he captained.[5]

Following the war's end in 1865, regiments of the U. S. Cavalry returned to service in Texas. Notable among these frontier troops were Colonel Ranald Mackenzie's Fourth Cavalry, which crossed the Mexican border several times in pursuit of Indian raiders, and Colonel Benjamin Grierson's Tenth Cavalry, a regiment composed entirely of black troops who proved themselves so well disciplined and capable in battle that the Indians openly showed their respect for these "buffalo soldiers."

The cavalryman's pride and his dependence on his horse often meant that his mount received first priority in care and equipage. The Confederate cavalry was often described as being well

Colonel Benjamin Grierson

mounted, but poorly equipped and armed. Every company recruited its own farrier, and many also had a saddler and a blacksmith on their muster rolls.[6] The Second Cavalry, in purchasing horses, chose a different color for each company. Captain Earl Van Dorn's Company A, mounted on grey steeds, became known as the Mobile Greys. This tradition continued after the Civil War. Captain Louis Carpenter's Company H, Tenth Cavalry received orders designating them the "black horse troop" in July 1867. Each trooper was to be provided a fresh black steed, fully equipped. In this case, discrimination against the African American soldiers surfaced in the matter of supply. As Carpenter later complained to Colonel Grierson, "Since our first mount in 1867 this regiment has received nothing but broken down horses and repaired equipment as I am willing to testify. . . ."[7] Some of the horses apparently were even rejected mounts from the Seventh Cavalry.

Horses were not the only animals common on a frontier outpost. Dogs followed the cavalry wherever they rode. Captain Robert G. Carter was presented a half-breed Chihuahua as a pet for his young child. The baby had just become comfortable with the dog when the Carters were presented with another pet by the men of his troop. This was "a wee, diminutive brown bear cub, but a few days old. He had small gimlet eyes and was all legs, head and hair. The baby loved both of her pets. . . ."[8] At this time, Fort Richardson where Carter was stationed had a menagerie consisting of "a deer, two fawns, three brown bear cubs, a buffalo calf, three old bears, one coyote, two wolf pups, an eagle, two wild cats or kittens, and many half-breed wolf dogs."[9]

The regiments of cavalry formed for frontier service were usually organized into ten companies or troops, designated by the letters A through K. There was no Company J, as the letters I and J were too similar and could be easily confused on a handwritten return or muster roll. Cavalry recruits came from every possible lifestyle and occupation. Many were immigrants from Ireland, Germany, Scandinavia, or Italy. Some enlisted rather than serving prison sentences.

Unfamiliarity with military procedures often produced amusing results. In learning the routine of drill, new noncommissioned officers were heard to order their squads, "Get into rows," or "Go endways." A novice officer attempted to order his column left or right by yelling "Gee" or "Haw." One raw recruit even reported to his commanding officer that he thought he heard the enemy "cocking" their cannons in preparation for the coming fight.[10]

Veterans sometimes broke the daily monotony by various means of initiating the new recruits. In the Fourth Cavalry riding the buffalo calf became a tradition. The calf's "hump made him so elusive that the recruit had no seat at any time. A camel would have been a luxurious rocking chair. By a series of wild plunges, sky rocket pitches, and catapults he . . . hit the ground with a cold dull thud."[11] No recruit ever fully mastered the buffalo calf.

In contrast to the large scale destruction and death experienced during the Civil War, service on the Texas frontier rarely led to death in battle. At the Battle of the Wichita Village in 1858, Captain Van Dorn lost one officer and four enlisted men. Yet, this engagement is believed to have dealt a blow from which the Comanches never recovered. Still, the possibility of death was always present and soldiers knew that they "might be killed before night, and it didn't do to let our minds rest too much on the solemnity of the fact."[12] In the first three-and-a-half years of active service at Fort Concho, only six soldiers died of gunshot wounds.

During the same period, five died from diarrhea and dysentery, and eight from typhoid. At Fort Davis, almost twice as many soldiers reported to sick call for diarrhea as for any other single disease. It appeared that the army rations of beef, bacon, hardtack, beans, and coffee were as likely a cause of disability and death as wounds received in an Indian attack.[13]

Beef and bacon became the staple of the soldiers' diet on the Texas frontier. While the meat was frequently tough, Surgeon Samuel Smith of Fort Concho attributed many of the dietary problems to the method of food preparation, lamenting, "Grease predominates and the spatter of the frying pan can be heard uttering its dulcet tones every morning, noon & night."[14] In the common folklore of some black regiments, the words to mess call soon became, "Soupy, soupy, soupy, widout a single bean, Po'ky, po'ky, po'ky widout a streak ob lean."[15] Hardtack or pilot biscuits were frequently used in frontier service due to the high cost and general unavailability of flour. This was a cause for constant discontent among the troops, who complained that the hardtack was infested by weevils, too hard to chew, and even that some portions of one issue were "distinctly dated 30 B.C." "But hardtack was not so bad an article of food, even when traversed by insects . . . eaten in the dark, no one could tell the difference between it and hardtack that was untenanted."[16]

In an attempt to vary the unappetizing ration, many gardens were cultivated on post. Officers would pool their extra funds in order to purchase occasional delicacies. Some of the items bought to make meals more appealing included clams, sardines, salmon, dried apples, dried peaches, raisins, prunes, pickles, jellies, preserves, canned milk, tomatoes, green corn, green peas, potatoes, asparagus, onions, peaches, pineapples, cranberry sauce, oysters, and various spices. Yet, the supply of fresh vegetables and items such as butter, honey, and lemons remained scarce. Hunting and fishing became very popular as methods to supplement the rations and to escape the boredom of post life. In Texas, extended hunting expeditions were organized for every type of game, from buffalo to rabbit.

Drinking and gambling were also common activities on any isolated army post. There was often no money for months in between pay periods, and gamblers were reduced to playing for tobacco, cartridges, or even clothing. When whiskey was scarce, soldiers resorted to various homemade concoctions such as "white-mule" whiskey. Its ingredients are unknown, but "it was clear and white to look upon . . . mixed with water it became milky and gave out an odor suggestive of a turpentine emulsion. Of its drunk producing properties no doubt can exist . . ."[17]

The arrival of the army paymaster was anticipated not only to supplement drinking and gambling habits, but as a welcome change in the routine of army life. Troops were scheduled to be paid every two months, but on the frontier it was normally six to eight months between paydays. In the Confederate Trans-Mississippi Department, soldiers were actually paid only once in 1863, once in 1864 and not at all in 1865.[18]

Even when it occurred at rare intervals, payday was a break in the monotony. Other attempts to provide a social life on post included dances, theatricals, and holiday celebrations. The Fourth of July, which was a favorite occasion at military posts across the nation, was often celebrated with horse races, foot races, and picnics. The Sixteenth Infantry band even provided entertainment for the first community Independence Day celebration in San Angelo. Cavalry troops frequently would alternate hosting dances on post, and abundant feasts of wild game were provided whenever successful hunters and fishermen returned from their expeditions.[19]

Music was another important diversion in the frontier army, even if its only accompaniment available was an occasional guitar or banjo played around the campfire. Before the Civil War, each regiment was authorized to have their own band. During the war, this became impractical and the authorization was reduced to one band for every brigade. After the war, bands were no longer authorized, but they had become so vital to morale that many commanders detailed soldiers with musical ability to band duty and used personal and regimental funds to provide band instruments. Despite government cutbacks, cavalry troops continued to perform their duties to such popular tunes as "The Girl I Left Behind Me" and "The Regular Army, Oh!" Some regiments had a mounted band that routinely traveled between the isolated outposts manned by the troopers. At various times during their periods of service, the Fourth and Tenth Cavalry each had a regimental band stationed at Fort Concho. Bands played when the troops entered the post or left, during formal parades, or just to entertain the garrison.[20] Colonel Mackenzie maintained an active band throughout the Fourth Cavalry's frontier service. While it has yet to be documented, there are tales that at least one of the band members also played the bagpipes for Mackenzie on appropriate occasions.

Colonel Ranald Mackenzie

All of these traditional activities helped ease the rigorous boredom of frontier life during almost forty years of cavalry service in Texas. By 1875, the Comanches had been confined to reservations in Indian Territory. In January 1881, a company of Texas Rangers rode into the Sierra Diablo, engaged, and defeated the remnants of Victorio's Apache band in the last Indian battle fought in the state of Texas. The Indian threat had vanished entirely from the Texas frontier. The rough, desolate cavalry life that had caused Robert E. Lee to despair of ever being able to have his wife join him while stationed in Texas was gone by 1890.[21]

In the old movies, the narrator states that wherever the cavalry went, that place became part of the United States of America. In truth, the survival of the frontier regulars on the rugged lands of West Texas did open to settlement such vast areas as the Big Bend, the Concho Valley, and the South Plains. Their outposts have long been abandoned, but in their place stand cities and towns such as San Angelo, El Paso, Abilene, Colorado City, and Jacksboro. The frontier experience was often difficult, tedious, and for most there was little glory involved. Despite these hardships, regiments like the Second, Fourth, and Tenth Cavalry and the Confederate irregulars did survive to bring settlement and civilization to the frontier regions of Texas.

Endnotes

1. W.W. Heartsill. *Fourteen Hundred and 91 Days in the Confederate Army*. Jackson, TN: McCowat-Mercer Press, 1953.
2. "Report of the Secretary of War," December 4, 1854, Thirty-third Congress, Second Session. Government Printing: Office, Washington, DC.
3. Harold B. Simpson. *Cry Comanche*. Hillsboro, TX: Hill Junior College Press, 1979. 19–25.
4. George W. Tyler. *The History of Bell County*. San Antonio, TX: The Naylor Company, 1936. 204–205.
5. *Confederate Veteran*. September, 1906. 34.

6. Confederate Muster Rolls for Lane's, Stone's, Baylor's and Phillips' Regiments. National Archives, Washington, DC; George Peris Brown. *Collin County in Pioneer Times.* McKinney, TX: Collin County Historical Society, 1975. 54.
7. Simpson. *Cry Comanche.* 31; Muster Roll for Company H, Tenth U.S. Cavalry, August 1867. U.S. Army Continental Commands, 1821–1920, RG 98 (National Archives); William H. Leckie. *The Buffalo Soldiers: A Narrative of the Negro Cavalry in the West.* Norman, OK: University of Oklahoma Press, 1967. 12–13, 51.
8. Robert G. Carter. *On the Border with Mackenzie.* Washington, DC: Eynon Printing Company, 1935. 330–331.
9. Ibid.
10. Edward Anderson. *Camp Fire Stories.* Chicago, IL: Star Publishing Company, 1896. 32–35.
11. Carter. 344–345.
12. Anderson. 166.
13. Medical Records for Fort Concho and Fort Davis, RG 94 (National Archives); Robert Wooster. *Soldiers, Sutlers and Settlers.* College Station, TX: Texas A&M University Press, 1987. 195–210.
14. Surgeon's Reports for 1877, 1878 and 1880, Medical History of Post, Fort Concho, RG 94 (National Archives).
15. John D. Billings. *Hardtack and Coffee.* Boston, MA: George M. Smith and Company, 1870. 114–116.
16. H.H. McConnell. *Five Years a Cavalryman.* Jacksboro, TX: J.N. Rogers and Company, 1889. 83.
17. Ibid. 60–61.
18. Ibid. 156–157.
19. Carter. 343.
20. Ibid. 332–340; McConnell. *Five Years a Cavalryman,* 91; Regimental Returns of the Fourth Cavalry, 1877–1889, RG 94 (National Archives).
21. Wooster. 38.

Johnny Campbell

4

GATHERING AT BILL'S: MAINTAINING THE FOLKLORE OF LIVE OAK COUNTY

by Mary Margaret Dougherty Campbell

Every evening about 5:45, a white pickup turns onto a caliche street on the edge of town in George West, Texas. The pickup creeps down the secluded street, turns to the right toward the fence, then backs into its self-assigned parking spot on the caliche driveway, almost but never quite hitting the small barbecue pit with its back bumper. The driver leisurely opens his door, eases out, and ambles to the bed of the pickup where he lifts one end of his ice chest lid and takes out two beers. He slides each into its own fat, Flying W Caprock Ranch rubber koozie (the only kind of koozie he'll use), closes the cooler, and walks toward the garage.

Just before reaching the garage, he sets the two beers on the stop-sign table, using the beer cans to anchor his scratch-off tickets. From there, he opens the garage door and takes out a white plastic chair. Back at the table, he sets the chair in front of the two beers, sits down, and waits—in the same spot every day. As he waits, he pops the top of one of the beers and takes a long sip. He takes his snuff can from his shirt-front pocket and arranges it on the table beside the koozies. Then, he takes out his pocket knife and scratches some of the tickets, which according to his superstition must be done while he's alone. That done, he sips again, scratches a few more tickets, and waits. (If he scratches them all at once, it's bad luck.) Each time he hears a vehicle on the paved road, he looks up to see if anyone is turning onto the caliche street. Meanwhile, he watches the birds and other wildlife in the yard and the goats across the fence. He also watches with a skeptical eye the neighbor to the north. He's convinced the man is part of the witness protection program because he lives behind three locked gates, has security cameras strategically placed on his property, and never acknowledges anyone. Thus, as he waits for company, he's got plenty to occupy his time: wildlife and secretive neighbors.

Sometimes the owner of the house at the end of this caliche street is home; sometimes he's not. It doesn't matter—Johnny Campbell's routine is the same whether Bill Phillips is there or not. Even if Bill is in the house, he may or may not sit with Johnny at the table in his driveway. Visitors have jokingly accused him more than once of being antisocial. When Bill is home, so is his dog. For a number of years he had Little Dog, who would join Johnny and the others in the evenings. Now it's Daisy, a fully grown black standard poodle who eagerly greets the late afternoon guests, chases her ball when someone will throw it, and chews Johnny's ABC gum after Johnny has chewed the flavor out. When pals Punkin and Dominga visit with their owners, young Daisy has a high time playing chase. One afternoon as Bill and Daisy puttered into the driveway in his 1987 faded-red Chevy pickup, Johnny observed with a grin, "That man and that dog do not go together."

In time, a vehicle turns off the paved road onto the caliche. Its occupant may be any one of many possible evening guests at Bill's. Regular visitors include Johnny's brother Billy the craftsman, David Huser the insurance salesman, Gene Chapline the attorney, Bobby Alaniz the restaurateur, neighbor Nona Schorp the landman, Johnny's son Cody the refinery worker/rancher, and me, Cody's wife the school teacher. Others are frequent visitors, like Johnny's son Casey and his fiancée Kody, or Gene's wife Josie the nurse/school board member. Representatives of other professions, families, and local color stop by once in a while for a visit, including cowboy Kenneth Gerfers, who might share a story about putting together a bunch of steers or having to ride some rank old horse no one else would ride, or offshore drilling rig motorman Randy "Mudcat" Bramblett and his girlfriend Pam, who may recount one of the four times she's been snake bitten. Even Bill's

A gathering of friends (Cody Campbell, Mudcat Bramblett, and Johnny Campbell) sharing stories, as Daisy watches

mother Lib graces the gathering now and then. Lib is known as "The Gray Lady," not so much for her beautiful hair but because, as Cody explains, "she's an unreconstructed Confederate; she's still convinced we won the war." Everyone snaps to attention when Lib is around. Discussing why people come over to Bill's, Billy observes that "the main reason people show up [is that] if you don't show up, they'll talk about you," to which Bill adds, "and you don't leave early." Occasionally Bill will look up, though, to find himself surrounded by Campbells. He rubs his head, chews on his cigar, and shrugs. He says, "Well, I was Charles Cecil's adopted son, anyway." He adds emphatically, "And besides, he left *me* his boots and hats—because they wouldn't fit either of you." (Charles

Cecil was Johnny and Billy's father.) Bill points out about the evening gatherings, however, that "it *happens* to be my house, but they're not comin' to *my house;* they're comin' to their grounds. If I ever sell this house, that's part of the deed."

This gathering has various monikers—the Round Table, the Twilight Gang, the Lagarto Club, the Liar's Club (a name, Gene points out, that is already taken by Mary Karr), the Board Meeting, and possibly more. Whatever it is called, the group is a delightful assemblage of knowledge, experience, expertise, education, and heritage. Passersby might wonder what this group does every day in that driveway. Well, they catch up on the latest community news, tell stories of days past, watch the birds that come to the yard each season, play with Daisy, have a few beers and, in general, relax and enjoy one another's company.

Whenever I have a local history question, I seek the collective memory and wisdom of this group. The regulars range in age from their mid-thirties to mid-sixties. What they have not lived through or personally experienced, they have heard from those who preceded them—or, they have made up. And they relish telling and retelling (and often retelling again) stories of people and events of their area. Billy contends that "it's interesting how many times you can hear the same story but it's never told the same way twice." They tell stories much like those who gather at the local Dairy Queen or coffee shop in George West or in any other town. The main difference in the make-up of the group at Bill's, though, is that they include women whereas most DQ and coffee shop groups are exclusively men. No one brings coffee, either. "It's bad for you," quips Johnny.

Their campfire (their front porch) is a driveway where they sit in plastic chairs—most of which have at least one duct-taped mended break. (Bill complains that his guests could at least buy him "chairs that don't break so easily.") They sit in these chairs around an old stop sign that used to sit atop a cable spool but now rests on a fancier white octagonal table David brought one day from a trash pile behind a local convenience store. Bill says that the old spool rotted, so when David saw the "old display table, [he] dug it up," loaded it into the back of his pickup, and hauled it over to Bill's. Most members have their usual places around the table. They are a predictable lot. Their feelings are hurt if anyone parks in their spot or sits in their place. Most people realize their mistake soon enough, however, from the looks on the regulars' face—and move.

They tell funny stories on others, on each other, and on themselves. Likewise, they speak of tragedy and loss. They offer advice to the younger ones. Together, they comprise a wealth of information—whether it is where to find good used tractor parts, who might have hay for sale at an affordable price, how much it rained in any given spot in the county last night, where so-and-so is buried, who built the first concrete water trough in the area, who ran for sheriff in 1946, how many children Henry and Gertrude had and whatever happened to each one. Maybe someone will ask a question such as, "Who started the saying around here 'He's all dressed up like Puss Erwin's hack driver'?" Inevitably someone in the group will remember. Once in a while, they are stumped, so to speak, on a question. "If a family branch is missing," muses Bill for example, "Bill Hardwick or Judge Holland has to be called in to set it straight." Robert "Judge" Holland knows all the family trees in all the neighboring counties. Bill also adds that if anybody needs to know the name of a local football player up to 1960, Bill Hardwick is the man with the answer. This group also discusses movies, often quoting entire sections of dialogue. They chat about whatever sport is in season (local teams, regional teams, national teams), about hunting of almost all kinds, current state and national events, how many cows were at the livestock sale that week and what the market was like (not to mention who brought in the biggest load), books, movies, relatives, and local gossip. If I have been out of town a few days, you can guess where I go to catch up on what I have missed.

Some of the storytellers are fond of center stage and will sabotage the story of another to gain or regain that attention. Recently,

David was telling about a young man from Beeville who wanted to be a rodeo clown until he met with an experience that made him change his mind. As David was relating the incident, Bill chimed in with a sly smirk, "Being a circus clown would have been a lot safer," folded his arms and placed his cigar back between his teeth, looking around to ensure that everybody had heard him. Distracted, and perhaps a bit perturbed, David looked at Bill with an almost hurt look and, with a sigh, resumed his story about the rodeo clown wannabe, the punch lost. One of David's storytelling assets is his uncanny ability to mimic the language and oral mannerisms of a host of individuals. He can have us doubled over in our chairs with our eyes watering from laughing hysterically at stories accompanied by his accurate personality portrayals of the characters. Bill maintains that another of David's assets is knowing where to find sweet corn. Bill says, "Huser pinpoints all the sweet corn in the county for the corn boil. Huser and the owner are the only ones in the county who know where it is, and sometimes only *Huser* knows where it is." And Huser does not reveal the secret. He does not keep all of the corn for himself; rather, he shares it with his friends.

To verify his corn authority, David tells of the time when two brothers near Beeville had quite a stand of sweet corn, and they had a family wedding one Saturday when the corn was ready. Since David had been invited to the wedding, he knew that the Mass was at 3:00 and the reception started at 5:00. He says, "I knew they may not all go to the wedding, *but* about 5:30 they'd ALL be at that reception drinkin' beer and not thinkin' about that corn." He laughs his jolly laugh: "*Every*body had corn that year!"

Poor Billy rarely can get a complete story told to the entire group because someone—usually his brother Johnny or his friend Bill—will start a story after Billy has begun his. Thus, two stories are going simultaneously. Others at the table will not get either complete story, trying to be polite to both tellers at once, looking back and forth from teller to teller as though watching a tennis match. Johnny and Bill apparently do this on purpose to make Billy mad, but he finishes his story despite their attempts at sabotage

All in good fun

and does not get mad because he is used to it. His view of the situation is "When they interrupt me it's usually because the other turd isn't listening or can't hear." Many of Billy's stories concern his days as a star athlete at George West High School and as a football player for the University of Houston Cougars. In fact, Billy was the first athlete from George West to ever play college ball. Other favorite topics of his pertain to his current leather or woodworking project or, as Johnny adds, "fighting major wars around the world since 1501." Sometimes, however, Billy and Bill turn on Johnny. Bill observes, "It kills Johnny because Billy and I team up on him sometimes. We high-five after a good comeback!" Gene, David, Bill, and Johnny come to Billy's creative defense by eagerly mentioning that Billy is the only one who makes rosaries out of horsehair and rawhide and that he is the "only living beer tab artist in the world—and he's running out of material."

Billy's not the only teller to have his stories interrupted. My son J. Michael observes that "Cody is funny, too, but when he tries to tell a story, Johnny or Bill interrupt with a funnier story than

Cody has. It is like a competition." It *is* a competition to them, but a friendly, entertaining one.

Having been a working cowboy most of his life and a ranch foreman, Johnny has many stories dealing with those experiences. In fact, he has published many of them in his two books of poetry and one novel (he has another on the way). Often his stories turn to day-working cattle with fellow cowboy and friend Bob Dougherty. Because they worked cattle together on ranches and smaller places throughout South Texas, Johnny has plenty of these tales. One, in particular, involves a group of spoiled cattle owned by a farmer of Polish descent. The cowboys had to rope each one in the herd, making for a long, tedious day. Johnny's finale to this story is: "Bohemians shouldn't be allowed to own cows. They can have all the pigs they want—but no cows." He also likes to talk about the days on the Ward Ranch near Vanderbilt where he was foreman. Actually, he speaks daily on a myriad of subjects.

But Johnny has stories told on himself, too. One of David's favorite Johnny stories is about the Christmas David talked Johnny into delivering sausage with him. Every year in December David goes to Karnes City and has sausage made, which he gives to his friends for Christmas. Their last stop that evening was at Bill's house (evidently no gathering that particular evening), already after dark. David could tell nobody was home, even though he saw Bill's wife Judy's car in the garage, so he got out of the pickup to leave some sausage in Bill's deep freeze. Since he thought nobody was home, Johnny paid no attention to what David was doing. David says, "He was fiddlin' with his snuff can or somethin' and wasn't watchin' what I was doin.'" When David returned to the pickup, he said, "Did you see Judy come to the door in that negligee? Man, you could see right through it!" Johnny never missed a beat. He said, "You don't have another link of that sausage, do you?"

Sometimes the Campbell brothers tell a story together. One family story they like to tell involves a relative and stolen horses. Sometime in the early 1900s, a cousin named Ethan stole a bunch of horses from the Army. He smeared mud across the US brand on

stories as well as adds the experiences we have had ourselves, to our own children—J. Michael and Maggie. Thus, oral history lives, legends grow, and oral tradition thrives. As long as that white pickup backs into that same spot every day and this group continues to gather, the folklore of Live Oak County will live.

[With approval by and contributions from the participants, June 2003.]

A WOMAN'S

TOUCH

Members of the Cooking Club: Mary Margaret Dougherty Campbell, Bill Phillips, Nona Schorp, and Dean Phillips

5

THE COOKING EXTRAVAGANZA: SEQUEL TO "GATHERING AT BILL'S"

by Mary Margaret Dougherty Campbell

The Lonely Hearts Supper Club, its original title, is a spin-off from the afternoon gathering at Bill's. Like a TV sitcom spin-off, the club's members are from the original group, with occasional guest appearances by members of the original cast.

The episode that sparked the spin-off involved one of Billy Campbell's creations in wood: a pasta drying rack crafted from a broken branch of a wild olive tree in Bill's front yard. E-Bay Bill had recently scored a pasta machine and was eager to put it to use; however, he had no means of drying the pasta—that is, until he casually mentioned to Billy that he would like to have a wooden drying rack AND just *happened* to have some wood for one. Always up for a creative challenge, Billy took the pasta rack instructions (which Bill also just *happened* to have), loaded up the wild olive branch, and went home, as Bill watched with his arms folded across his chest, wearing a satisfied smirk.

Upon his regular arrival at Bill's, Billy commonly emerges from his vehicle with some handicraft he wants to show off to the group—some type of leather or horse hair or wooden creation—so nobody was surprised when he arrived a few days later holding a wooden frame and a bunch of little sticks that looked like miniature dowel rods. Without a word, he set the frame on the stop-sign table and began laying the sticks across the frame in the grooves, examining the group with his peripheral vision to make sure everyone was watching. Curiosity killing these cats, Johnny finally asked, "What the hell *is* it?"

Before Billy could utter his answer, Bill appeared from the dark garage, quickly shuffling toward the table saying, "My drying rack!"

"Your *what?*" Johnny asked, as he wiped the tobacco juice from his chin.

"My drying rack for the pasta I'm gonna make with my new pasta machine!" Bill said as he grabbed the rack and began his examination.

Silent stares all around.

Intrigued, Nona wanted to know how it all worked. She had never eaten homemade pasta because her Scandinavian mother's cooking lessons had not included it. Nona remembers, "Bill had been bragging for months about his excellent pasta, and we challenged him about WHEN we were going to be invited." I have always been a pasta fan, but the only experience I had had with homemade pasta was vicarious—the steamy pasta scene from *The Godfather Part IV,* or whatever number it is when Michael Corleone's daughter is all grown up. Besides, I have a fascination with wild olive trees, so the idea of homemade pasta drying on a wild olive tree rack was just too much for me.

When Bill invited Nona and me over the following Saturday night to make homemade pasta, we eagerly accepted. Cody would be working, and J. Michael would be with his father (where J. was quickly learning he really did not think he liked milking cows or the schedule dairy farming dictates), thus leaving me home alone. Nona was not dating anyone at the time (as usual) and was glad for an outing. Bill spends most Saturday nights with only his dog Daisy for company because his wife resides in Houston, but that is another story. So, to alleviate loneliness and boredom, plus gain a new culinary experience, we decided that Bill would be in charge of the main dish, Nona would make a side dish, and I would make a salad. We would also have wine and bread.

By the time Saturday rolled around, we had each shopped for our groceries and excitedly assembled to cook our meal. We created the pasta on Bill's kitchen island, a wooden chopping block situated in the middle of his rather small kitchen. The drying rack worked perfectly, as did the shiny pasta machine with all its parts and settings. Our boiled pasta was the whitest pasta I had ever seen and tasted like no store-bought pasta can. Bill's sauce that night was a garlicky shrimp creation, and Nona's side dish of okra and tomatoes proved interesting coupled with Bill's pasta dish. My colorful salad tasted crisp—texturizing our collective meal. We toasted with a glass from the fourth or fifth bottle of red wine and complimented each other on a successful culinary experience.

As we ate our meal at the table I had set using Bill's everyday dishes and flatware, we decided that we should make our collective cooking a monthly experience. We would take turns being in charge of the menu and cooking the main dish. The rule, though, was that we had to cook something we had never cooked before. So, not only would we alleviate loneliness and boredom, we would learn to cook new dishes.

Apparently, Bill told his wife Judy about our first cooking adventure because the next time we cooked, he told me we had been instructed by Judy to use the china and silver flatware for our table. She had said, "Oh no! You *must* use the china." Her reasoning was if we were going to all that trouble to cook such fine meals, then we needed a suitable table. So, he took me into the adjoining room, pointed out the box of silver flatware, and opened a hutch, revealing multiple sets of china. From that moment, I gained another official duty on cooking nights: I was in charge of the table. Each month I experimented with different table creations. After all, Bill had four or five sets of china and two drawers full of placemats and napkins. Subsequently, he has even found yet another set of china he did not even know about in his closet! As I set the table time after time, I thank my mother and my grandmothers for teaching me about china and silver, and my homemaking teacher Donna Wallace for teaching me the proper way to set a table.

That month, Nona achieved her reputation for laughing at a recipe and doing it her own way. She and Bill had eaten a dish at a Corpus Christi Italian restaurant, a dish she had enjoyed so much that she wanted to try her hand at recreating it. Scouring her cookbooks, she found a suitable recipe; however, she made a few alterations. When the recipe called for bell pepper, she substituted jalapenos. For parsley, she used cilantro. Thus, her Italian dish turned out to be South Texas Italian—a la Nona. Another successful cooking and dining experience.

For my turn at the menu, I wanted to cook fish and risotto. Bill had fish he had caught in the gulf waiting in the deep freeze, so that took care of procuring the fish. Bill knew of a risotto dish that called for saffron. I said, "I have saffron threads Mother brought to me from Spain," to which Bill gasped, "God Almighty! That's gold!" So I was set—nervous about the fish, but set nonetheless. Bill's son Dean came down unexpectedly from San Antonio for the evening. When he tasted the risotto, Dean discovered a whole new taste experience. He exclaimed, "The flavors just *burst* in my mouth!" None of the rest of us knew what he was talking about. Bill's diagnosis: "He watches *The Food Channel* too much." Not only did Dean join us for dinner, but he saved me by taking over the fish, so we dubbed him "Guest Chef," to which he exclaimed, "Guest, hell! This is *my* house! I'm part of this group." Thus, we gained our fourth member, who renamed our group. When we told him that we called ourselves The Lonely Hearts Supper Club, he exclaimed, "That's *pathetic!* This is too much fun. It ought to be called 'The Cooking Extravaganza!' " Who could argue with that?

In San Antonio, Dean has the privilege of going to Central Market, a grocery store with anything any chef might need to prepare even the trickiest of recipes. One of Dean's chosen recipes called for "fresh hearts of palm," so he went to Central Market in search of this obscure ingredient. After an unsuccessful search, he asked a store employee for assistance. This particular employee had never heard of fresh hearts of palm, so he left in search of the expert-on-duty. Momentarily, Dean heard on the store's loud speaker, "We've got a foodie on aisle 9." Dean looked up at the closest aisle sign: 9. Upon arrival, the expert, whom Dean said looked like "she'd been there since they erected the building," asked him, "Where are you going with this recipe?" Dean said, "I'm part of a cooking group, and I've got this recipe from a

French guy in New Orleans. . . ." Before he could finish his explanation, she cut him off and disgustedly informed him that there is no such thing as "fresh" hearts of palm, that if he wanted "fresh" hearts of palm, he needed to be "on the plantation waiting while they cut it down." She handed him a *can* of hearts of palm, and Dean promptly left the store.

Because most of us live in a small rural community, obtaining fresh herbs locally is out of the question—or was, at least, until Bill decided to create his own supply. He has planted tarragon, dill, sage, three kinds of oregano, cilantro, two types of parsley, a bay tree, and four basils. They grow in swimming pool chemical buckets obtained from The Widow Hubert, but that is yet another story. His long-time friend Pete Hamel noted, "If you've got all of your herbs staked in swimming pool chemical buckets, you might be a redneck." Pete simply disregards the fact that these buckets are resting on an old wrought-iron bed frame, complete with the headboard, that has been turned into a bench. However, the bench legs have rusted, so to improvise, Bill has set the bench across two mesquite log stumps to keep out the red ants. Bill says tongue-in-cheek of Pete's observation: "That snob!" Let's just overlook, then, his six or eight tomato plants—in bright red cattle feed tubs scattered throughout his backyard. To Bill's defense, he has unsuccessfully tried growing herbs in his flower bed. The only herb that has survived—and thrived—is his rosemary. It is a bush as big as his plumbago. Bill says that even though he has an abundance of rosemary, "Dean always brings rosemary, and I can't understand it. I tell him, 'Dean, I'm up to my ass in rosemary' but he still brings it. He might as well be bringing salt and pepper." Dean explains that he's "just trying to help. I'm just trying to bring fresh herbs from the city."

The meals we share on these evenings are not typical family meals, with the exception of a few. Mainly we choose to experiment with recipes that intrigue us but that we might not attempt for a weeknight family meal. Take, for example, the time-consuming homemade pasta, which sparked these monthly culinary adventures. We have made several different types of pasta, including ravioli, which took *all four of us* to prepare. One of my favorite dishes to order at an Italian restaurant is veal picatta, so when it was my turn one month, I cooked veal picatta. While experimenting with these out-of-the-ordinary foods, we have learned what Dean calls some "fancy food terms from researching new menu items." He provides these examples: "When one of Bill's pasta dishes called for a '*béchamel*,' we learned it's the same damn thing we pour over chicken fried steak . . . white gravy! Or, if you're using carrot, onion, and celery, you're using a '*mar aqua*' and that onion, bell pepper, and celery make up what foodies call 'the trinity.' " Being an official foodie, as he was labeled over the Central Market intercom, Dean should know. We have also learned some "dos and don'ts" associated with cooking. For example, we learned that first night that putting oil in with fresh pasta when it is cooking makes the pasta mushy because it absorbs the oil more readily.

In all the months of cooking, we have had only one real fiasco: the lamb. Dean worked diligently on his lamb dish, which he cooked to perfection, as far as preparing lamb goes. However, we were not as enthusiastic about this dish as we had been about the others. When Bill looked for the leftovers the next morning, he found them over the fence in the horse trap. According to Bill, "Dean does not like failure." Since then, Dean has been accused of practicing his recipes before coming to George West, which is illegal in our little club. Club members agree with Bill, though: "Nobody will ever fix lamb in this house again."

Cooking is not all we do at The Cooking Extravaganza. We listen to music via DirecTV in the background. When Bill cooks, we listen to classic country as a rule; Nona's choice is the blues. Dean and I prefer '80s rock. While dining, though, Bill tends to insist on what Dean and I call "elevator music." Nona seems also to enjoy it as we dine. On occasion we have been known to dance in the living room after dinner, thankfully only to classic country. Nona is a talented singer and musician. While learning to play the fiddle, she demonstrated her progress over several extravaganzas, proving marked monthly progress. Bill asked Nona to play a song that he and his mother Lib particularly liked, a song called "Ashokan

Farewell" from a Civil War documentary. Bill gave the tape to Nona, who took musical dictation, and played it for the group the next time we met. Everyone was astonished to know that she had listened to it and written it out like that.

One evening, the conversation somehow turned to Native American literature. Sometime into the discussion, Bill announced that he had a book of Native American poetry. After retrieving it from his bookshelf, we took turns reading the poetry aloud, except for Dean, of course, who just listened and commented. Wine tasting is among our regular activities. Since Dean lives in San Antonio, he has a better selection of wines, so he always brings two or three bottles of different wines for us to sample. Much to Dean's disgust, his father always likes the cheapest ones the best. Also, we discuss recipes we are considering for future meals. One in particular that Dean was considering demanded thirty-one hours of preparation, to which Bill offered: "Imagine how drunk we'll be." Finally, we tell stories on ourselves, on each other, on unsuspecting absent others. In general, we have fun.

Another discovery in Bill's cupboards, in addition to multiple sets of china, was a set of Irish coffee glasses. Of course, we had to utilize them. "Nona has discovered a palate for Irish coffee. Her desserts dictate Irish coffee," notes Bill. Since I do not drink coffee at all, my glass has only the whiskey—just like the true Irishman I am. Speaking of glasses, we all learned from Bill that wine tastes differently when drunk from glass than from crystal. He had learned this on the Hill Country wine tour. On the occasion he imparted this knowledge to us, his daughter Diane was visiting. She wanted to know if wine would taste even differently drunk from sterling. It does—and much better! Nona notes, "Gene, our distinguished neighbor, can attest to that. *And* that it tends to go to the system faster."

At most of our cooking Saturdays we have had at least one guest. Of course, we had our first surprise guest, Dean, who took over the fish, declared himself a member, and renamed our group. Additionally, all three of Nona's children—Kate, Hannah, and Zane—have dined with us at least once or dropped by to check on

Toasting good food and good company

us. Some members of the evening gathering gang have also dined with us: Gene and Josie Chapline, and Billy Campbell. Diane, whose husband is a civilian working in Iraq for an American company, brings her two young sons down to visit quite often, and they join in on the evening's fun. Cody, not scheduled to work a time or two when we have cooked, joined us, realizing that we were not scheduling our Saturdays just to exclude him. He always gets the rewards of the cooking, though, because I bring him a sample of what we have cooked. Nona's kids like the leftovers, too. J. Michael has been with us but not eaten because he is too finicky. Both my cousin Mike Powell from Banquete and my brother-in-law Billy Chapa have dropped by for a visit, only to find us cooking. Each stayed and ate food they had never eaten before—and may not eat again. In fact, when Mike saw Nona a few months later at the county fair, he pointed at her and said, "That woman'll make you eat *spinach*." Imagine: the former Heart of Texas Queen making someone eat spinach!

A few days before a monthly cooking night, Jeff Hubert learned that I would be making crawfish étouffée. Jeff just happened to show up at the evening stop-sign gathering and stayed to oversee my making of the roux because, he said, a roux is easy to foul up. This was after he had made a ten-mile trip home and back to get his *own* recipe. He wound up staying for the evening's duration. When I thanked him for helping me, he said, "Mur, you cooked it; I just did the prep work." However, he coached me all the way and did, indeed, chop all of the vegetables, taste the dish occasionally, add salt, etc. That makes twice I have been saved by my old buddies! We told Jeff over dinner about the lamb fiasco, which reminded him of when he ordered lamb at Outback Steakhouse "out of curiosity." He says of his experience: "I would have just as soon had my socks grilled. With a little rosemary, I'd have had some pretty damn good socks." Even though they may be a bit skeptical to try our dishes, our guests have been complimentary of the food served them—with the exception of one of Dean's friends who happened to stop by only for appetizers. Dean had prepared a crabmeat spread served with crackers. To Dean's disgust, his friend Tina said, "That's too crabby." Dean had used lump crab, which is quite costly, and told us after she had left, "At $11 for eight ounces, it's SUPPOSED to taste crabby! I guess steak would taste too *steaky*." Bill's comment: "That just goes to show you: People in Live Oak County are not ready for our palate." We have had other guests—some invited, some by happenstance; however, our guests generally do not participate in the meal's creation but enjoy the end results of our labor and have fun telling stories, laughing, and visiting in the meantime. Bill says, "It's all about the food. You don't sweep the floor; you don't think about the house." However, Nona and I maintain that yes, the food is what brought us together and is the official focal point, but it is also the camaraderie and the fun that give us pleasure and keep us coming back each month.

Our cooking group is beginning to get a reputation. Various community members have asked to join the group. Bill sums it up for us all when he says, "It's a closed society, and the only entry into it is if someone dies." We welcome guests, but guests they shall remain.

During the time we have gathered to cook one Saturday a month, I have cooked dishes I have always wanted to cook but had not the courage to attempt (fortune cookies, for example). I have eaten meals the finest metropolitan restaurants could not match. Indeed, I have come to appreciate the art of cooking. Dr. Meredith E. Abarca said, "The practice of cooking is a mode of expression just as valuable as the written word or the painted image."[1] The experiences Nona, Bill, Dean, and I have had cooking together have, indeed, heightened our awareness of the true artistry of cooking and the intrinsic value of enjoying that artistry with friends.

ENDNOTE

1. This observation is quoted in the following article: Lucy Fischer-West. "A Tortilla is Never 'Just' a Tortilla." *Both Sides of the Border: A Scattering of Texas Folklore.* Denton: University of North Texas Press, 2004. 93–99.

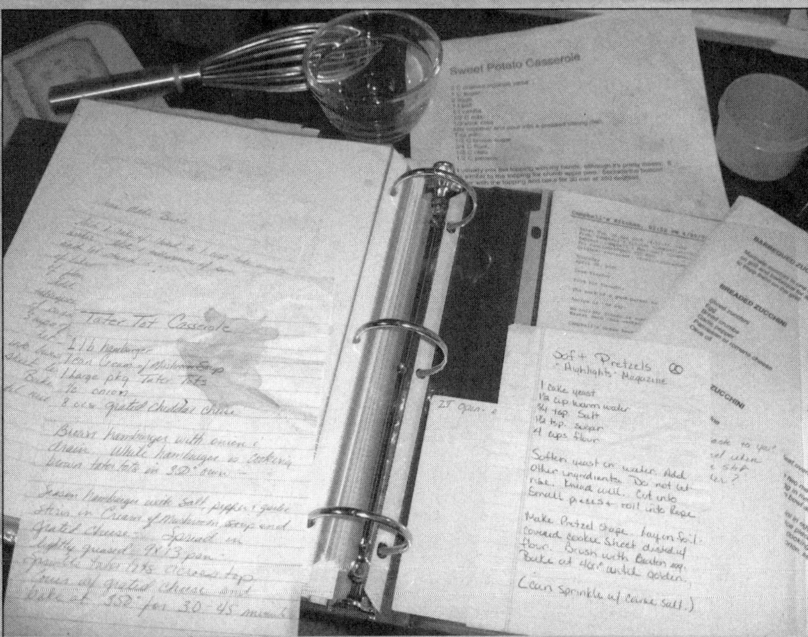

Favorite family recipes

Kelly Mosel-Talavera and escort Nathan Walker, ready for the evening wear competition

6

GROWING UP FEMALE IN TEXAS: THE IMPORTANCE OF BEAUTY PAGEANTS IN TEXAS COMMUNITIES

by Kelly M. Mosel-Talavera

I am standing on stage in my high school auditorium wearing the most expensive dress I have ever bought from Foley's, waiting for the announcer to call my name. Everyone told me I was a shoo-in to win the title. I was not even nervous as she called out the runners-up, still thinking my name would be next. "And the winner is . . ." What?! Not me? How could this happen? The girl from Future Farmers of America won? But I am in the drama club!

As I have grown older, many of the women I have met have shared similar experiences. Some did have their names called, and others went on to compete in numerous other pageants; many, like me, ended their pageant experience in one night of disappointment. It surprises me how many of my friends competed in beauty pageants in their hometowns. It is also interesting how the pageants are similar in some ways and different in others, and what they mean to the contestants.

"The results of beauty pageants are not going to greatly alter the course of world history. The same can be said about the Super Bowl and the World Series, most movies and books, the circus, and small-town celebrations, but few people would argue to abolish these events."[1] Including county fairs, high school homecomings, and preliminaries, there are approximately 750,000 beauty pageants a year in the United States.[2] The Miss America pageant alone awards over $5,000,000 annually in scholarships at all levels of competition.[3] Audiences are now asked to vote for their favorite contestant in the televised *Miss America* pageant and the votes are included in the contestants' scores.[4] Beauty pageants, while criticized by some feminist scholars, continue to flourish in communities and contribute to both their local and national identities. By looking at the role of beauty pageants in communities that organize them, one may determine the appeal of beauty pageants to the contestants, how the judges determine who is the best representative of the community, and the overall role of the pageant in the community. Beauty pageants take place within the context of a particular community, including communities all around us. Therefore, it is important to consider the role these pageants play in the lives of Texas women.

When a Texas debutante bows her forehead to the floor in the famous "Texas dip," society columnists all across the country speculate interminably over what it is that sets Texas women apart. But really, how could they know? Even the women born and bred in Texas can't always answer that question.[5] The ideal "Texas woman" is a combination of confidence, BIG hair, flashy jewelry, wry wit, shoulder pads, artificial fingernails, bold make-up and an unmistakable charm that can catch anyone's attention. Not all Texas women possess every quality; however, they each have a distinct combination of physical characteristics and personality. Public figures such as Lady Bird Johnson, Phyllis George (Miss America, 1971), Farrah Fawcett, Ann Richards, Molly Ivins, Barbara Bush, and Laura Bush, possess many of the characteristics of the ideal "Texas woman." Even popular cultural representations of Texas women such as the Dallas Cowboy Cheerleaders and the characters on the long-running television series *Dallas* reinforce this image.

In beauty pageants, contestants are expected to have impeccable hair and make-up, quick and intelligent answers, poise, and charm that distinguishes them from other competitors.[6] The qualities that are used to describe beauty pageant contestants are similar to the qualities that Texas women hold as an ideal. As a young girl grows up in Texas, she sees women presenting themselves to the public in a way that is reminiscent of the behavior rewarded in

Beauty facts card

beauty pageants. When young girls reach an age where they can make informed decisions about their willingness to participate in pageants, they can enter into this rite of passage that leads to becoming the "ideal Texas woman." Through this rite of passage young women prepare themselves to not only be seen as beautiful, but also as intelligent, well composed, and empowered individuals.[7] This rite of passage occurs on a community level in order to create young women who will be ambassadors for their home towns and, perhaps, go on to become Miss America, a movie star, or even the next governor of Texas.

Methodology and Results

This study is limited to beauty pageants with contestants in high school. Although many towns have beauty pageants that have categories from infants on up, studying those younger contestants is problematic. The contestants in high school are more often making a conscious decision to participate in this rite of passage. That does not mean that there is never any peer pressure or encouragement from parents to enter; however, the young woman in high school is old enough to refuse to participate. High school students are also old enough to fill out surveys about why they entered without influence from a parent.

Collecting Data

The intent of this study is to describe the Texas beauty pageant from a number of different perspectives: the contestants, the judges, and the organizers. The results from this study come from my own experience judging two of the pageants, personal interviews, questionnaires passed out to other judges and contestants, and the documents received by pageant officials in various communities. I sent out seventy-one letters to various Chambers of Commerce and received twenty-nine responses. Two asked me to be a judge, and one personally invited me to their beauty pageant based on my letter of inquiry. In total I was present at five beauty pageants. The collected data demonstrates three things: how beauty pageants serve as a rite of passage for young Texas women, what beauty pageants contribute to communities, and the role beauty pageants play in the lives of the young women who compete in them.

The results of this study can be interpreted by taking a closer look at the responses to my inquiry about local beauty pageants, an analysis of the concept of beauty in beauty pageants, how the community chooses a representative, the rite of passage to becoming an "ideal Texas woman," and how our view of pageants must change based on this study. Each of these areas of inquiry provides a more in-depth look at the pageant world and the people who participate in it here in Texas.

Littletown and Smalltown are two of the places I visited during this study. The organizers of the Littletown beauty pageant invited me to judge, and also asked if I could bring a friend to help judge as well; we did not discover our judging assignments until we arrived. Smalltown invited me to judge both the "Junior Miss" and "Miss Smalltown" categories. Both of these beauty pageants allowed me to see what goes on during the competition from a slightly different perspective.

Littletown

My first experience in being a judge began when my friend and I arrived in Littletown. We were quickly welcomed with "which one of you is writing the paper?" They were very nice and seemed genuinely interested in my research. There were six judges in all: three for the "Junior Miss" and "Miss Littletown" beauty pageants, and three for the contestants under the age of twelve. Five judges were female, including me and my friend and, surprisingly, there was one male. We all mingled around for about fifteen minutes before we had our "judges luncheon" with the volunteers. The organizer of the beauty pageant, Jennifer, called all of the judges and volunteers together to say a prayer before lunch. We blessed the food and prayed for the contestants, and also for the judges to have the "strength to make the right decision." Jennifer also gave thanks for us being able to come up to judge, and she asked God to guide everyone home safely afterwards.

After lunch it was announced that Jim, Amy, and myself would be judging the older girls. It was time to decide who would be the "head judge" for each of the sections. We were to choose among ourselves. I think Jim was prepared to take on the role, but the sixteen-year-old judge handed me the folder with the "head judge" material, and I didn't give it away. My duties were tough; I had to be the one who wrote the winner's name on the paper that would go to the announcer at the end of the pageant. My judging folder had a gold star on the front to set it apart from the others, but other than that, my duties were equal.

The pianist began to play, giving us the cue the beauty pageant was about to start. The president of the organization that was sponsoring the beauty pageant came out first, welcoming everyone and introducing the emcee. The first competition occurred immediately after that, with my groups coming on stage in their "sportswear." I was as nervous as they were, trying to look for something within them instead of looking at what was on them. The emcee read the contestants's short biographies from the information provided on their entry forms. As the emcee was reading, the contestant moved across the stage modeling her outfit. When the emcee was done, the contestant walked over to answer a question. The questions asked at this time were easy: "What activities are you involved in?" "What type of music do you listen to?" "Where do you plan to attend college?" I tried to listen carefully to the biography, watch the contestant, listen to her response, and write down scores at the same time—but it was really hard to do. The contestant was only on stage for a total of about three minutes at that point, and the next one came out right after, so I quickly figured out a scoring system for myself. I would write down a number and then go back at the end and re-analyze the score I had given them.

Once my two groups of beauty pageant contestants were done, the two other judges and I left the table to go back to the hallway for the interviews. I had imagined that in the interview portion of the competition I would be provided with a list of possible questions, or perhaps the contestants had something that they knew they were going to be asked. I was wrong, however, and I had to quickly come up with some of my own questions to ask the contestants. It was much easier to think of questions for the younger contestants in the "Junior Miss" pageant. At that age girls do not have too many future plans, worries or achievements, so I asked them more about what might be going on in their lives currently. I asked them to tell me about their favorite movie or actor, or to tell me a story about their best friend. The two other judges asked similar questions; some were a little too hard I thought, but I did not say anything.

The older contestants competing for "Miss Littletown" were mature enough to handle "issue-oriented" questions. The other judges asked them to tell us what some of the problems were in their schools, such as drug use, drinking, or gang membership. I still tried to keep things light, so I asked them to tell me about their most embarrassing moment, or what three people they most likely would invite to dinner if they could invite anyone. We talked to each of the contestants for about five minutes. We generally would ask a few questions and then pass to someone else. Occasionally I would step out of turn, or they would, but it was not a big deal. We all were struggling to think of questions together. By the time the kids' competitions were over and we were finished interviewing, we went back out for the final competition: formal wear.

The cafeteria was now really loud, with lots of children and parents talking. We took our seats in front of the stage, and tried to drown the noise behind us. The contestants came out on stage again, in the same fashion as they had for sportswear. We were to judge them by the same criteria as before. When that competition was over, we excused ourselves back into the hallway to make our final decision. We tallied our points and each came up with a winner. Luckily, the winner was the same for all of us, and we only had to decide on First Runner-Up, which was done easily and quickly.

I completed my "head judge" duties by filling in the winner's name and giving it to the organizer. The contestants were all sitting down in the audience and were not on stage, so when a name was called they had to walk all the way up to the front. I thought I would be more excited, seeing someone happy because of my influence. Actually, I was just tired . . . and really hungry. On our way out we did receive a small gift of candy and goodies from the community, as well as many "thank you's" and warm wishes on my research.

Smalltown

For the pageant in Smalltown, the judges were told to meet at a designated location in town. I saw an itinerary for the first time in the Suburban that was to take us to our various locations. We were going to different houses during the day for "tea" and interviews, then to another house for dinner before the beauty pageant.

Like the beauty pageant I judged previously, we were given no specific questions to ask in the interview. These interviews were, however, limited to three minutes, so we did not have to ask as many questions. I found out later that the houses where we were doing the interviews belonged to women in various "women's" organizations in town. Apparently, the organization would agree on a member's house in which to have the tea, and then the rest of the volunteers from the organization would come and help with the party. This seemed to get more of the community involved than any one organization.

During the interviews we asked the same standard questions as before, but this time we decided we would ask them all one question that was the same. We made it an odd question for which they could have no prepared response. I thought of the question, "Who is your favorite Superhero, and why?" I certainly was hoping they would say Wonder Woman, because she was the only female Superhero. Only two fulfilled my wish. Some cited Superman or Spiderman, saying they were their favorites because they had special powers to help people. I guess I am getting too old to relate to the rest of the contestants, because the remainder of the contestants did not take Superhero to mean cartoon characters on television, but instead referred to their favorite Superhero as an actual person. With this, a few named Michael Jordan to be their favorite Superhero, while others mentioned their mother. Oddly, more than one noted God to be their favorite Superhero, and even stranger, they repeated the same reasons that were mentioned for Superman and Spiderman.

The pageant was being held in the junior high school gym, which had been dressed up nicely with decorations that represented the theme of the pageant. The pageant began with the contestants coming out in their formal wear. The "Junior Miss" competitors wore really nice dresses that were not too "mature." The "Miss Smalltown" contestants, however, wore dresses that they would probably wear to the prom. The contestants came from the back of the gym up to the stage after their names were announced. Once they got on stage they modeled while the emcee read their biography. When he finished, the competitors walked to the front of the stage where there was a microphone and said,

"Good evening, Smalltown, my name is _____." Other than that one moment, the contestants did not speak while they were on stage. After this event, a person came from back stage and took our ballots. Apparently, they have their own volunteers who tally the scores. The other judges and I were never able to discuss or compromise a winner as I had been able to do previously.

The "Junior Miss" competition was disappointing for me. As it turned out, the one African-American contestant was clearly a beauty pageant veteran. She was the most articulate and relaxed in the interview, and she was the most poised and confident on stage. Despite this being painfully clear to me, the other judges refused to give her high scores. When she did not win (because I was outvoted), sighs of disbelief could be heard in the audience. I was embarrassed and ashamed at what I had witnessed and been a part of. I am quite certain that racism steered the fate of this particular competition. I learned later that she has several titles from other pageants, so my thoughts were even further confirmed.

When the beauty pageant was over, I was given more goodies from the community. I had developed much more of a rapport—and even friendship—with the women involved with this pageant, both among the volunteers and the judges. I think this had much to do with how it was set up throughout the day. This pageant, even more than the pageant in Littletown, seemed to weave women's rituals into its preparation, organization, and celebration. We gathered at women's homes for tea, dessert, and other snacks. We were encouraged to socialize in our intimate environments, calmed from the awkwardness of the situation by refreshments. We even got to celebrate with the other judges and volunteers by toasting with wine to a hard day that was almost over. When the event *was* over, we all exchanged phone numbers for future pageants and even hugged each other good-bye. With my disappointment I had for my fellow judges, it was a bittersweet moment when I was leaving. To quote one of the contestants, "I had a good day of just spending time with other girls."

The "Beauty" in Pageants: Judges and Contestants

One of the most interesting aspects of studying beauty pageants is discovering how "beauty" is defined. While many contend that pageants have moved away from physical beauty,[8] others assert that the definition depends on the community's notion of what is beautiful.[9] In order to determine how beauty is defined in the beauty pageants that this study encompasses, I looked at information from both the judges and the contestants themselves.

Judges were given a questionnaire. Only four of the judges cited physical appearance as being important to their decision on a winning contestant. Most mentioned personality or something having to do with the interview portion. Judges were also more often interested in confidence and eye contact than they were of height or weight. A contestant who appeared to be natural and not putting on an act could be more representative of members of the community. This seems to support information about the importance of factors other than beauty that go into the selection of a winner.[10] The judges themselves were clearly looking for a variety of factors, and in the pageants I attended the winner was never the young woman who was easily identified as the prettiest among the group. Instead, each pageant winner stood apart from the others during interviews. Therefore, the judges' choices reflected their answers to the questionnaire, in that they did not choose the winning contestant solely on her physical attractiveness.

Not only is the way the judges see the pageant important, but the contestants' reasoning behind entering a "beauty pageant" should be examined as well. Therefore, a questionnaire was also given to contestants. When I asked contestants why they entered the pageant and what the pageant meant to them, each put down roughly the same answer. Half answered that they entered the pageant for fun. Only one admitted that she entered to win. Nobody said that they entered because they thought they were pretty, nor did they say anything about physical appearance at all. I was trying to think of what I would have said had someone questioned me when I was in a small-town pageant. I think I would have responded in a manner similar to what these young women did. Even now when asked about my own experience in a beauty pageant I tend to discount my experience and tell my friends I entered because the high school drama coach forced me into it. The truth is, I thought I would win—I thought I was pretty, talented, and articulate. But like the contestants I questioned eight years later, I told the judges at the time that I wanted to have fun and experience something new.

What I am remembering about why I failed to tell the truth was the peer pressure surrounding me, as a young woman unable to acknowledge or accept my appearance. To say that I entered a beauty pageant because I thought I could win is saying I was pretty and self-confident, which is socially unacceptable among young women. With these memories I can assume that many of my respondents answered with the same thoughts. While many thought they were talented, funny, smart, or pretty, most would not admit that to be the reason they entered the pageant. I imagine that most entered with hopes of winning, but they can only say they entered for fun. This is ironic, considering that the pageant is one of the only rituals in which young women can publicly highlight their accomplishments.

Choosing a "Representative" of the Community

Not only do beauty pageants help define what a community considers beautiful, they also put forth a representative who will attend events in neighboring communities.[11] It is for this reason that the community develops the ritual. However, part of the ritual is ensuring that the representative reflects the values of the community. In order to analyze how a community chooses the most appropriate individual, I looked closely at the pageant rules, as well as at characteristics of the contestants themselves.

There were many different rules listed among the materials I received from various pageants that responded to my initial inquiry. The majority of the rules I obtained, however, described what type of young woman may enter. The variations I saw of rules concerning a contestants' marital status included being either single, never married, or having had a marriage annulled in one instance. Several but not all also said that the contestant must not have children. These rules expose much about the values of the community.[12] The pageant that allowed annulments had an age limit of twenty-one. This community recognized that young women can make mistakes early in their life and that perhaps they should not be punished for it by being banned from entering the local beauty pageant. Those that have rules for being never married tended to also have rules about being enrolled at the high school within the local community, so there was a lower chance of this being a problem. Those communities that included the rule of having no children have recognized that young women can and do have children out of wedlock and even in high school. Communities that did not include this rule overlooked this fact. Being a representative young woman of a small town does not include having a child at age sixteen. Still, by not specifying no children as a rule, organizers simply would argue that it was implied.

The rules are not the only way to determine how a young woman will represent her community. Most of the pageants also ask the contestants to list the activities in which they participate. The activities contestants responded with included everything from sports to academic associations or honors clubs, and various other extracurricular activities.

Finally, it is interesting to note the ethnicity and class of the pageant winners. According to Lavenda,[13] beauty pageant winners are more likely to reflect the dominant race of the community and are more likely to represent the class with power in the community. Only one contestant in the beauty pageants reported she was not Anglo, and most of the contestants responded that they are upper-middle class. The African-American contestant I judged was not the winner. Each of the pageants was dominated by contestants who represented those who held power in the community and the ethnicity of the majority.

Becoming the "Ideal Texas Woman"

Not only has the community established this ritual to choose a representative of the community, it has also provided a rite of passage for the young women, a way for them to become "the ideal Texas woman." What is overwhelming about attending the beauty pageants is the way the young women are presented. They put on their nicest clothes, put a great deal of time and effort into their hair, make-up and jewelry, and they discuss what they would like to do in the future. The beauty pageant itself gives a view of young women we rarely get the opportunity to see. Not only is it about confidence, poise and speaking ability, but we learn about their accomplishments in school and in extracurricular activities, and about how they volunteer their time. I kept thinking while attending these pageants that these young women demonstrate many of the skills required to be a star in business, government, Hollywood, or anywhere else a girl dreams about succeeding. More importantly, though, the categories listed on the score sheets and the characteristics judges look for are qualities that can lead to success in any walk of life, especially for women in Texas.

It is not enough for Texas women to be attractive, intelligent, and well educated. In order to climb your way to the top in Texas, a woman must be able to deal with the "good-old-boys." The use of categories such as "Stage Presence," "Poise," "Personality," and "Response to Questions" allows young women to demonstrate their confidence, talk about their abilities, and answer tough questions from interviewers. The score sheets themselves establish criteria on which young women must present themselves as more than attractive. The young woman who gets the highest score in all of the categories will be the winner; therefore, the winner must have a combination of qualities from attractiveness to intelligence to win.

The judges indicated they were looking for things such as verbal skills, eye contact, confidence, sincerity, and desire. The mostly female judges were all professionals in a variety of professions from nurses to paralegals. While the score sheets set up rather broad categories such as "Stage Presence," the judges narrowed what they were looking for to more specific qualities such as eye contact. The qualities that the judges say they were looking for are also qualities you would expect to be mentioned by employers interviewing perspective employees. Attributes such as communication, honesty, ambition, assertiveness, and enthusiasm are among the top ten things that employers look for in an employee. Winning contestants appear to be young women who will go on to achieve their goals throughout their lives.

Reframing Our View of Beauty Pageants

For many years, beauty pageants have been discounted as merely parading young women on stage for men to see. However, this study suggests that new conclusions must be drawn about the function of beauty pageants in communities. In order to do that, one must understand that pageants are not simply about physical "beauty," that contestants who win possess qualities that make them outstanding individuals who are articulate and intelligent, and that pageants allow young women a much needed place to highlight their accomplishments. It is also important to consider the role women in the community play in organizing pageants, encouraging young women to enter, judging pageants, and also watching them.

Beauty pageants help to dispel the myth that it is not "ladylike" to compete and not acceptable to, in the eyes of Phil Donahue, "compete with each other, and that the prize is men."[14] Wolf disagrees, calling for the acknowledgement of competitiveness as part of female identity.[15] Teaching young women how to compete based on their skills is an important lesson a community can provide to its young women. The skills these young women learn in competition with one another help prepare them for competing later in life for specific jobs, to keep their business on top, and to achieve financial success. "Beauty pageants provide another arena in which women can compete if they choose. Through this competition, women gain recognition and improve skills that can also be utilized to achieve other goals."[16]

Conclusion

This study shows that pageants can expand our notions of beauty beyond physical attractiveness to include personality, intelligence, poise, and confidence. It also demonstrates how a community chooses a winner who can represent it in other communities, thereby imposing rules for contestants that reflect the values of the community. Next, it presents information which suggests that, in Texas, the beauty pageant is a rite of passage that may help a young woman become the "ideal Texas woman." Finally, the study calls for a reframing of societies' view of beauty pageants, from an objectification of women to a source of power and advancement for women.

Future studies should focus on the positive aspects of beauty pageants that have been made apparent in this research. By studying the events in this manner, researchers can change the way beauty pageants are viewed. The young women in this study were unable to admit that they entered because they were pretty or wanted to win. Changing the way society views beauty pageants will allow these young women to be proud of their accomplishments—even if one of those accomplishments is winning a beauty pageant. Because this qualitative research lays groundwork by which to understand the beauty pageant process, future studies can look quantitatively at specific characteristics of contestants, judges, organizers, and beauty pageants as a whole. Longitudinal studies to determine if pageant participants go on to achieve their goals, and research that looks at the confidence of pageant participants before and after their pageant experience can enhance our understanding of the role beauty pageants may play in the lives of individual young women.

I sure was disappointed that night I lost the "Miss Gregory-Portland" pageant. Truthfully, I am still a little bitter. What I have learned in the years that followed my upset is that most young women who do enter beauty pageants lose. The process and the experience of the beauty pageants are what come to be the important factors that move young women from one point in their life to another. I am not sure if the beauty pageant I entered has anything to do with what all I have accomplished thus far in my life, but I do know that it has had an effect on the way I present myself today. It has also sharpened my wit, both because of being bitter over losing and because of my acquired sense of being able to laugh things off. Both of these qualities are part of the wide array of characteristics associated with the "ideal Texas woman."

An announcement for the Miss Gregory-Portland Beauty Pageant

Endnotes

1. Barbara Peterson Burwell and Polly Peterson Bowles. *Becoming a Beauty Queen*. New York: Prentice Hall Press, 1987. xi.
2. Melinda Beck, Shawn Doherty, Nikki Finke Greenberg, David Frienly, Diane Weathers, and John McCormick. "A Controversial 'Spectator Sport'." *Newsweek* September 17, 1984, 56.
3. Anna Stanley. *Producing Beauty Pageants*. San Diego: Box of Ideas Publishing, 1989. xix.
4. Richard Corliss. "Dream Girls." *Time* September 18, 1995. 103.
5. Prudence Mackintosh. *Just As We Were: A Narrow Slice of Texas Womanhood*. Austin: University of Texas Press, 1996. i.
6. Burwell and Bowles. xiv–xvi.
7. Beck, et al. 56; Stanley. 5.
8. Stanley. 5.
9. Denise Lawrence. "Parades, Politics, and Competing Urban Images: Doo Dah and Roses." *Urban Anthropology* 11: 1982. 156.
10. Burwell and Bowles. xiv–xvi.
11. Robert H. Lavenda. "Minnesota Queen Pageants: Play, Fun, and Dead Seriousness in a Festive Mode." *Journal of American Folklore* 101: 1988. 170.
12. Lawrence. 156–157.
13. Lavenda. 171–174.
14. Burwell and Bowles. xiv.
15. Naomi Wolf. *Fire With Fire*. New York: Random House, 1993.
16. Burwell and Bowles. xiv.

Henry Wolff, Jr. *Photo by David A. Smith*

7

MADAME BLACKLEY: SEER OF SOUTH TEXAS

by Henry Wolff, Jr.

Madame Blackley could see things that other people couldn't see. During her time, the Victoria, Texas, clairvoyant was the "Seer of South Texas" and was particularly adept at finding lost and stolen horses and other livestock. Ranchers and cowboys from throughout the region sought her services, and their stories have become legend.

I first heard of Madame Blackley in 1981, when Oscar Roemer of Port Lavaca[1] got to telling me one day about how she had helped his father find a horse. Roemer said it was about 1914, and his dad had never seen the woman before, but that when he walked up on her porch she invited him in by name. "You think someone stole your horse," she said, "but they didn't." She then began to draw some landmarks on a piece of paper to show him where the body of the horse could be found in a pasture on the old Thomas Ranch, and sure enough it was there. "The brand was still readable," according to Roemer. He told another story of how Madame Blackley had helped locate some gold in a house that had burned, and how she had once worked in a popular old Victoria eatery, the Manhattan Café. She could set a table for people before they had even come in the door, knowing how many would be there before they arrived.

Mrs. Charlie "Alma" Beck grew up in the Diamond Hill area of Victoria, a hill overlooking the flats along the Guadalupe River where Blackley had property. Mrs. Beck said her father had property joining that of Blackley and that she called him "Sonny" even after he was grown. "We called her Aunt Annie," she recalled.

Blackley was known to everyone on Diamond Hill, an old section of town that had been mostly settled early on by German families, but was then a mixture of blacks and whites, with a black school and churches. Many other black families lived down below the hill in "the flats" that spread out from the Guadalupe River where Blackley had property and where there is a public housing development named for her.

"She didn't like being called a fortune teller," Mrs. Beck said, "and didn't charge for her services, accepting donations instead." "My mother never believed in fortune tellers," she recalled, "but when Aunt Annie told her something she believed it." Her father, Charlie Miller Jr., who operated sprinkler wagons on the streets of Victoria for years, went to Madame Blackley after somebody had stolen his horse from where a city watering trough was located on Market Square, now better known as City Hall Square. "Why silly," Mrs. Beck quoted Blackley as having told her father, "why didn't you come to me sooner because you knew I'd know where it was at." Then she told him "exactly how to get to it, that somebody from Yorktown had taken it."

Charlie Beck, a Victoria County rancher, remembered his mama telling how her daddy had lost a cow and Blackley told him to go on a certain day to a certain spot in the river where she said the cow was coming for water each day. He did, and the cow did, along with a calf that she had given birth to after straying or being stolen a year or so before.

Blackley could also have a sense of humor at times, like when Mrs. Beck's sister, Annie Miller, lost a ring and asked her to help find it. "There is no need to find it," Blackley told her. "You would just lose it again." "And," Mrs. Beck recalls, "she didn't tell her either."

While many of the stories about Madame Blackley involve her expertise at locating livestock, she had quite a reputation by the time she had arrived in Victoria in 1882 (at the age of 42), according to her obituary. It was said she had known presidents and had even warned Lincoln of his impending assassination. "Anna P. Blackley, 87, colored, credited with supernatural powers by many people and widely known as a fortune teller, died at her home at

703 S. Depot Street in this city Sunday afternoon at 1:45 o'clock after a long illness,"[2] *The Victoria Advocate* reported in her obituary. "Madam[3] Blackley as she was generally known, was born in Falmouth, Virginia, and reared in Washington. Her alleged power to foretell events early demonstrated itself and for this reason she was spared the hardships of slavery. She was personally acquainted with Presidents Lincoln and Grant and is said to have warned Lincoln of his impending assassination."[4]

It was further noted that she claimed to be a close relative of Frederick Douglass, the anti-slavery orator and journalist who was reared as a slave although his father was a white man. "During the 45 years that Madam Blackley lived in Victoria thousands of people came here from far and near to seek her advice as to love affairs and business transactions," it was noted in her obituary. "She could have accumulated a large fortune but for her many acts of charity, which represented substantial contributions to religious institutions and the needy. As it was, she left a handsome estate."[5] Her husband, Fleming Blackley, died in 1918, and she was survived by one nephew, Isaiah Arthur of Victoria, and a number of relatives in Washington, D.C., where her body was sent for burial by her dying request. There were funeral services at Palestine Baptist Church in Victoria where she was among the earliest members. Mrs. Ron "Celeste" Brown said a maid in her parents' home, Alice Epps, recalled an incident that happened during Blackley's wake when a black cat ran under the coffin. Epps said the mourners "flew out of the windows."

One of the best physical descriptions of Madame Blackley appears in one of Leon Hale's columns from the *Houston Post*, reprinted in his book, *A Smile From Katie Hattan and Other Natural Wonders*. In Hale's interview with Leonard Chappell of El Campo, Chappell described visiting Blackley with his father in 1917 to get the clairvoyant's advice on finding a work horse that was missing from their rice farm at Nada. "She was a big woman," Chappell told Hale, "six feet tall or better, and had this long face. And she had curly hairs growing to the side of her nose. The hairs were curled up so they made you think of a watch spring."[6] Chappell noted that he had seen such facial hair on the faces of other mulattos.

"She kept her eyes about half closed," he recalled. "She said to Dad, 'You've lost a horse.' And then she said, 'I have a presentiment. I see your horse in a village with white houses. He is grazing in grass up to his knees, and he is in a pasture with a gray tick mare and a pair of line-backed dun mules. You will hear from your horse by Friday.' "[7] Despite that being during the 1917 drought when there wasn't a lot of grass, the following Friday while seventeen-year-old Chappell was in Garwood with his brother Earl, a man was asking if anybody had lost a big black horse with four white feet and a star on its forehead. Sure enough, it was old "Charlie," grazing in a pasture along the Colorado River beside a gray tick mare. "And," Chappell said, "in the pasture with him was a pair of little old line-back dun Spanish rat mules."[8]

In his autobiography, *Some Part of Myself,* J. Frank Dobie mentions his Uncle Ed Dubose looking for treasure with some specific directions from a Negro fortuneteller in Victoria.[9] But, it was probably a man since the account was in reference to a story that he had detailed more thoroughly in his earlier book on Texas treasure, *Coronado's Children.* In a chapter titled "The Facts About Fort Ramírez," referring to the old Spanish ruins on the ranch where he was born in southern Live Oak County, Dobie mentions that his Uncle Ed consulted "a noted mulatto fortune teller in Victoria."[10] Dobie describes the fortuneteller as being a man who offered to find the fortune for $500 and was taken to the site by Dubose. When it wasn't found and payment was refused, the man declared that "spirits would move the box" and it would never be found.[11] That fortuneteller might have been a Mr. Kitchen, who was active in Victoria during some of the same years as Madame Blackley.

Born and raised on the Oliver Ranch at Nursery just north of Victoria, George Oliver said his Grandfather George Frank Oliver once bought a fine Brahman bull from the Hudgins Ranch in Wharton County. He had planned to keep the bull up for a week or two before turning him out to pasture. "The bull disappeared," Oliver said, "and he couldn't find him anyplace." He heard the story from his father, Jesse L. Oliver, who recalled that his father finally decided to send him into Victoria to see Madame Blackley.

"Grandfather always sent my father for some reason," Oliver noted. "He rode horseback into Victoria, tied up his horse and sat on Madame Blackley's porch until she had finished with someone else. She saw him and told him that she knew why he was there." "Tell your daddy that bull is in an anaqua mott about a half-mile from the house," she said. Sure enough, the bull was found just where she said. "He would come out and feed and get water and then go back into the mott," Oliver noted. "That's why he was so hard to find."

There are the occasional stories that relate to subjects other than livestock, like one that is told about a prominent Victoria County rancher's love and marriage. Supposedly, Madame Blackley had predicted the marriage of Al McFaddin and Ada Pettus. Agnes Jewell, whose mother worked for McFaddin, had heard the story and that Blackley had also predicted McFaddin would come into a fortune and that his wife would become an invalid. Jewell had done some research on Blackley when a historical marker was being obtained for Palestine Baptist Church and recalled that there was another black fortuneteller in Victoria. Not a mulatto like Blackley, his name was Kitchen and he dealt more in death and such things while Blackley concentrated on money and property.

George Oliver remembered another story about a bachelor who sharecropped for his grandfather on a piece of land known as "the island" on the Guadalupe River. The man was found dead and his cabin ransacked. "Grandfather told my father to go into town and talk to Madame Blackley," he said. "Some money had been stolen and food items taken in the process. Dad rode into Victoria in the dark, and if I'm not mistaken got her out of bed. She asked, 'What's the problem?' " His dad explained the situation. "It's not a problem," Blackley said. "None of the local people did this." She went on to say that three Mexicans passing through the area had done it and were camped out beneath a large oak tree. She told him the location, how the culprits were dressed and that they had buried what they had stolen on the south side of the tree. "There was some bread, canned goods and some money," Oliver said. "It was just like she had said."

During the dedication of an official Texas State Historical Marker at Palestine Baptist Church, Mrs. Charlottie Dement said she had lived with Madame Blackley for a time in the early 1920s. "She lived on Second Street and had a whole block there across from where the projects are now," she noted, referring to the Annie Blackley Apartments. Mrs. Dement, who helped unveil the historical marker, remembered how Aunt Annie once helped a man on Pleasant Green Drive to find a couple of lost mules in the Guadalupe River bottom, "down near where the syrup mill was located." She told him they would be found snagged in the brush because he had them tied together when they ran off, Mrs. Dement recalled. Blackley then chastised the man for tying his mules that way. "She would tell them beforehand what they did wrong," Dement noted.

It would appear from what was said during the dedication that Blackley had been in Victoria more than the forty-five years noted by *The Advocate* when she died in 1927. The impression given was that she was present on June 27, 1868, when the church was started by twenty-one devoted Christians and a circuit riding preacher beneath an old oak tree believed to be one still standing near the church. When a second church building was constructed in 1873, Blackley supposedly gave a large donation and later a church bell that was hauled from Indianola to Victoria following the storm of 1886 that destroyed the once thriving seaport on Matagorda Bay.

There is a letter from John L. Cunningham of Watsonville, California, in Victoria County historian Sidney Weisiger's files in the Regional History Center, Victoria College/University of Houston-Victoria Library, describing how Blackley told his dad that money was buried in a barn on the family ranch at the northwest edge of Victoria. She told his father that "a spirit wanted him to get it."[12] Blackley then gave his father a verse from the Bible that he should say, but warned him not to mention the Holy Ghost. His father was afraid and would not do it, so any treasure evidently went with the sale of the ranch to A. L. Thurmond in 1902.

Robert D. King of San Antonio told a story about his grandfather Bob Willemin asking Blackley about when he was going to die.

"Mr. Bob," she said, "you won't be living 30 days from now." While she might not have been one who dealt in death, King said that his grandfather went home and threw his boots behind the bed. "I won't need these anymore," he told his wife, explaining what Blackley had told him. "Grandpa then crawled into bed and never got out," King said. "He stayed right there and died of pneumonia."

"You have been writing about the Negro woman, mind reader of Victoria," Mrs. Ruby Mays of Edna wrote after I had made some mention of Blackley in my column in *The Victoria Advocate*. "Yes, I remember about her. One time my uncle was missing when we lived at Red Bluff. My brother, James Gilmore, and my husband, Dewey Mays, came to Edna to talk to Mr. Huie White, the sheriff of Jackson County, about his being missing. White sent them to Victoria to talk to the Negro lady." She says Madame Blackley asked if they had a child missing. "No," they replied, "a man." "You go on back home," she told them, "when you get there he will be sitting in a chair reading a paper." Mrs. Mays said, sure enough, when they got home her uncle had been found, that a Mr. Brandes had found him in Ganado in a café eating a bowl of chili and brought him home. She said Sheriff White was a believer in Blackley and would sometimes seek her advice when he had a big decision to make.

Wayne Hillyer of Victoria remembered how his dad, D. D. Hillyer, once sought her advice when he had lost a bunch of cattle in the early 1920s from his place near Louise in Wharton County. "On Christmas eve night," he recalled, "there was lots of sleet and someone drove off 50 head." That would have been the blizzard of 1924. With the ground covered with sleet and snow, there was no way to tell which way they had gone. Hillyer decided to go to Victoria to see if Madame Blackley could help him and got another man to ride with him. "You can come in," Blackley told Hillyer when he arrived, "but I don't want that man in my house. He's a crook. You wanted to see about your cattle," she continued. "Someone took them a long ways off and I doubt you will get them back." She went on to describe the rustler. "To a T," Hillyer said, "just who papa suspected." He said she only charged a dollar for a hearing, an amount sometimes quoted in other accounts as well, while yet others indicate that rather than charging she accepted "donations" for her services.

There were definitely people she would not talk to, claims Mildred Davidek of Boling, recalling a story that involved her Uncle Ben Caraway who was known to be somewhat of a tease. He and some friends rode horseback to Madame Blackley's house to ask her some questions. On the ride Caraway had made some derogatory remarks about her. When they arrived at her gate, she came to the porch, pointed at him, and said, "He's not coming in because he just called me an ugly name." You didn't want to mess with Madame Blackley unless you were serious about something. Davidek's grandfather, Dennis Caraway, had two white mules that had wandered away from their pasture. Blackley told him where to look and they were exactly where she said they would be. Caraway once lost a suitcase that was tied with some twine on a train ride from Victoria to Bay City and Madame Blackley not only told him where to find it, but what he had in it.

Somewhere around 1920, Mrs. Garland "Lucy" Rather said her father, W. B. Hamilton of Telferner, received an inheritance from his parents in Iowa and lost $400 in newly purchased government bonds, for which he sought the help of Madame Blackley. She told him "to go right home and look behind a stack of lumber." "They were there," Mrs. Rather said.

Velma Warner's father, Zilmon Boothe Jones, along with his brother John and two friends once came from Choate in Karnes County to see "a fortune teller in Victoria," evidently Madame Blackley, after he had lost his best saddle horse. They went home and found the horse right where she had told them to look. Here again, Blackley would not talk to any of those with her father because "they had been making fun of her on the way to Victoria, doubting her word."

"She also told my dad who he was going to marry," Mrs. Warner said. "My mother's name was Maude Smith and she already knew that. Daddy did not tell her. My daddy used to say that the fortune teller was the reason there were so many rich people in Victoria. She could tell them to make the best decisions about business, or trading, what they were to do and it would be the best choice."

Jerome Hubalek of Fredericksburg recalled a story of his grandparents losing two mules near Salem when moving in a wagon caravan from Lavaca County to Victoria County in 1911. Upon reaching Victoria County, someone told them of Blackley and they rode on horseback to see her. "Upon moving toward the porch," he said, "she greeted them, saying 'you are looking for two mules.' She took paper and pencil and drew a map to direct them." They found the mules where she said they would be in a pen near Inez, not far from where the family had settled in southeastern Victoria County.

E. L "Scrub" Kelley of Refugio, who put out a little book of local history and lore from columns that he had written for the Refugio Press, described Blackley as a brown-skinned Negro woman whose abilities were nothing short of miraculous. "In none of the visits to her that I heard of did she resort to tea leaves or palm reading or any other gimmicks," he wrote. "She simply told the visitors what they would ask of her."[13] As a boy, he remembered hearing many times of ranchers and businessmen who would never close a deal of any kind without first talking it over with Madame Blackley.

In *Ever Since I Remember . . . Refugio Recollections,* Kelley tells a story about his father, who was a freighter hauling goods by wagon and mule team from the nearest railroads that were at Beeville, Goliad, and Victoria, and also from the old port of St. Mary's on Copano Bay. His father had several teams of mules which, when he was not on the road, he grazed on the town commons north of Refugio. One morning a pair of his mules failed to show up with the rest. After searching and making inquiries for about a week, his father decided to visit Madame Blackley. "Her home was a modest frame house," he recalled, "with a small front porch enclosed by an old picket fence with a swinging gate."[14] As soon as his father entered the yard, Blackley came out and said, "Yeah, you come over here to get me to tell you who stole your mules. Ain't nobody stole them; they off in a man's pasture and he don't know who they belongs to, so you go on home and in about two weeks a red-faced man gonna bring your mules back."[15] "Sure enough," Kelley said, "in a couple of weeks a Mr. Williams from Blanconia drove up leading the mules."[16]

He recalled another time when his brother-in-law, Rufus H. Winsor, and a couple of others visited Blackley in an effort to locate some treasure that was supposedly buried at a mott of trees in eastern Refugio County where mysterious lights appeared on dark nights. The trio rode horseback to Victoria and had no sooner tied up in front of Blackley's home when she appeared on the porch shaking with laughter. "You silly boys come up here to get me to tell you where some money's buried," she said. "You gonna get some money all right, but you gonna get it the same way you been getting it—six bits or a dollar a day working cattle."

They might not have realized it at the time, but she had just proven what she wanted people to believe about Madame Blackley. The seer of South Texas was a clairvoyant, not a fortuneteller.

Endnotes

1. Most of the information about Victoria clairvoyant Madame Blackley comes from personal interviews and correspondence with readers of my newspaper column, "Henry's Journal," in *The Victoria Advocate.* The sources included Oscar Roemer, Mrs. Charlie "Alma" Beck, Mrs. Ron "Celeste" Brown, George Oliver, Agnes Jewell, Mrs. Charlottie Dement, Wayne Hillyer, Robert D. King, Mrs. Ruby Mays, Mildred Davidek, Virgil Sparks, Mrs. Garland "Lucy" Rather, Velma Warner, and Jerome Hubalek. The columns relating to Madame Blackley appeared on July 17, 1981; May 4, 1984; July 31, 1991; October 31, 1991; December 12, 1991; February 19, 1992; February 27, 1992; March 5, 1992; February 6, 1998; February 12, 1998; February 13, 1998; November 3, 2000; November 16, 2000; and November 22, 2000. Other sources consulted but not specifically cited are: Sidney Weisiger. "Sidney's Vignettes." Victoria: *The Victoria Advocate,* October 11, 1970; and my own "Henry's Journal, Volume II." Victoria: *The Victoria Advocate,* 1991.

2. "Madam Blackley," obituary. *The Victoria Advocate*, Sept. 19, 1927.
3. The newspaper used the title Madam, where I prefer the French title of courtesy Madame.
4. "Madam Blackley," obituary.
5. Ibid.
6. Leon Hale. *A Smile From Katie Hattan & Other Natural Wonders.* Bryan: Shearer Publishing Co., 1982.
7. Ibid.
8. Ibid.
9. J. Frank Dobie. *Some Part of Myself.* 1952. Austin: University of Texas Press, 1986.
10. J. Frank Dobie. *Coronado's Children.* Dallas: The Southwest Press, 1930.
11. Ibid.
12. Sidney Weisiger. Letter from John L. Cunningham. Regional History Center, Victoria College/University of Houston-Victoria Library, 1994.
13. E. L. "Scrub" Kelley. *Ever Since I Remember . . . Refugio Recollections.* Refugio: Refugio Publishing, 1971.
14. Ibid.
15. Ibid.
16. Ibid.

An original painting of La Llorona by the author, Gloria Duarte

8

LA LLORONA'S ANCESTRY: CROSSING CULTURAL BOUNDARIES

by Gloria Duarte

La Llorona, the Weeping Woman, is probably one of the most popular cultural icons in the Mexican-American culture. Myth, fantasy, and perhaps some history have merged into creating such a well-known archetypal character, whose appearance in Francis Edward Abernethy's *Legendary Ladies of Texas* attests to her popularity. A few common essential details of La Llorona exist regardless of geographical region: a cultural or racial difference between the lovers, the killing of a child or children, and ultimate madness. Ambiguity exists regarding the physical appearance of La Llorona, ranging anywhere from a beautiful woman dressed in white to a horrifying monster clothed in black, or even to death itself. Essentially, La Llorona fits a pattern: she had a sexual relationship with a man outside her social class, which produced a child or children; he abandoned her for a woman from a higher social status; she killed her children, usually by drowning; and now she haunts water areas looking for the souls of her dead children so that she can find peace and enter the kingdom of God. The legend of La Llorona has been used to teach lessons in the Hispanic culture: to young Hispanic females not to fool around outside their social class, to young children as a scare tactic to gather into the home before dark, and to wayward husbands not to stray outside their marriage. Although the legend of the Hispanic La Llorona probably originated in the European culture, she has crossed cultural boundaries with similar legends appearing in the Philippino, German, Greek, and Jewish cultures, providing some of the most interesting variations of the legend.

A typical Hispanic version of La Llorona appears in *Mexican Ghost Tales of the Southwest.* In this version, a Mexican widow is left with three small children who became a burden to her social life. She left them alone while she pursued an escape from her responsibilities by going to fiestas. The children cried frequently because they were hungry and because the mother beat them. When she grew tired of hearing them weeping and begging for food, the woman placed them in a sack and dragged them to a nearby river where she dumped their bodies. She heard the crying and pleading of the children, but she turned a deaf ear. She continued her dissolute life until her death, at which point she appeared before God for judgment. He condemned her to roam the rivers until she found her children. She would not find rest until the end of the world.[1]

The first appearance of La Llorona may have been in 1502 in Mexico before the appearance of Hernando Cortés and the Spanish conquistadores. The Mayas, in what was then known as Meso-America, heard a woman crying a forewarning about some terrible occurrence upon the land. The Mayans heeded the warning and retreated into the forest, thus escaping most of the brutality of the Spanish influence.[2] Meanwhile, Moctezuma supposedly received word of the premonition; however, he was not convinced of the impending danger because Cortés' appearance resembled that of their God Quetzalcoatl.

In the Aztec version, Doña Marina/La Malinche is associated with La Llorona and at times merges with her. According to Blea, Moctezuma sent a group of women as a peace offering to the conquistadores, but the females were distributed among the men as gifts with Doña Marina going to one of the soldiers. When the soldier discovered her abilities with languages, he informed Cortés who then assumed possession of her. Because he used her knowledge of the land and of the people to help him conquer the empire, she has been referred to as *La Malinche,* or Traitor. However, the circumstances surrounding her assistance seem clouded in ambiguity since there is no clear knowledge about her involvement with Cortés.[3]

Supposedly, myth takes over history as the story reveals that Doña Marina had a son by Cortés. When he was ordered to return to his wife in Spain, Cortés naturally wanted to take his son with him. In one version, he does take his son with him. In another, Doña Marina refused to part with her son, and fearful that the youngster might die on the voyage she performed the ultimate sacrifice, condemning herself as she drowned him to ensure that his spirit would remain in his homeland. The worst thing that could happen would be that her son would die away from his land, and his spirit would wander and never rest. The account continues that when Doña Marina died, God would not allow her through the gates until she returned with the soul of her son. Legend has it that her son's soul had floated away, and she continues to wander the river and its tributaries on a relentless quest.[4]

According to Rick Hernandez, the Philippines have at least two versions of La Llorona: the Siren and the White Woman. In the first, some believe that the Weeping Woman was a siren, similar to a mermaid, who gave birth to children who were mer-people like her. On their fourteenth birthday, they chose whether to become human or to remain mer-people. On one occasion, one of her children chose to become human but was inadvertently killed by fishermen. Now whenever a child drowns or disappears, many believe that the Weeping Woman has taken her revenge. When they hear her wailing at night, they realize someone has drowned. Another version presents the White Woman, "the stealer of souls." Very beautiful and alluring, she lives among the clouds of fog that drift along at night, enticing men to follow her into the mists where they are lost forever. Belief has it that she steals the soul of a young girl every year during a May parade. The wind heard howling at night is her crying.[5]

A variation of La Llorona appears in German folklore, as well. John O. West provides a brief account in which a peasant girl, deceived and then abandoned by a naughty nobleman, gives birth to a child. In a rage, she killed their child, stabbed the father to death with his own sword, and then hanged herself. Supposedly, she returns to haunt the place of the double murder.[6] In another German legend, the White Lady (Die Weisse Frau) emerges as a ghostly figure, haunting the castles of the dynasty of the Hohenzollern and brings bad luck or foreshadows misfortune.[7] After the death of her husband, the Countess Kunigunde wished to marry Albrecht von Hohenzollern, who reportedly stated he would if not for "four eyes between [them]." He meant his parents, but the Countess misinterpreted and thought he meant her two children. Determined to kill them and make it appear as if they died naturally, she used a "golden needle" to pierce their skulls. Punished by her conscience, she went before the Pope in Rome, who promised her forgiveness if she devoted her life to monastic work. In some versions of the legend, she died in her attempt to establish a monastery, while in others she did found a monastery but died shortly thereafter.[8] Legend has it, she continues to haunt the castles of the Hohenzollern dynasty as a malevolent specter.

Two Greek versions associated with La Llorona include the stories of Lamia and of Medea. According to Greek mythology, Lamia, one of Zeus' paramours, produced several children from her liaison with the god of gods. As usual Hera, Zeus' wife, found out about the affair and in a jealous rage killed Lamia's children. Hera punished Lamia for her relationship with Zeus by making Lamia unable to close her eyes so that the horrifying image of her dead children would continuously haunt her. According to legend, Lamia's grief turned her into a monster, who in revenge stole and devoured the children of other mothers. Zeus pitied Lamia and granted her the ability to remove her eyes and put them back, thus allowing her rest from her grief.[9] Lamia has the face and breast of a beautiful woman and the body of a serpent.[10] She is sometimes referred to as a male or a hermaphrodite, but she is believed to have the ability to change herself into a beautiful young woman. Like La Llorona, Lamia wreaks vengeance on other women by stealing their children from them. In addition, both women find no rest from the loss of their beloved children.

A second Greek relative of La Llorona is Medea (431 B.C.). Euripides' drama of the same name presents a story of revenge as

Medea assists Jason to steal the Golden Fleece, betrays her father, leaves her country to follow Jason, and then is herself betrayed. In Corinth, Jason lives with Medea, and the couple produces two children. But he abandons her to marry a princess, explaining that the royal marriage will benefit them all. In retaliation, Medea murders their children. Euripides' masterpiece reveals how anger and jealousy consume the powerful Medea, who is torn between her love for her children and her hatred for their father. She explains the murders as a sacrifice on her part because she refuses to allow her enemies to exact revenge on them. Her act is similar to Doña Marina's, who likewise drowned her son to assure his spirit remain in his homeland.

From Jewish folklore comes one of the oldest and most interesting connections to La Llorona in the form of Lilith, the first woman created by God, and thus the predecessor of Eve. According to Ausubel, Adam and Lilith never found peace together because she refuted Adam's claim to be her superior, in particular in having to lie beneath him.[11] She argued that because they were created simultaneously from the same dust, they were equal. She insisted there was no justification for his supremacy. Rather than accept subjugation, Lilith left Adam to live alone by the Red Sea, where she found peace making love with satyrs, minotaurs, and centaurs. Subsequently, Adam appealed to God, who sent forth three angels to persuade Lilith to return. The woman preferred life without a mate like Adam, to giving up her integrity and independence. The angels threatened her with death for her refusal, but she provided a logical response: "Don't you know, I've been created for the purpose of weakening and punishing little children, infants and babes? I have power over them, from the day they are born until they are eight days old if they are boys and until the twentieth day if they are girls."[12] Angered by her defiance, the angels grabbed her with intentions of drowning her, but Lilith promised that if she entered a home where a woman was giving birth and she saw an amulet on each wall bearing the angels' names or images, she would spare the newborn. They let her go, and God thus created Eve as Adam's mate. Since then, Lilith roams the world, "howling her hatred of mankind through the night and vowing vengeance because of the shabby treatment she had received at the hands of Adam."[13]

According to Lilly Rivlin, "In medieval Europe (especially Germany), Lilith became a popular man-devouring creature, a threat to Christian and Jewish homes. She is the envious estranged wife and mother who covets other women's children and threatens to steal them, unless prevented by charms."[14] Like La Llorona, Lilith also underwent a physical change from a beautiful woman to a hag, who preyed on sleeping men. She appears in numerous guises. At times, she is a wicked harlot and the pinnacle of evil. She serves as a scapegoat for both men and women to blame unexplained desires and frustrations. She can also be a female demon and move in the night, "visiting women in childbirth and trying to strangle their newborn babies."[15] Women who deviated from the norm of being submissive and showed characteristics of being outspoken must be Lilith in disguise; otherwise, there was no other explanation.

Myth and fantasy blend in the creations of such a fascinating character as La Llorona. And while many Hispanics claim La Llorona as their own, her ancestry blurs cultural boundaries as similarities abound in other versions of women much like her. In most instances, her name is associated with evil; however, ambiguity abounds in her legend, and new perspectives tend to view her as a victim.

Endnotes

1. Alfred Avila. *Mexican Ghost Tales of the Southwest.* Houston: Piñata Books, 1994. 11–12.
2. Irene I. Blea. "Spanish Impact on the Changing Role of New World Women." *La Chicana and the Intersection of Race, Class, and Gender.* Westport: Praeger, 1992. 30.
3. Ibid. 31.
4. Ibid. 32.
5. Rick Hernandez. "La Llorona in Other Cultures." 15 Nov. 2003. *http://www.lallorona.com/siren_white.html.*

6. John O. West, "The Weeping Woman: LaLlorona." *Legendary Ladies of Texas.* F. E. Abernethy, Ed. Dallas: E-Heart Press. 1981. 31.
7. Joe Nickell. "Legend of the White Lady." 1 December 2003 *http://www.csicop.org.*
8. Ibid.
9. "Lamia." 26 November 2003 *http://www.pantheon.org/articles/l/lamia.html.*
10. Gertrude Jobes, Ed. *Dictionary of Mythology, Folklore and Symbols.* New York: Scarecrow Press, 1962. 967.
11. Nathan Ausubel, Ed. *A Treasury of Jewish Folklore.* New York: Crown Publishers, 1948.
12. Ibid. 593.
13. Ibid. 594.
14. Lilly Rivlin. "Lilith." *Ms.* December 1972: 96.
15. Ibid. 114.

Donna Meletio

9

BURNING BRIGHTLY: THE EASTER FIRES OF MATERNAL NECESSITY

by Donna Meletio

"Freedom is not free—It is costly."—John O. Meusebach

Imagine if you will that the season is late winter in the year 1847. The night air is cold outside a woman's small cabin in a new settlement in the Pedernales valley in the Texas Hill Country west of Austin. She is alone in the dark with her young children; many women in her small German community are likewise alone, having fended for themselves since late January, when the men had gone northwest to try to negotiate a treaty with the Comanche Indians. The men's purpose in leaving was to secure their community from Indian raids, but the women are alone, vulnerable and frightened, even as they try to keep up a brave front for the sake of their children. Up in the hills surrounding the valley, they can see the glow of Indian campfires, and each one wonders as the night passes if her husband is still alive, if she will survive another night.

This woman has braved other challenges before and survived. Just a year earlier, in 1846, she had come with 120 other emigrants from Germany to settle this new colony called Fredericksburg. Her group had landed in Indianola, on the Texas Gulf coast, and had traveled for sixteen days to reach this area. During the journey, friends and fellow colonists died of cholera; in fact, one in every ten perished, but she was one of the lucky ones. This night, she prays that she will endure once again if there is another Indian raid.

While the plight of these women who were left alone in the winter of 1847 has been passed down primarily through oral history, the accounts of German Texans have been well documented. The new colony was led by the 34-year-old, red-headed Baron Ottfried Hans, Freiherr von Meusebach who had changed his name to John O. Meusebach when he arrived in Texas.[1] He had been appointed commissioner of the Adelsverein (the Noble Society, or the Society for the Protection of German Emigrants to Texas) that had been "organized between April 12, 1842, and March 24, 1844"[2] to secure the safe voyage and settlement of colonists who were leaving Germany to seek religious freedom and to escape the laws of primogeniture. Within two years, "thirty-six ships carrying 7,400 settlers arrived in Texas [but . . .] 4,600 (62%) of these groups died within two years."[3] The Adelsverein had purchased land from the Fisher-Miller grant, but in order to secure title to these lands they had to survey the land before September 1, 1847. The Adelsverein were hindered, however, from traveling past the Llano River because of hostilities with the Penateka Comanche Indians and other Indian groups.

Meusebach knew that he had to survey the land and to find a solution to the constant threat of Indian raids. As community leader, he organized a group of approximately forty men to meet with the Comanches to see if he could effect a treaty in order to co-exist peacefully. On January 22, 1847, he arranged to travel to San Saba to meet with the Comanches who had a winter encampment there. On February 5, 1847, he made friendly contact with Chief Ketumse near what is now Mason, Texas, and on February 9, he was joined by "veteran treaty-maker Major Robert S. Neighbors and Jim Shaw [Bear Head], a Delaware who knew the Comanche language."[4] Neighbors had won the respect and trust of the Comanches when he had helped with the United States Treaty with the Indians in Texas in 1846.

Towards the end of February or "on March 1 and 2, Meusebach and his party met with the Comanches who were headed by Chiefs Buffalo Hump, Santana [or Santa Anna] and Mopechucope [Old Owl],"[5] and they began treaty negotiations. During the time that the men were gone on this mission, however, the women and children in Fredericksburg were left with scant protection, but Meusebach believed so strongly in the success of his undertaking that he considered that the greater risk lay in allowing the current situation to continue, and he even went so far as to ignore the Indian agent, Major Neighbors, who had been sent by Governor J. Pinckney Henderson to warn the colonists.

The Indians had good reason to distrust any overtures made by white settlers. In many other situations, Indian leaders had been lured to treaty negotiations not realizing that cavalry soldiers were en route to massacre them. In order to protect themselves, the Comanche leaders sent scouts to look for soldiers who might be following Meusebach's group. They also sent warriors to watch over the German settlers, and these warriors lit fires in the hills surrounding Fredericksburg in order to exchange smoke signals with their leaders. If the treaty failed or if the Comanche leaders were ambushed, the Indians were to attack the settlement.

In the valley below; the women and children watched those fires anxiously, fearing for their safety. During the long winter nights, the children would become afraid, and according to accounts passed down by the survivors, one mother alone with her children, creatively found a way to calm her children's fears. Because Easter was approaching, she told them that the fires in the hills had been lit by the Easter bunnies who had picked wildflowers, such as bluebonnets, pink primroses, yellow buttercups, purple verbena, and scarlet Indian Paintbrush, and that the bunnies were boiling the flowers in pots of water to make dyes to color Easter eggs. Because the story was so successful, it soon spread throughout the community.

Soon thereafter, Meusebach and his contingency returned on March 7, 1847, and the peace treaty was ratified on May 9, 1847, in Fredericksburg.[6] The Germans agreed to give the Comanche $1,000 in Spanish dollars and $2,000 in gifts for the right to survey and hunt in the land north of the Llano River; the Indians would also be granted access to enter and trade in Fredericksburg. The treaty was signed by "J. O. Meusebach, R. S. Neighbors,

F. Schubert, J. Torrey, Jim Shaw, John Connor, Santa Anna, Buffalo Hump, Old Owl and Ketumse . . ." and "copies of the treaty are in the Solms-Braunfels Archive, the Library of The University of Texas, Archives Division."[7] The success of the treaty over the next few years was due in large part to the benevolent power of Chief Santana. As successful as this treaty was, however, what the people of Fredericksburg chose to celebrate every year thereafter was not just the treaty, but also the Easter fire story told to the children.

From a folklore perspective, the most intriguing aspect of this story is its combination of cultural, religious, and pragmatic elements. In Germany, there are legends about "märchen" of fairies who light fires on the hillside forests to celebrate the new birth of spring. As a practical matter, the accumulation of dry brush is collected and burned every spring to facilitate new forest growth. In the *Handbook of Texas,* Terry G. Jordan states that this practice can be traced to the "provinces of Westphalia and Lower Saxony in northern Germany" and that these "Hanoverians were one of the two largest groups in early Fredericksburg."[8] Thus, this cultural heritage was imported into a new world context wherein the German tradition was merged into the popular lore of the Easter Bunny, who dyed eggs and brought them to the children at Easter. The result was a combination of Christian and pagan traditions.

Ruth Reichman at Purdue University states that there has been much speculation about the connection between pagan and Christian rituals and symbols. The bunny or the hare (the Osterhase) is a symbol of fertility, and the egg is a symbol of the beginning of new life—two ancient symbols connected to Eostre, the Anglo-Saxon goddess of fertility (and from which we get the words "estrus" or "estrogen," the female hormone).[9] According to some sources, in Europe in 1682, these symbols were incorporated into the Christian celebration of the new life of Christ who arose from the dead at Easter. Thus, the ancient pagan symbols and the Christian ones were synthesized into a common celebration of new life that arises out of the seeming dead of winter.

This story told by the German mothers is a creative adaptation born out of maternal necessity to protect their young, and it is one that combines pagan, Christian, old world, new world, religious, and folk icons into a new legend that is emblematic of the synthesis the new world represents, one where all faiths, walks of life, and cultures combine, and where people work together to secure survival. The woman's story is as much about the peace treaty as the treaty itself: it takes what is known and recasts it into a workable solution to secure peace for the children, just as the men secured peace for the community. Both address personal fears and overcome them to secure a workable solution, utilizing life experience and assembling strength in order to find creative ways of recognizing opportunity and to find new ways of seeing the world and securing a place in it. In a strange new land, these settlers took the raw material of their cultural heritage and blended it with the novel experiences of their new world, and formed a new identity, and with the clay of maternal necessity cast a new monument.

Today, Fredericksburg still serves as testament to those cultural values represented by the legend born in 1847, and each year the citizens celebrate their treaty with the Comanche and the story told to the children in the form of an Easter Fires Pageant. For 155 years the entire community has come together to collect wood and stack bonfires in the hills surrounding the town, and the same duties are often passed down from generation to generation. The Easter Fires Pageant began in 1946, and is a community project involving the Boy Scouts, local choirs, civic clubs, and schools. As a result of the work of many families and groups the final production is held at the local grandstand not far from downtown, and continues to draw large crowds today. The contributing cast members are often as many as 600 people.

At the pageant, the history of the Treaty and the Easter Fires is read over a loudspeaker while the Pageant is presented in several sections. First, the story is told of the Indians and the tale of a little girl who placed her prized blue corn husk doll into the sacrificial fires in order to bring rain to the dry region. According to legend, when the rains came, bluebonnets bloomed everywhere as nature's tribute to the little girl's sacrifice. To honor this tale, young pageant participants dress up as wildflowers and dance a ballet. Another section of the pageant depicts the story of the treaty and its negotiations, as well as the story of the mother who first told the tale of the Easter Bunny's fires in the hills. There is also a section devoted to the story of the first church (Vereinskirche), which was a "community church for all creeds,"[10] and they ring the evening bells (Abendglocken) with the original church bell. A men's chorus sings songs in German, and there are American patriotic songs included. At the end of the pageant, many townspeople of all ages enter the pageant grounds wearing Easter Bunny outfits in a variety of bright colors.

Ultimately, the pageant represents a synthesis of Indian and German cultures, Christian and Pagan rituals, and legend and lore, all achieved by the combined efforts of the townspeople who come not merely to be entertained but to enjoy a sense of pride and belonging, knowing that their hard-working hands have made the final production possible. No one is an un-invested observer: on that stage is a husband, brother, wife and daughter, sister and cousin, teacher and boss, employee and neighbor, co-worker and friend—and therein lies the success of this pageant. It is less about the production and more about the people behind it, those who have learned to create a life for themselves and sustain it for over a century, even in times when their peaceful co-existence with the Indians sometimes failed, and later when they struggled to create industry to support their community. If the study of folklore reveals anything, it shows the values, morals, and beliefs that underlie any cultural practice, and a study of the celebration of the Easter fires reveals that Fredericksburg is a tale of synthesis and survival. Even as the people of Fredericksburg have maintained the rich cultural heritage of Germany, they have incorporated the raw material of a new world and created something new.

The Pioneer Museum in Fredericksburg

If one were to look beyond the pageant itself, one would see that this sense of survival through synthesis resides throughout this community. While many small towns across this nation decline and disappear, Fredericksburg continues to flourish: it has museums, boutiques, restaurants, and businesses. It has a successful peach industry, wildflower and herb farms, wineries, sausage, chocolate, and fruit preserve manufacturing companies, a booming bed and breakfast business, and a publishing firm. Taking the raw material of their natural surroundings and incorporating the pride and hard-working industry of their German heritage, they have formed a new identity in a new world whose success began 155 years ago, when far-sighted men decided to work towards the success and survival of their community, and when a mother, facing the dark unknown and uncertainty of a new land, took what she knew of religion and lore—of her homeland and her new land—and formed a new story that at its core is the key to the success of these people.

Endnotes

1. Rudolph L. Biesele. "The Relations Between the German Settlers and the Indians of Texas 1844–1860." *Southwestern Historical Quarterly 41.* Oct 1927. 116n–117n.
2. Kenneth F. Neighbours. "The German-Commanche Treaty of 1847." *Texana 2.4.* Winter 1964. 311.
3. "Fredericksburg: Popular and Surviving in Spite of It." *Texas Southwest.* 24 (Pioneer Museum Archives). 24.
4. Karl A. Hoerig. "The Relationship between German Immigrants and the Native Peoples in Western Texas." *Southwestern Historical Quarterly* 97.3. Jan. 3, 1994. 429.
5. Ibid. 429.
6. Ibid. 430.
7. Neighbours. 322.
8. Terry G. Jordan. "Easter Fires." *The Handbook of Texas Online.* (March 5, 2002). *http://www.tsha.utexas.edu/handbook/online/articles/EE/lke2.html.*
9. Ruth M. Reichman. "Ostern/Easter." *Max Kade German-American Studies.* Indiana University-Purdue University Indianapolis. (March 5, 2002). *http://www.serve.com/shea/germusa/ostern.htm.*
10. William Petmecky. *Easter Fires of Fredericksburg Seventh Edition.* Fredericksburg Texas: Fredericksburg Publishing, 1979.

Additional Sources

Abernethy, Francis Edward. *Folklore of Texan Cultures.* 1974. Denton: University of North Texas Press, 2000.

Adams, Don. "Relived: Fredericksburg Early History." *The Austin American-Statesman.* (Pioneer Museum Archives).

"Cross Mountain Texas Historical Marker Dedicated." *Radio Post.* May 19, 1977. "Easter Fires Story, Legend Comes Alive at Annual Pageant Saturday Night."

"Easter in the Hills: Traditional Easter Fires are Re-kindled each Year." *Dallas Morning News: The Texas Star.* April 2, 1972.

Fredericksburg Standard-Radio Post. April 3, 2002.

King, Irene Marshall. *John O. Meusebach: German Colonizer in Texas.* Austin: University of Texas Press, 1967.

Knopp, Kenn, "Easter Fires Festival of Fredericksburg" and "The Fredericksburg Easter Fires Pageant." *News from Fredericksburg.* (Pioneer Museum Archives).

"Meusebach's Expedition into the Territory of the Commanche Indians in January, 1847." (From an old number of the *Magazine of Literature From Abroad*).

"Meusebach's Peace Treaty with the Indians." (Pioneer Museum Archives).

Penniger, Robert. *Fredericksburg Texas. The First Fifty Years: a translation of Penniger's 50th Anniversary Festival Edition*. Trans. Dr. Charles L. Wisseman. Fredericksburg: Fredericksburg Publishing, 1971.

Syers, Ed. "Fredericksburg's Fires of Easter: Pease Story." *San Antonio Express News*. April 11, 1965.

Tatsch, Ruth. "Legend and History Clasp Hands in Fredericksburg." *Texas Historian*. Jan. 1971.

FOLKLORE AT WORK:

OCCUPATIONAL LORE

A drilling rig with several stands of drill pipe in the derrick

10

FIVE STANDS OFF BOTTOM

by Lew Schnitz, P.E., P.G.

[Drill pipe is usually run into a well or pulled out of a well in "stands" of two joints or three joints, depending on the height of the derrick. A joint of drill pipe measures approximately 30 feet in length.—*Schnitz*]

We were five stands off bottom when it happened. The mud tanks started running over. The well started kicking over the bell nipple. It was the derrick man's fault because he's supposed to take care of the mud! Most of these stories that started with "five stands off bottom" went rapidly downhill from there.

This paper is about some of the early day drillers, toolpushers, bosses, and service people who had come from boom days drilling at Spindletop, Kilgore, Ranger, Desdemona, King Ranch Stratton, and other famous oilfields. The stories are about a few of us who interfaced with them as we entered a phase of deep high pressure drilling on South Texas' large ranches. My forty years in the Texas oil patch before I retired from Exxon gave me the opportunity to meet and work with several old-time drillers and toolpushers whose work ethic, wisdom, wit, and humor is legend.

Almost everyone had a nickname, and you will hear several of them as these stories are told. There was "The Gray Fox," "Jew" Ober, and "Fwop Down" (because he would flop down almost anywhere on the rig floor or catwalk and sleep). There was "Blister," who always showed up after the work was over, or "Gavilan," the chicken hawk. My nickname was "Coyote." They said I had shifty "coyote" eyes and I had lived in the brush country so long I thought more like a coyote than a human.

"Jew" Ober was a rotund, Mr. "Five by Five" driller with a big booming voice and a ton of humor. You could hear him holding court in the bunkhouse chow hall long before you got to the door. He told a story about being in a poker game in East Texas, where they called a Bowie knife a "Bow-wee Runner." He said the betting had come to an end and the players were declaring their hands. One said, "I've got three sixes" and another declared that he had a full house. One man sitting by Jew said, "I've got two deuces and a Bow-wee Runner!" The player with the full house said, "You lucky son-of-a-gun. You always draw out on me."

C. L. "Smokey" Starnes was a toolpusher when I was associated with him. He was very dedicated, hard-working, and handled the Company (Humble Oil & Refining Company, later Exxon Corporation) rigs and equipment like they were his own. In the early 1940s, a well blew out in the Greta Field between Victoria and Refugio. The well caught fire and the rig cratered; that is, it fell into the hole created by the blowout. Highway 77 had to be re-routed around the blowout for years, but one could see the crater from the highway. Several important events occurred because of that blowout that still impact drilling and producing operations today. Since the well was blowing out underground and was charging all the shallow sands in the area, even water wells were blowing out and it made all drilling operations very dicey. Smokey Starnes moved to Greta in the mid-1950s with a company rig to drill several wells. He knew the history of the field through information he got from other rig hands and drillers, and from company knowledge of the blowout history. I arrived at the location and stepped out of the company car with my hard hat and boots to help Smokey drill this particular well. He met me halfway to the toolhouse and said, "Boy, don't you dare pull up a weed out here. It'll blowout on you. Why, look: all the crawdad holes are blowing out"—and they were. The sands were charged so shallow that the crawdad holes were bubbling and blowing natural gas. There was at least one incident where someone stepped out of a car, lit a cigarette and threw a match to the ground, causing a flash fire as the lighted match ignited the natural gas at ground level.

Old drilling friends: Lew "Coyote" Schnitz, Leonard "Gray Fox" Kemp, and R. L. "Junior" Westbrook, Jr.

When radios first started being used to communicate between the rigs and the District Office, there were some very funny conversations that took place—some of them tellable in polite company; some of them not. Smokey had been at the rig all night, maybe several days, having trouble with the well "kicking" (that is, trying to blow the drilling mud out of the hole). Chester Burrage was the warehouseman, the person the toolpusher called when they needed supplies or equipment. One morning Smokey called Chester on the radio and the conversation went something like this:

> Smokey: Chester, this old well has been kicking on me all night and I need you to send me some Baroid out here right now.
>
> Chester: How much of this Baroid do you need, Smokey?
>
> Smokey: Hell, Chester, that ain't near enough!

Smokey was used to the warehouseman trying to cut back on supplying equipment and materials to keep costs down.

We developed a form of communication meant to get the point across without stirring up others who might hear. For example, I would tell Gigi, who was the radio and telephone communicator at the office, "I'll be out at Arroyo Conejo this afternoon." She knew where to reach me. Arroyo Conejo sounded like many other South Texas ranch pasture leases. Actually, it was the nickname we had for the golf course, or "Rabbit Run."

H. H. "Clearwater" Howell was a wildcatter in South Texas. He was nicknamed "Clearwater" because he didn't believe in spending money on weighting material for his drilling mud and had his rigs drill wells with clear water. Anyone who has been around the oilfield at all knows that there is something wrong with this picture. A wildcatter in South Texas with the nickname "Clearwater" adds up to a lot of well control problems—to be brutally honest—blowouts. Mr. Howell had his drillers trained in his ways. The story goes about one driller who called in on the radio and said, "Mr. Howell, this well has been kicking on us and right now it is flowing up to the first girt on the derrick. We need some weight material to kill it." Clearwater replied, "Hank, I'm going to send you two sacks of Baroid and I want you to kill that well if it takes every damn bit of it!" A thousand sacks wouldn't have been enough!

Chris Dowden was a toolpusher in charge of Company Rig 44. Chris was a good toolpusher and tried very hard to achieve efficiency, efficiency in drilling and in moving the rig to minimize lost motion. Chris talked with a slight lisp and had a kind of sing-song voice that earned him the name of "Crying Chris" Dowden.

When a roughneck worked himself up the rig hierarchy to the status of "Morning Tour Driller" (working morning tour), he was rewarded by getting to be in charge of moving the rig. R. L. "Junior" Westbrook got to that point on Rig 44. He was trying his best to make rig moves go smoothly with little lost motion. But he didn't please Chris. After observing several of Junior's rig moves and on a day when nothing pleased him, Chris told Junior in his unmistakable voice: "Dod Dammit Junior, the first two things you move are the coffee pot and the shit house."

"My Good Man" Thompson was a pot-fireman on Rig 11 when I knew him and worked with him. I don't know what his first name was, but he addressed everybody as "My Good Man"—and that's what we called him. Jody Skaggs transferred to Rig 11 as a driller and he wanted to be sure his pot fireman always had enough good steam so he wouldn't be short of steam to drill or pull out of the hole when he had to. He was ragging "My Good Man" around about how he wanted plenty of steam available when he wanted it—no mistakes. The old pot fireman replied, "My Good Man, I could keep plenty steam up by firing these three boilers with goose feathers—and pick my own geese!"

Oilfields operated somewhat differently in the days before OSHA. A contractor roughneck dropped a piece of "spinning" chain in the casing on S. K. East B-13 in Kenedy County. We fished for several days for the chain with no progress. We decided that we needed to pick up on the casing and get the slips out to nipple up blow-out preventers and improve our fishing results. The rig pulled on the casing with a spear until the driller and toolpusher refused to pull any more, fearing they would pull the derrick down, resulting in fatalities—especially theirs. The next step was to pull on the casing with hydraulic jacks. In this way, an operator could work several yards away from the rig with hydraulic controls without much hazard to personnel. With this operation, we pulled up to 400,000 pounds on the casing to no avail.

Homco was on location, ready to "string-shot" the casing loose downhole whenever we got the slips out. The string-shot method used an explosive (prima-cord) to jar the casing connection at a depth where it was free and allow us to back off the casing. The operator on that truck was "Peewee Hodges." Peewee said he had idea how we could get those slips loose if we could come around to his plan. His plan was to wrap three wraps of prima-cord (an explosive used exclusively in downhole operations) around the casing head and run the detonator controls over behind the pipe racks where he promised we could all hunker in relative safety. "Relative to what?" we asked. No comment from

Peewee. This was at a time when the bosses in the office didn't want to hear about your problems, especially in the middle of the night, and didn't care how you did the job. They just looked at the results, good or bad. Why did all that change when I got to be the boss in the office?

We took a strain on the casing with the hydraulic jacks. Peewee wrapped three wraps of prima-cord around the casinghead and put the detonator cap in place. He then ran the electric firing line a distance of about 40 yards behind the pipe racks. We company men, roughnecks, lease crews, and any others on location were behind the racks long before Peewee got there. He warned us to expect a very loud noise and to stay hunkered under the pipe to avoid any miscellaneous flying iron particles. We braced ourselves, put our fingers in our ears (state-of-the-art ear protection) and Peewee fired the shot. There was a very loud noise and iron rattled for 30 seconds, but the slips came loose!

The radio conversation to the District Office was called in the next morning at 5:30 A.M. (No one wanted to hear anything in the middle of the night, only at morning report time). The radio conversation was short and without any embellishment. "We got the slips loose on S. K. East B-13 and we're preparing to nipple up blowout preventers and resume fishing." I'm sure the engineers and operations supervisors went into the morning meeting in the District Office and said only, "We got those slips loose." DON'T ASK. DON'T TELL.

They called him "Fwop Down" because he would frequently "fwop down" behind the draw works and go to sleep. But this story is not so much about Fwop Down as it is about Junior Westbrook's "new development" and beating Coots Matthews of Boots & Coots out of a blowout control job. A Flournoy rig was drilling S. K. East 28 at about 9000 feet with surface casing set at 1000 feet. Fwop Down was overall co-ordinator of the rig operations but Junior Westbrook was the on-site supervisor. I was the Drilling Engineer Specialist. This meant whenever and wherever a rig was in trouble (blowouts, lost returns, etc.) I went to the rig until we got it under control. The well started to kicking and they had to close the hydril blowout preventer to contain the well, build mud weight, and pump in to try to kill the well. Junior mixed mud and pumped in for two days and nights with no returns and no results as far as killing the well. He would call in periodically and tell what his mud weight was and how much mud he had pumped in the drillpipe without seeing any results. Fwop Down would take the radio, call, laugh, and tell Junior to keep at it.

One morning Junior was calling in a routine report and in the middle of his conversation, he said, "Wait a minute. I've got a new development. I found out where my mud's been going." The well was blowing out underground at the surface casing seat and had broached to the surface through shallow faults, blowing small geysers of gas and condensate in Junior's mud pits and all around the rig.

The District Superintendent called Boots and Coots and they dispatched Coots Mathews to Kingsville. He came to town, checked into the local motel and prepared to meet with the District Superintendent the next day to discuss his plans to kill the well. My boss, Jerry Bullock, called me in and told me to get Weldon Whitaker and go down there and work with Junior and get that well under control.

We called Halliburton to be on location ASAP with four pump trucks, 5000 sacks of barite, and 5000 sacks of cement. They arrived about dark and tied into the drill pipe and annulus. Halliburton started mixing barite and cement, pumping barite down the drill pipe and cement down the annulus, with me on one pump truck and Junior on the other. Weldon had his explosimeter held at hip level and was checking for explosive limits because the exhausts on Halliburton's trucks were cherry red from the extensive pumping. Weldon signaled us that we had explosive limits at hip level all around the rig. Junior and I certainly knew the danger we were in, and I'm sure the Halliburton crew knew it from the look on our faces. One Halliburton cementer later told Junior, "You big son-of-a-bitch, if you hadn't been blocking my way to the ladder, I would have shut down the pumps and vacated that location." We continued pumping until we had the barite and cement used up, and those minutes really dragged. But activities really picked up when we finished pumping and told Halliburton to rig down.

I've never seen Halliburton crews knock loose and spool-up faster in my life. They rigged down and we all retreated to the sandhill above the rig. It was about 5 A.M. by then, and not yet time to call in the morning report, so we sat back in our cars and took a short nap. We called in the morning report about 6:00 A.M. and I'll bet by now you can write the script for the radio call: "We got that well dead on S. K. East 28. You can send Coots Mathews back to Houston." Then, we all went to Riviera and had chicken fried steak and eggs for breakfast. I'm not sure but it could have been a few Lone Stars on the table.

S. K. East 37 blew out. Now, not every well we drilled blew out. I'm just telling about the ones that were the most fun. The well was blowing gas, water and sand—so much water that the gas did not catch fire. It appeared from a distance (about seventy-five yards) that the blowout had almost cut the blowout preventer stack off the drill pipe.

Coots Mathews, Leonard Kemp, and I were standing by the toolhouse watching the rig substructure as the well was blowing wild, threatening to crater. Coots said, "You know, we need to walk down there under that substructure and see if that HCR valve is open. If it is, we could close it and maybe that would stop the flow from the annulus." The Gray Fox looked at me, then over to Coots and said, "Where do you get that 'we' sh—? Who is the one pulling down the big bucks here?" We walked down there and found the HCR valve had been cut off by the blowout and was lying on the ground. So that was the end of that good plan. We drilled a relief well, but by the time we got halfway down, the blowout had bridged over and quit flowing.

Nowadays, new employees of oil companies must undergo considerable training. First, they read a lengthy Safety Manual, then the Ethics Manual and others. Things were different back while I was in college in the late 1940s. I went to work for Humble

Oil & Refining Company in the Imogene District near Pleasanton. My training and orientation session was by Superintendent A. B. Van Heuser. His words of training were, "Boy, pay attention to those old heads out there so you don't get yourself hurt or killed, and watch out for those rattlesnakes." End of training.

Well, with all that wisdom, training and advice about drilling oil and gas wells, I'm going to leave you "five stands off bottom." You have a new drilling bit on and your mud man and driller are among the best. Go back to drilling. Don't call me until morning report time, make a lot of hole, and don't screw it up.

The author acknowledges the following referents: Leonard D. Kemp, Carroll Starnes, Georgia Clancy "Gigi" Starnes, R. L. "Junior" Westbrook, George Dabney, Weldon Whitaker, and The Halliburton Company.

Charles Williams

11

DISPATCHES FROM THE ELECTRONIC FRONT LINES

by Charles Williams

The reporter knocked on the door a little after 6:00 A.M. The tall, slightly stooped elderly man who answered the door had obviously just gotten up, and he was still dressed in a worn bathrobe. The reporter excitedly asked what he was going to do next. The man paused and thought about it, and then answered that he thought he'd make a pot of coffee. The reporter pressed on, until it became obvious the man had no idea what he was talking about, or why this should be any kind of a special day. Finally, the reporter broke the news to him—he had just won the Nobel Prize for Physics. It turns out that Jack Kilby, who was the man who had answered the door, had taken out his hearing aids when going to sleep and had missed the official call from Sweden.

This is only the latest in a continuing line of dispatches from one of the most exciting areas of new folktales, the electronic front lines. It is peopled by exciting, eccentric, energetic, enthusiastic, entrepreneurial, egotistic, exuberant explorers who are inventing a new industry and changing our very world while they do it. They are engineers, dreamers, medicine show pitchmen, computer geeks (and isn't it interesting how much carnival slang has drifted over into this industry), sleight-of-hand (or perhaps sleight-of-mind) artists, and other assorted types who have embraced the latest of the get-rich-quick mother lodes. It is a profoundly young industry, and to this point, no one has written the definitive biography of it. Tracy Kidder has come the closest, but he has only captured a moment in time, which was largely obsolete by the time his books were published. It is a profoundly mobile industry, where employees have a loyalty to the industry rather than to a company, and no one expects to spend their entire career working for one company. Quite the opposite—there's a curious stigma attached to that, like "How come you never moved, aren't you good enough to work somewhere else?" The successful firms have countered this by encouraging movement within the company, so very few have worked with the same people in the same group more than a decade. The net result of this is that corporate (and industry) culture get transmitted by story—kind of a classic definition of folklore and folktales.

This paper will share some of those folktales. I make no pretense of presenting a scholarly examination of the way traditions developed, nor any coherent tracing of their growth. It is instead a collection of those stories garnered from thirty-plus years working in the industry. Actually, I've had the incredible good fortune to have worked for two of the deepest lodes of the electronic story mines, Fairchild Semiconductor and Texas Instruments. So, let me launch off in the way I do when introducing the history of TI to TIers, with a little bit of swing music.

What does the music of Artie Shaw have to do with semiconductors? To understand the answer to that question, you have to go back to Christmas Eve in 1947 to a small town in New Jersey. The world had just been through a devastating world war, a war that in the minds of the public had largely been won through the efforts of the scientists. Further, the people expected the scientists to now lead them into an era of unprecedented peace and prosperity. On that snowy December afternoon, many of those hopes were about to be realized.

Three men were gathered around a crude piece of scientific apparatus. The tall, shy-looking man in the back was John Bardeen, probably the most outstanding physicist America has ever produced. He would go on to win two Nobel prizes—one for his work here, and one in another, separate field. The kindly looking man standing next to him was Walter Britain, experimenter extraordinaire, and the man who actually constructed the apparatus of interest. The man sitting down at the microscope was William

Shockley, who was to play a key role in the industry being born in that room. He was the leader of that extraordinary group of scientists, and they were putting on a dog-and-pony show for him.

The object beneath the scope was a piece of grayish metal with an odd looking arrow-head of Lucite covered with gold foil pressed down against it. It was connected (with a bent paper clip) to a microphone, forming a crude amplifier. Shockley picked up the microphone, said "Hello" into it, "Hello" boomed back from a speaker across the room, and the world was forever changed.

Not, however, right away. The grayish metal was germanium, and the scientists at Bell Labs in Murray Hill, New Jersey (which was the name of the small town) had just demonstrated the world's first point contact transistor. The world reacted—with monumental indifference. In point of fact, Bell Labs had somewhat of a problem figuring out what to do with it. They had been locked in a tight race with several other labs, most notably Purdue University, to demonstrate the transistor. The idea was not new; the first patents on the transistor go back to the 1920s. Bell Labs did some characterization, and announced it at the end of June in 1948. The *New York Times* gave it a short paragraph, right below the times for the Boston Braves/Brooklyn Dodgers and Philadelphia Athletics/St. Louis Browns double headers and traffic reports for the upcoming Fourth of July weekend. Bell decided to issue some licenses and let others figure out how to use it.

Among those applying for a license was a small company in Dallas, Texas. They had been an oilfield service company, specializing in seismographic work. During the war, they had worked closely with the navy developing anti-submarine technology, and they were ready to expand. One of the contacts they had made at the Department of the Navy was instrumental in overcoming Bell Lab's reluctance to grant a license to this newcomer, and he even agreed to become their president. They had changed their name to Texas Instruments, and Pat Haggerty believed in them enough to join them. TI promptly hired a Bell Labs scientist name Gordon Teale and boldly launched off in a new direction: silicon.

The first transistors were germanium, but germanium has some severe technical limitations, mostly in temperature range. Everyone knew that the silicon was the more promising material, but it was hard to work with and very difficult to process. Every so often, Bell sponsored a meeting of all the license holders and, in 1954, Gordon sat and listened as all the big companies—DuMont, RCA, General Electric, Zenith, etc.—explained that while silicon was obviously the material of choice, it was at least two years away. No, another speaker would say, it's four years away, and another would say it's at least ten years away. That afternoon, Gordon Teale calmly got up and announced that TI had silicon transistors in production and pulled some out of his pocket. He then arranged a demonstration. A record player was set up next to a glass of hot oil. A germanium transistor was put in the circuit, and when it was plunged into the hot oil, the music stopped. Teale then unplugged the germanium transistor and plugged in a silicon transistor. When he plunged that into the hot oil, in Teale's words, "The swinging notes of 'Summit Ridge Drive' continued unabated." The meeting broke up in pandemonium amid calls for samples and prices, and a small company in Texas had set the world on its ear.

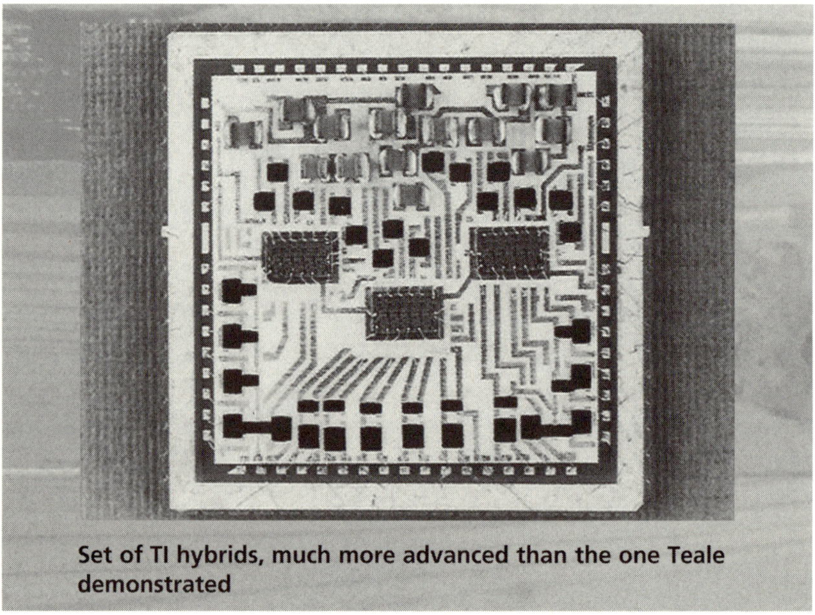

Set of TI hybrids, much more advanced than the one Teale demonstrated

But the story does not end there. Most people saw the transistor as a super small vacuum tube, and that was the way it was produced and sold. However, the Air Force saw it in a slightly different light. They were in the midst of designing the Minuteman missile, and needed everything small, smaller, and smallest. The thing that got in their way was what was called the tyranny of numbers. All the components had to be soldered together, and solder joints were only 98% or so reliable. If you have hundreds of joints, that means your chance of anything working on the first try was slim or none—not a good thing if you're talking about a missile with a lifetime of one shot. In the summer of 1958, TI hired a young engineer away from Centralab in Wisconsin. They told him to work on the interconnection problem, and then left him alone for two weeks. That happened because in those days, TI had mass vacation the first two weeks of July, and since the new guy didn't have any vacation, he was left alone in the lab. It was at that time that he had the flash of insight that was to lead to the Nobel Prize forty years later. That young engineer, who was of course Jack Kilby, reasoned that if he could make all of the circuit components out of silicon, he could interconnect them with thin metal layers, which are orders of magnitude more reliable than wires. He built a sample circuit, and on September 12, 1958, he hooked up a crude device to a battery and an oscilloscope. A perfect curve showed up on the oscilloscope, and in that quiet moment, the world was forever changed. Jack had demonstrated the first integrated circuit, and the rest, as they say, is history. By the way, to give you some concept of just how much it has changed, if a digital cell phone were made with vacuum tubes, it would be the size of the Washington Monument.

Speaking of Jack and cell phones and the general uses to which his invention has been put, it is somewhat ironic that Jack did not own a cell phone, nor for that matter, much advanced technology. Jack has commented, "Communication between people has become much easier. Cell phones, that sort of thing, are now very common. If you don't like the telephone much, and I don't, you may not consider that a plus." Once, when asked what he thought was the best thing to have come out of the invention of the IC,

Jack, who is hard of hearing, replied that the hearing aid had to be up there. Jack also developed the hand-held calculator. Later, when I had the privilege of working with him on another project, we would sometimes meet in his office. Whenever a question came up that needed calculation, Jack would reach into his desk drawer and pull out a circular slide rule and figure the answer. Now, as far as I am concerned, being able to use a circular slide rule is proof enough of genius, but we asked Jack one day why he used the slide rule when he had invented the hand-held calculator. In his careful, soft-spoken way, he replied that while the answer might be more exact with a calculator, you had no way of knowing if you had put the number in correctly, and you might be off by an order of magnitude. On the other hand, his answer on the slide rule might not be as exact, but it was going to be awfully close.

Jack Kilby with the solar energy system he invented

Jack was a gentleman in every sense of that word, and it is somewhat ironic that even if he had known he had won the Nobel Prize, his reply to the reporter at six in the morning might well have been the same. Not that he can't be a little ironic himself on occasion. Tom Engibous, the present CEO of TI, tells of the time that he and some of his fellow vice-presidents made a pitch to Jerry Junkins, who was then president. At the time, business was in a downturn, and TI was scrambling to recover. The pitch was impressive, with full-color foils and dynamic action plans. After it had been made, Jerry went around the table and asked for comments. Everyone said how impressed they were, until he got to Jack. Jack leaned back and asked, "Aren't these the same guys who got us into the ditch in the first place?" (Since this paper was presented, Jack Kilby has passed away. The world is a poorer place.)

In many ways, TI culture was the antithesis of Jack's personality. Born in the oilfields of the '30s, it started life as a seismographic oil exploration company called GSI. There is a story about a visiting number-cruncher who was pressed into emergency service at a drilling site, to lend a hand turning a hand auger. The disconcerted and momentarily demoted professional cursed and grumbled that when he joined GSI, he was supposed to be a numbers man and that he hadn't hired out as a field hand for a beastly job like that. "And neither did I," mumbled the mud-stained man on the other end of the auger handle. "What job did they hire you for?" asked the computer man sympathetically. "President," croaked J. Clarance "Doc" Karcher, Ph.D. and co-founder, as he strained to bear down on the auger.

That tradition of hard work and rough-and-tumble tactics carried over into the new company Texas Instruments. Hours were long—twelve- and fourteen-hour days were common, and weekend work was more likely than not. Meetings were often adventures where the faint-hearted dare not go, and disputes were settled by who had the loudest voice. Old timers talk in awe of a meeting where Mark Shepard got so mad he threw a chair through a window, and another one where another high-ranking officer got up on the table and mooned the other participants. I had a female tech who told about being in meetings with the Department Manager and Head of Silicon Production over die sizes. Things would get heated and the language would get rougher and rougher. Finally, when they were mad enough to get up and stomp and pound, they would notice the girls and tell them they were excused.

They also used to tell about Head of the Hermetic Seal Department Paul Goundry. (Hermetic Seals are small packages with vacuum-tight seals made for electronic components; they particularly keep out moisture, which is very detrimental to reliability.) He would have weekly production meetings in HSD where he would verbally beat up on his line foremen when they were behind in production, which they inevitably were. One of them, however, would always tell Paul he was right on schedule until the last week of the month, when he, too would be behind. His fellow supervisors asked him one time why he did that, and he told them that while they got beat up four times a month, he only got it once.

Not all was rough, and there were plenty of opportunities for fun. Pat Haggerty was pushing hard one time to get an order shipped. The production engineer and foreman had had enough of it, and they loaded all the rejects into a wheelbarrow. After the order was safely in shipping, they rushed the wheelbarrow into Pat's office, dumped them on the floor and said here they were, what did he want to do with them? For a long time, the company also provided free donuts and coffee at break time, and nearly twenty years later, some of those old donuts were still around, kept as mementos along with old packages and rejected silicon slices.

And then there was The Creek. The TI plant was in a dry area, and the nearest bar was a ramshackle joint on Greenville Avenue called The Creek. The Dallas Cowboys were in their early years at that time as well, and the Cowboy coaches and TI engineers spent many an interesting evening telling war stories while sitting on the empty beer cases that were the seating at The Creek. Unfortunately, it burned before I had a chance to go there, but I did see the end of one of the other institutions, The Dallas Inn. It was right across the freeway from TI, and it was the sort of place where you rented rooms by the hour, clean sheets extra. It was heavily used during the day for that purpose, and for card games at night. TI Security sponsored a workshop on plant protection one time, and invited an FBI agent to be the main speaker. His secretary, being totally unfamiliar with Dallas, booked him into the closest motel to TI—The Dallas Inn. The next day, one of the local law officers took him aside, quietly explained to him they had him on surveillance tape, and suggested he might want to find more suitable quarters. He did. It changed hands soon after I moved to Dallas and three nights after it changed hands, it burned in a rather spectacular fire.

But TI was a quiet haven compared to the West Coast, and Silicon Valley. My days at Fairchild were amazing to a sheltered farm boy from upstate New York who thought that because he'd gone to college, worked in the Atomic Energy Commission and for Coors Porcelain that he was a man of the world. Wrong. Silicon Valley was the wildest place I have ever worked. Fairchild was full of brilliant people, good line supervisors and top management, but was totally mismanaged at the mid-levels. I worked in the Hybrid Department, which had three groups: Sales, Production, and Engineering. The Sales Manager and the Production Manager were continually at each other's throats. So, one day the Department Manager called a meeting and announced that the Sales Manager was now head of production and the Production Manager was now head of sales. It was a disaster. While they were suited by personality for their original jobs, they were totally unsuited for their new ones, and the department never recovered.

To give you some flavor of the Production guy, Fairchild won a program to produce units for the 747 in-seat entertainment module. It was a big job, both in terms of the size of the contract and the size of the module. The production floor didn't have a screen printer large enough to handle the module, so this guy went out to a screen printer vendor and told them he was interested in buying one of their larger machines, and could he try it out for a while?

They were most happy to do so, and he brought it in and ran the production across it. Then, when he had finished, he brought in the salesman, told him the machine was a pile of crap, and to get it out of his sight. That was fine until some of the modules came back and he had to replace them. He then called the screen printer company back, told them he had been hasty, and asked could he borrow it again? They declined.

Not that it made a lot of difference to the engineers. My office-mate in my time in Mountain View was a young engineer who had developed an interesting twist on a product. Instead of trying to get it produced at Fairchild (which admittedly would have been difficult), he spent most of his time during the day calling potential investors to start his own company. The most interested investor was . . . Sherman Fairchild. And while Dallas had The Creek, Silicon Valley had Walker's Wagon Wheel and Ricky's. They were sort of industry conference rooms, where engineers from all companies could meet and work out problems, with the added bonus of picking up line girls when the technical talk got boring. This camaraderie fostered a loyalty to the industry, which was good for the technical progress of semiconductors, but poor for any individual company. Fairchild does not exist anymore, but the entrepreneurial spirit is alive and well. Of the eight engineers in my section, one year later, only four were still in engineering (one of them owned a motorcycle dealership in New Jersey and the rest were in supervision), and none of us worked for Fairchild in Mountain View. Two had started their own companies, neither of which exists anymore.

In this paper, I have only scratched the surface of the vein of stories leading to the mother lode. I could have told about the guy who used to regularly send parts out of Fairchild to National to help them get started, and then got fired from Fairchild for taking a door out of the scrap heap. Or how TI got started in the crystal pulling business, when a scientist from a national lab told a TIer that he had some single crystals on his desk, that he didn't have them counted, and would the Tier excuse him while he went to the bathroom? (I should explain here that in the early days, single crystal silicon was very difficult to grow, and only a few people knew how. Now, it's the basis for the industry.) Or I could have told about the stuffed squirrel award a TI plant manager used to pass around to his underlings whom he thought had done a particularly dumb thing. But those are different stories for a different day.

Milt McAfee

12

A RURAL MAIL CARRIER

by Milt McAfee (as told by Ben Mead)

About February 1, 1954, Ben Mead, a former Texas Folklore Society member, rode with rural mailman Leroy McAfee on his last round of Route 5 in Navarro County, attempting to capture the essence of Leroy's nearly fifty years of postal service. This is Ben's story:

On May 1, 1907, the postmaster at Corsicana, Texas, hoped that one of his problems had been solved. He needed a reliable mail carrier for Route 5, a rough-and-rugged twenty-four-mile route that sprawled around, between, and through the blackland, creek-bottom farms east of town.

During the year past, a young substitute carrier named Leroy McAfee had occasionally delivered the mail on Route 5 when the regular man had been unable to make the trip. Now the twenty-two-year-old McAfee had received the appointment as the Route 5 regular carrier. The postmaster hoped the young man would be able to handle the route well—and Leroy hoped that at last he had found a permanent position.

Just how "permanent" the position would be was shown nearly half a century later. Six different postmasters in turn had administered the affairs of the Corsicana Post Office before it became necessary to replace Leroy McAfee on Route 5. In January 1954, Leroy reached the age of seventy, and postal regulations required his retirement. For forty-eight years he had delivered the mail along Route 5 to the friends he made there . . . and to their children . . . and their children's children. Other men have spent such a span in the postal service, of course. But so far as is known, no other man has ever retired after such a period of serving the *same* route with which he started.

The postman's identity was one of the very few things that did not change during his five decades along Route 5. Children grew up, married, and built new homes along the route; farms were split up and sold and new people moved in. The great oil discovery was made—Leroy watched the first gusher from his buggy on one of the roads on his route. Then, the first refinery west of the Mississippi was built and with it came more people to live in the area. Leroy added to the population himself. In 1905, Leroy had married Johnnie Emmons, an attractive girl who lived near the McAfee home. They started a family that grew until there were ten children in the household.

World War I came and Leroy delivered draft notices and letters and news. Parcel Post delivery on rural routes began, and now the postman brought packages as well as word from loved ones. Prosperous times were followed by Depression times, and then World War II. Again, he carried draft notices, now to the children of the previous recipients, along with mail-order catalogs, papers, and magazines. He got to know all his patrons very well.

The route itself changed somewhat from time to time. Roads occasionally were moved to provide a more favorable location for a bridge across a creek; roads were graded, straightened, widened, and graveled. Finally, roads began to be paved. The postman kept pace with the changing times. Eventually, horses were exchanged for a Model T; the Model T gave way to something better. As delivery became faster and easier, more miles were added to Route 5. By 1940, it had grown from twenty-four to sixty-two miles. As the population increased and the mail sacks bulged and became too heavy, miles were lopped off and Route 5 shrunk to forty-five miles. But in the main, it served the same area for the entire time that Leroy McAfee traveled it.

When appointed regular carrier in 1907, Leroy delivered the mail in a horse-drawn two-wheel gig and Route 5 was about a normal day's work when the weather was good. He always kept an extra horse or two, and by alternating, a fresh "spare" was always ready. The route—and the postman—seemed to have an effect on horses. Maybe it was the long hours in the harness and the fre-

Leroy McAfee (far right) and his family

quent commands to start and stop. Maybe it was the companionship between a man and his animal. Whatever the reason, a nervous horse would become wonderfully gentle after a few weeks on the mail route.

Leroy sold one of his gentled horses for a much higher price than he had originally paid. After that he kept a sharp eye open for good horses that could be bought cheaply because they were not gentle enough for ordinary use. Route 5 tamed and taught good manners to horses that might otherwise have become outlaws; and Leroy had plenty of uses for his horse-trading profits.

The young postman had always been a hunter, and many of his friends along the route were hunters, too. Horse trading enabled him to acquire a pack of dogs of which any hunter could be proud. When you say "hunter" in this part of Texas, you don't necessarily mean one who goes out with a gun to shoot ducks or squirrels, although this type of hunting is also well known here. A hunter—as the term was used by Leroy and his friends—is a man who hunts or "runs" wolves with highly trained dogs at night over the hills and through the creek bottoms, when the moon and the dew are right for trailing. Strangers may call this type of hunting a hobby. Actually, it is more like an incurable malady—the victim who once gets the fever never seems to get over it. The advent of fences, roads, and settlements hampered the activities of the wolf hunters to a great extent, but Leroy and many of his friends still hunted regularly. The worth of a good hunting dog and the hunter's pride is shown in this old story: "There goes so-and-so; when he first came here 20 years ago he didn't have a thing, and now he owns nine dogs!"

Besides the two-wheel gig, Leroy also used a buggy on Route 5, especially in good weather. For bad weather the most important and necessary part of the postman's equipment was his saddle and saddle-bags. In the early days of Route 5, some of the roads were simply trails beaten into the ground by years of iron-rimmed wagon wheels rolling behind countless hooves. Ungraded and undrained, the rutted paths wound around the blackland cotton fields and meandered through the creek bottoms. Here and there a lesser-used path joined the main track, and at these junctions could usually be seen the weather-beaten mail box on a post; or, several boxes might be fastened to an old wagon wheel whose broken axle was set into the ground. The postman could turn the wheel and reach all the boxes without leaving his seat.

In good weather the dry earth was ground into dust which arose in clouds to trail each vehicle on its journey, or sometimes travel slightly ahead if there was a good tail-wind. Rain changed these black roads into a weird, unbelievable morass of gumbo that could make any attempt to travel a nightmare. Even a two-wheel cart like Leroy had would collect enough mud on the wheels that finally they would refuse to turn at all, and he would have to leave the cart mired to the axle and slog back to the post office astride his tired, mud-caked horse. If he got back early enough, he would saddle a fresh mount and set out again to finish the route, hoping to make his way back across Chambers Creek before the water became too deep.

"That mud was hard on man and horse," Leroy said. "Why, it would wear all the hair off a horse's legs. On each step he would go down in the mud to his knees. He would have to pull each leg up, one at a time, then put it down in the mud to the knees again. Sometimes a man could not walk in it at all—his boots would just come off and stay in the mud." One rainy season Leroy delivered the mail from his saddle-bags for 40 successive days—each day an ordeal for man and horse.

"The mail just *had* to be delivered to those folks," he said. "That was the carrier's job. It didn't make any difference what the weather was like. We just didn't let anything stop us." In winter the postman might have to drive through sleet or freezing drizzle. Frozen ruts make rough riding for a cart or buggy. Sometimes there would be some snow, but it was not a problem. On the whole, winters were not too severe in the Corsicana area. Mud was the real enemy of the postman!

"Not *all* the weather was bad," Leroy said. "We've been talking about the *worst* of the times. Most of the time it was a mighty pleasant job! You got to where you knew every foot of the road. It's a nice way to spend the day, driving a buggy—or a car—on a sunshiny spring day when the fields are turning green. The bottoms are tree-shaded and there are plenty of squirrels and birds." Leroy pulled up to a rusty mail box, tossed in a couple of letters, and tightened the strap on the remainder. He flipped the mail box lid shut with one hand as he shifted gears with the other, then ground through the gravel back to the solid footing of the pavement.

"Now you take that big pecan tree over there," he waved. "Spotted a big timber wolf one time in a thicket that used to be just the other side before they cleared it out and plowed there. I just got a glimpse of him, but that night I came back here with the dogs. We had a whale of a race down that creek bottom. Dogs caught him about a mile-and-a-half down; see, where that big bluff is, right where the creek turns back west! He put up quite a fight, too, but I had a big Walker dog that was too much for him."

"If you want to tell the story of Route 5 and me," Leroy said, "you just tell the folks that I delivered the mail and hunted wolves for forty-eight years along Route 5 and enjoyed all forty-eight of them." Another mail box lid was banged shut, then Leroy turned. "Say, up at this next house here, on the left, there's an old man I want you to meet. He's lived on this route over thirty years. I'll get him to tell you the story of the big hunt!"

We met W. H. Mitchell and his son Pleas. They came out to see Leroy and talk awhile, knowing that the next mail delivery would be brought by a stranger, and that never again would they see their friend under the same circumstances. This meeting could have been sad, but Leroy wouldn't have it that way. "Pleas," said Leroy after the introductions, "we've been talking about hunting on the way up here. I want you to tell this fellow all about the Big Hunt for the Varmint of Tupelo. Every time I think about how bad the folks were scared around here, I get to laughing all over again!"

"You don't need to laugh," Pleas said. "There wasn't anybody here as worked up as *you* were when you saw those tracks! Why, Leroy couldn't wait to get home and get his dogs. Excited? He brought every dog he had and some he borrowed."

"Me excited?" Leroy returned. "Why, I was just aiming to help you folks out by tracking down the varmint! You didn't see me with a hog-leg pistol three feet long hanging on my hip like Pleas had! But I can't blame them for being scared around here. Mr. Mitchell told me himself the darn thing was killing his chickens every night. 'Leroy,' he said, 'something's just got to be done! It killed two chickens last night and three the night before. You should have heard the mules taking on while the thing was in the barn gettin' the chickens—why it's liable to kill one of my mules tonight!' "

Mr. Mitchell laughed. "Well, I guess everybody *was* a little worked up, all right. A lot of the neighbors *did* get out their pistols and rifles. Work just about stopped. Everybody gathered at the Tupelo store to look at the tracks of the varmint and try to figure out what it was. The tracks looked bad, too. About the size of the palm of your hand, and plain as day in places where the dirt was soft and damp.

Ben Mead, whose ride with Leroy McAfee inspired this account

"Some thought it was a big panther, but the print of his toes was not plain. Some said the toes must have been cut off in a trap. The prints were close together, as if it had been slinking around, step-by-step. But the puzzling thing was that the prints just led up to the wall of the store and then stopped. Leroy's dogs just couldn't seem to pick up the scent. In fact, they never did get very interested—just milled around curious-like, watching all the folks talking!"

"Were you out here the first day Leroy?" asked Pleas. "Or, was that the second day when you brought your dogs?"

"I came out the second day," Leroy told him. "Remember, after the first day, you fellows stayed up all night on guard—or maybe you *slept* all night on guard. The next morning when you found the fresh tracks right up to your car was when you *really* got excited."

"Honest, we didn't sleep a wink," Pleas said. "We drank too much coffee for that. We talked all night long there in the car, real low so it wouldn't scare the varmint. That's why we couldn't understand those fresh tracks the next morning!"

"You ought to have seen this bunch," Leroy said. "They covered up the tracks with buckets and tubs and pig troughs, and folks came from all over the neighborhood. They would uncover the tracks and study them, and the mystery got bigger and the excitement worse! By sundown, word had spread all over the county and people began to drive in from everywhere—why, we had an army that could have whipped anything that would stand and fight!"

"Yeah, and just about sundown," Mr. Mitchell said, "that little kid found the varmint! It was just dark enough to turn on the store lights, and it was cool and damp outside. The men were all drinking coffee in the store when this little fellow came running in with a bucket in his hands, yelling, 'I've caught the varmint!' Sure enough he had! It was a big *toad* that had been staying under the store all day and hopping around after dark to catch bugs attracted by the light from the store windows! Every time he hopped, he left a print as big as your hand!"

The old man was laughing hard now. "You should have seen Leroy and his dogs when they looked at that toad!"

"Oh, yeah! What about those chickens that were killed, and your mules?"

"Aw, you just made that up, Leroy!"

After a round of back-slapping and handshakes, we said goodbye and set out for the next mail box down the road. "Don't have any 'box-holders' today," Leroy said. "So we'll make good time since we don't have to stop at every box." I asked him to explain. "You know, those ads that are addressed to 'Box-holder' or 'Patron' that have to be put into every single box on the route. Didn't have them in the old days, or we'd *never* have gotten through the mud with the load. Some days there are six or eight different ones, with one of each to go into every box. Always run late on those days because it takes so long to sort out the mail and make up the 'ties'; sometimes there's a lot more 'box-holder' mail than first-class mail."

"Now we have a package for the next place, so we'll drive up to the house and you can meet Mrs. Louis Szeansy. She has lived on the route for thirty-two years. When she was a little girl she lived on the other side of the road, but when she married Louis they moved to this side of the route." The package was delivered to Mrs. Szeansy. She and the postman talked over old times and said their goodbyes.

"The folks in the next house have been on the route for over thirty years, too," Leroy said. "I have to stop in and see how Mrs. Townes is—she's been sick in bed for several months. Marie, her daughter-in-law, has also lived on the route since she was four years old. That's Marie, coming down the steps to meet us now." We went in and talked with Mrs. Townes and with Marie and her husband. It was a rather sad occasion. Similar farewell visits were made a good many times along the route. Most of the times, the goodbyes were said with a lot of kidding and laughter, but always with a touch of sadness.

"Now, we're coming to the Roane Post Office," Leroy said. "I have to leave a bag of mail there. There's no railroad. I've brought the mail here from Corsicana ever since they set up this post office forty-seven years ago." It was a one-room frame building. A small vestibule in front was separated by a wooden slatted screen from the back part, with a mail delivery in the screen. There was a wood-burning stove in the back, along with sticks of firewood. We met the postmaster and several visitors, went through the goodbyes again, and left.

"Right here at Post Oak Creek is where I had my worst experience, I guess," Leroy said a few minutes later. "Must have been about 1912 or '13. Old Post Oak was flooded and still rising. Didn't know whether I could get across it or not. I asked the folks at the Harris house where I made my last delivery about it, and they told me John Harris had made it across a few minutes before on horseback. They suggested I follow his tracks in the mud and cross at the same place he did. It was still drizzling, but I found my way to the old bridge across the creek where all I could see was the railing sticking up out of the water. Some of the road had washed out and my horse had to swim part of the way before we got on the bridge. I was afraid to go on across—but when I looked back, I was afraid to go that way too.

"We got across the bridge and there I found a barbed-wire fence had washed down toward the end of the bridge and was tangled across the road. A negro boy had watched me go out to the bridge, so I turned and shouted back to him to get me an axe, but he didn't hear me. The water was coming up faster now, and I began to wonder if the bridge would go out with me on it.

"Finally, I got off the horse, pushed one of the fence posts down under the water, then stood on it to hold it down. That horse seemed to know just what the situation was; he waded right up to the fence and picked his way across it, stepping carefully between each wire down under the water, and got across without a scratch, making it the rest of the way. I sure was *proud* of that horse!" he said.

"Once when Chambers Creek was flooded for four or five weeks, I had to take the mail over to Powell on the train and deliver that end of the route with a borrowed horse and buggy; then I'd catch another train back and deliver this end of the route. Speaking of the Powell community, they had a cyclone down there once. I was on the route not very far from where it hit. The wind was awful bad and the rain would beat into your face like gravel. The horse just couldn't face it, so we turned and tried to make it back to a big cottonwood tree to get what shelter we could. Just a little before we reached the tree, lightning struck and tore it all to pieces.

"The new bridge across Chambers is mighty nice," Leroy said. "I remember once when the old bridge was under water and I couldn't make it across. I rode two miles up the creek to Hogan's Bridge, hoping I could get across there. Then I saw a fellow named Dick Baxter who told me I couldn't make it across Hogan's, either. Then two men rode up, one on a bay mare and one on a mule. We talked it over and they decided to ride with me just to keep me company. I hung my mail bags around my neck to keep them out of the water. The horse swam part of the way and waded part of it. I got to thinking about my lace boots and the mail bags around my neck and hoping the horse wouldn't stumble. But we crossed without trouble."

* * *

Other rural carriers have had similar experiences, of course. Even the ancient Persians had a system of mounted postal couriers who carried out their work faithfully. Herodotus described their work so well in one line of his writings that this sentence was chosen to be inscribed on the front of the General Post Office in New York City, as a tribute to the fidelity of today's mail carrier:

> Neither snow nor rain nor heat nor gloom of night stays these couriers from the swift completion of their appointed rounds.[1]

Another inscription is in the Post Office Department of Washington, D.C., which, after seeing Leroy McAfee's close friendship and affection for his patrons on Route 5, seems particularly appropriate:

> The Post Office Department, in its ceaseless labors, pervades every channel of commerce and every theatre of human enterprise, and, while visiting, as it does kindly, every fireside, mingles with the throbbings of almost every heart in the land. In the amplitude of its beneficence, it ministers to all climes, and creeds, and pursuits, with the same eager readiness and with equal fullness of fidelity. It is the delicate ear trump through which alike nations and families and isolated individuals whisper their joys and their sorrows, their convictions and their sympathies, to all who listen for their coming.[2]

Endnotes

1. *Herodotus,* Book 8, par. 98, describes the expedition of the Greeks against the Persians during the reign of Cyrus, 500 B.C.
2. Other inscriptions to the left and right of this one list dates on which various postal services began.

[A version of this story can be found on the Navarro County web site.]

Mildred Boren Sentell

13

THE TRIALS AND TRIBULATIONS OF A DIRT ROAD COUNTRY DOCTOR

by Mildred Boren Sentell

Dr. J. D. Davis, an early Fisher County doctor, wrote for his family and friends a recollection of his experiences in the early part of the century. He finished his narrative in August of 1935, when he was seventy-four, and it has been passed through the generations to his great-grandson, Gaza Seabolt, who has kindly allowed me to use it as a basis for this paper. His family were unreconstructed Confederates, and they carried on the traditions and views of those in the region of Georgia from which they drew their heritage.

Dr. Davis' parents immigrated to Texas from Georgia in 1857, making the move with an ox wagon and team. "The day they landed in Winnsboro, Father had the total sum of $20 in money and a family of twenty." Mr. Davis and the older boys worked in a saw-mill, hunted for meat and farmed for a living, and built a home on 269 acres of timbered land. On August 14, 1861 (the opening year of the War Between the States), J. D. Davis was born. He was named for Jefferson Davis.

After his mother's death in 1868, Davis remained at home until his father re-married eighteen years later. During the years following the War, J. D. recalled many occasions of his father and older brothers being jailed, though never convicted or disarmed, for finding it "necessary to whip a negro. I was instructed as a little boy to immediately let Father or the older brothers know if any man ever came in sight riding a gray horse, for the reason that the Yankee police always rode a big gray horse." He continues, "The Yankees usually had someone in each community to report to them any violation of . . . rules which had been laid down by them. . . . In our neighborhood, this 'spy' was a man and his son by the name of Musgrove. . . . Both were later killed by a Southern sympathizer. . . ."

During Davis' teenage years, he "would go to town on Saturdays and . . . swap horses and perhaps have two or three fights." Once he "hooked up with one Bill Miller . . . who, although proving to be a hard customer at fisticuffs, I finally got the best of him in a hard and long-fought battle. . . . Some two or three months elapsed before I encountered a man named George Redding, George losing. . . . Later I hooked up with Bill Miller and his brother. In the ensuing fight Bill was shot. . . ." The bullet encircled his waist, burning a place between his clothing and skin. Davis was indicted for assault with intent to murder, tried for aggravated assault, convicted, and fined $25.

Deciding on a medical career in the spring of 1884, Davis took two courses in the Louisville Medical College at Lewisville, Kentucky. He finished a two-year course in eighteen months. Returning home, he was examined by a medical board, and granted a license to practice medicine on February 13, 1886, at the age of twenty-seven.

Davis' first year of practicing medicine alternated with bronc busting, which he did for extra money. In November of 1887, Davis totaled his assets, counted $2300 in uncollected debts, and decided that he should re-locate. He began collecting his accounts, and "would accept anything I could get or anything one would offer, at his price, and if he had nothing, I would make him a gift of his account." On the 28th, he bought a ticket for Abilene, Texas, and from there took a freight wagon to Jones County, Texas, where he had a sister and brother living.

Davis' brother, "Uncle Dick" Davis, gave him "an old cow-pony with a big sore on his back about the size of a big red rose and with wind-galls on his legs about the size of hen eggs. With this dear old pony tied behind Uncle Dick's buggy and team, we headed for Roby in Fisher County to begin the practice of my profession."

Several passages from Dr. Davis' narrative provide insight to his medical career. Here, he describes his first cases upon settling in his new home:

> We found lodging at the Patterson Hotel on the night of our arrival. After we had retired for the night, I was aroused by a knock at the door and upon investigation, I met Mr. Sam Chalk who was a State surveyor employed by the state in surveying State school land in Fisher County. Mr. Chalk asked if there was a doctor in the house, and of course, I was not long in informing him that I would fill the bill. He stated that his wife would be confined at any time and we immediately left for his home. This was my first case in Fisher County. About the 3rd or 4th day from my arrival, I delivered a fine baby girl for Mrs. Chalk.
>
> The next morning I secured permanent board and lodging at the home of Mrs. W.W. Anderson, who was at that time post-mistress of the town. Being favorably impressed with the country and its fine people, I decided definitely I had found a permanent home. An inventory of my estate at that time consisted of $19.85 in cash of which $15.00 went for a month's board in advance. This left me with $4.85 in cash and my dear and trusted old horse, Bob. I spent 85 cents for a stake-rope and $1.50 for a sack of corn. My clothes were in good shape; I had a nice black broadcloth suit, and black derby hat. I also had a pair of square toed alligator shoes and they were long ones. I remember being accosted one day by Allen Chalk, an old cow puncher, who came up to me and sized me up from head to foot, taking into account my Derby hat and swell broadcloth suit. He had been partaking of plenty of strong "refreshments" and his breath was loud with "barrel licker." He took special

> note of my long squared-toed alligator shoes, as I sat there astride my old horse, Bob, and he wanted to know what I charged in breaking in a horse with shafts, indicating that my alligator shoes were long enough to resemble buggy shafts.
>
> My next case of importance was that of Mrs. Alax Shipp, of whom I delivered a fine baby boy. This was about 10 miles northwest of Roby on the old Crowley Ranch. These two cases that I have mentioned were the first girl and boy born in Fisher County.

Dr. Davis' practice grew in numbers and area, and he became a leader of his expanding community, imparting on his clients and neighbors his high morals and forceful nature:

> In the next few years my practice extended to a large section of West Texas. To Aspermont in Stonewall County, Anson in Jones County, Sweetwater in Nolan County, Colorado City in Mitchell County, and Snyder in Scurry County, and Jayton and Clairmont in Kent County. This was accomplished on horseback or in a double buggy.
>
> During the early days of my practice, I came in contact with all of the character and class of its people. I remember the first incident in Roby, one M. K. Kendall attempted to force me to take a drink of whiskey from his bottle. Being a young man that had not participated in any form of dissipation I was big and strong. I simply grabbed him by the hand and turned it so the bottle was emptied. That was the last time any one tried to force a drink on me.

It wasn't always easy to balance his personal, political, and ethical beliefs:

> During the Clark and Hogg campaign for Governor, which was one of the hottest Texas ever saw, the inter-

est waxed as warm in Roby as in any other section. The County Convention was held at Roby about June that summer. There was a big crowd in the court house and it was soon in an up-roar and a general free-for-all fight ensued. One John Peter Goggin and myself ran together. I had John bent back across the table and someone pulled me off him. John immediately grabbed the water bucket on the Judge's desk and struck me across the forehead cutting a "Fourth-of-July" about six inches long. Friends interfered and we were separated. It was necessary for me to get another doctor to stitch me up. For about two years after that we carried guns for each other. It seemed to me that we would have to fight or shoot it out most any day. One cold February morning John was severely injured in a gun fight. He received a pistol ball behind his shoulder blade and it passed out just to the left of his left nipple, penetrating close to the heart region, and leaving old John nigh unto death. Notwithstanding that we had been at each other's throat for several years, he sent for me to come. Not realizing the serious nature of his wounds and being somewhat doubtful of the sincerity of his message, I was at first loath to go. Upon second thought the ethics of my profession made me decide to go to his aid. I had my wife to load my pistol with fresh greased cartridges, I saddled old Brownie and rode up to the door of the house in which he lay. Having my pistol in my belt with the two lower buttons of my vest unbuttoned, I walked around in front of him. Every breath he took, he spat out blood.

He looked at me for a moment and asked if I would kill him. I said, "John, did you ever know me to take the advantage of any man?" He said, "No." I said, "Did you send for me?" He said, "Yes." I got right down beside him after placing my pistol on the mantle piece directly in front of him, and immediately gave

> him two doses of medicine. Staying with him for the next ten days, both day and night, with close attention, he finally pulled through to a complete recovery. After getting on his feet and able to ride his famous little old chestnut mare, called Kid, and going southwest across the street, he met me astride Brownie, going northeast. He motioned me by, and said, "Doc, what do I owe you?" I told him and he turned to the horn of his saddle and wrote me a check and handed it over and I thanked him kindly. He continued to look at me with tears rolling down his weather-beaten cheeks saying "what are we going to do?" I said, "By God, it is solely up to you." He reached over with his right hand and returned, "By God, I want to be your friend and I want you to be mine." I returned his hearty handshake and accepted the sincerity of his voice. Just here I want to say that I am satisfied that tears as large as a pecan or an apple passed down the cheeks of both of us. The simple fact was that my mind was made up that if our trouble was renewed, I intended to kill or be killed. I continued to be his friend from that day until July 2, 1935, when he was buried at the mouth of Duck Creek where it empties into Salt Fork, some fifty miles away.

While most cases were the usual sort any doctor might expect to see, some were more dramatic:

> For the next three or four years, my practice increased steadily but was uneventful. The next case of importance was the amputation of a limb for a Miss Ellen Kelly. In the spring of 1892, Miss Ellen, a beautiful 12-year-old daughter of A. P. Kelly, was bitten by a rattlesnake. I was called in and did not arrive until rather late. They had scarified the wound and bandaged the lower leg in such a manner that the lower part of the limb was in a paralyzed condition, making amputation

> necessary after three or four days of a futile effort to save it. I called in to consultation, old Doctor Davidson, an old Army surgeon and a noble old fellow, who has now gone on to his reward, and R. C. Crane, . . . the postmaster, . . . to accompany me. I had no instruments except sharp knives and a tourniquet and artery forceps, and used a common saw to cut the bone. I cut a half-circle in the middle third of the thigh . . . pulled the flesh back as far as possible, and sawed the bone in two. I tied up all the arteries, sewed up the wound, plastered it with a starch solution. . . . Mr. Crane gave the anesthetic. I am writing this from memory and may have gotten some little of it wrong, but to say the least of it, the young lady completely recovered and developed into a fine and useful life, serving as a school teacher and later District Clerk of this county.

Other cases of importance were cases of rattlesnake bites to old Grandmaw Foster and another woman about a mile down the road. In both cases, Davis applied tourniquets and the women set their respective feet in buckets of coal oil for four or five days. Later, Davis was called to doctor a case of a child with diphtheria, whose family lived in a dug-out, the walls of which were lined with skunk hides, one of which was hanging over the fire, dripping skunk grease into a pan. Every hour the family gave the child a tablespoon of skunk grease. Davis diagnosed the ailment as spasmodic croup and purged the child night and morning with a purgative followed by oil. The next morning the child was making "rapid recovery," and Davis departed for home.

Often Davis faced floods, lobo wolves, panthers, irate relatives bound on vengeance after a shooting, and sometimes mischievous children. On one occasion, Davis was called to treat one Dixon English, who was waylaid and shot while going to court to be tried for shooting the sheriff of Nolan County. English had been carried to a home near Roby and Davis feared that his assailants, if they were hanging around, would shoot the doctor by mistake. Davis had always been known for his whistling, and he said that he "whistled plenty of familiar tunes so that he could be recognized. . . . I have whistled more since that time than I ever did before, as I had plenty of practice attending English."

It was not all work for Dr. Davis. He also recalls some of the social events and customs of the times:

> During the period of development, there were lots of hardships for all, but it was spiced with some amusements and pleasures. I remember one instance during the year, 1890, one Victor Anderson and Layton Wood gave an ice cream supper in the old wooden court house. I was asked by the old ladies sponsoring same to escort a Miss Jose Foster to this entertainment. The custom then was to purchase said ice cream by the saucer, for 15 cents straight, the revenue, of course, accruing to the sponsors. On this occasion Miss Foster and myself had one saucer. I asked her to have another, which she did. Then the third, then the fourth, and by the time she had consumed this, I was left way behind. The boys giving the supper would come back each time and ask her to have another saucer, which she did until she had consumed eight big saucers at 15 cents each, becoming the center of attraction, and incidentally, costing me a lot of money for those days. I secretly thought that during the consuming process, that I would get that money back before daylight, treating her for "Ice Cream-Itis" or something, but strange to say, she was not the least bit affected or upset.
>
> This Layton Wood referred to above was about 12 years of age, and about this time I was sparking his widowed mother. I remember one night I called on Mrs. Wood, and we were unable to enjoy each other's company for being pestered by her son Layton, who

insisted on hanging around. I hinted several times for him to leave and also mentioned to her that "two was company and three was a crowd," but Layton, being a petted and pampered only-child, paid no attention to either his mother or me. At last I hinted that I or Layton would have to go. This aroused her ire and in vexation she jerked off her slipper and threw it at the boy. And when she saw it was going to hit him, she hollered, "Dodge, Layton, Dodge."

The same winter of this year, we had a big dance about 13 miles southwest of Roby above the old 18 Ranch at a Mr. Willbanks'. There was some 150 people present and one in particular named George Cochran, a cow-puncher who lived near Hobbs. George had a good case of the measles, which was contracted by some 100 of the guests. In fact, he scattered it all over this section of the country. I had some 100 cases on my books at one time. One case in particular was that of a little man in Roby, named Fesuire, who operated a little furniture store. "Fes" as we called him was in love with a pretty little girl named Nina Roberts. Fes had a pretty good case of measles and thought he was going to die. There was nothing unusual about his case and I was not concerned about his mental attitude. He would call about two or three times each day, and as I was very busy, I told him to leave me alone. He called me one evening after I had had a hard day, and told me he was going to die. I told him to go right ahead and make a good job of it and die. With tears running down his cheeks he said he would "not mind dying if it were not for leaving Miss Nina for some other fellow to get." Of course he did not die, and he and Miss Nina eventually married.

In addition to practicing medicine, Davis continued to be involved in fisticuffs and "run-ins." In a battle with a certain character named E. P. Boyce, Boyce pulled a long knife and in the ensuing fight, cut Davis in the side and on the arm. Although indicted for assault and tried in Fisher County, Boyce was not convicted. Davis said, "Two years later he contracted typhoid fever. His wife and two grown sons tried to get him to agree to call me to treat him. He was too stubborn to do this and he died soon after."

An old cowpuncher off the DE Ranch in New Mexico, named Tom Polk, also picked an apparently unprovoked fight with Dr. Davis in about 1902. A pretty tough customer in and around those parts, Polk attempted to give Davis a good whipping with a walking cane. In that altercation, Davis had to treat only his badly bitten thumb, and later, on at least four occasions, Polk pointed a gun at Davis, though he didn't shoot. Davis refused to take legal action against Polk, and later two very dear friends finally effected a truce between the two. The two gentlemen and Davis "talked our trouble over. They then conferred with Polk and reached an agreement for us to let the matter rest, with Polk and I agreeing to pass each other with friendly greetings, and that neither of us would ever mention the matter again. Polk is now dead and his brothers who live in this section of the country are good friends of mine."

Davis concludes "Trials and Tribulations" with a catalogue of the progress of Fisher County and his part in its ranching, printing press, banking, railroading, and civic activities. In his conclusion he states, "I have been a life long Democrat . . . I have practiced prohibition, but have also voted an anti-prohibition ticket. I have never taken a chew of tobacco, smoked a cigarette or cigar, nor have I ever tasted coffee, Home-brew, Iced-tea, or old fashioned Beer or '3-2.' I have drunk enough sweetmilk to run Palo Duro Canyon. If all the cactus along the Rio Grande was good corn bread pones and the old Rio Grande was honest-to-God Sweetmilk, I would eat my way from El Paso to the Gulf of Mexico in three days."

The last page of Davis' hand-typed narrative ends with this partial reference to Robert Burns' poem, "A Grace Before Dinner":

> 'Tis Oh, Thou who kindly dost provide,
> For every creature's wants,
> We bless Thee God of nature's wide
> For all Thy goodness lent,
> And if it please the heavenly guide,
> May never worse be sent.

I hope the incidents I have related will give you some idea of the trials and tribulations of the life of a West Texas dirt-road doctor of the early days. J. D. Davis' narrative of his experiences provide valuable insight to his life and profession, as well as to the lives and ways of other folk in and around Fisher County.

Joseph Edwin Fitzgerald speaking to a convention of nursery-men at the Ross Wolfe nursery in Stephenville, circa 1936

14

JOE FITZGERALD, NURSERYMAN AND PHILOSOPHER

by Mary Joe (Fitzgerald) Clendenin

Joe Fitzgerald was born in Erath County in 1876, only three miles from where he lived the rest of his life and died. His family, Johnathan Clint and Sara Elizabeth (Nelson) Fitzgerald, settled near the head of Alarm Creek when the county was young. Writing for the local paper and many other publications, including *Country Gentleman*, *Time*, and *The Rural New Yorker*, became a hobby to him after he established a nursery business in 1900.

Joe Fitzgerald began a nursery in Central Texas when predictors said it couldn't be done. He told a part of his own story in this excerpt from an article to the *Stephenville Tribune:* "Many years ago I remember the old apple wagons that came through the country. That must have been forty years ago (would be about 1895). The man who drove the wagon would always have an apple sticking on a stick to advertise, and from that I resolved some day to own an apple orchard."

Mr. Joe walked eight miles to John Tarleton College, got the education necessary, and taught school five years, saving money for the time when he could buy a bit of land and fulfill his dream. He married Ellen Carraway in 1898 and then, about 1899, he bought the first of several worn-out farms, fifty-two acres of land eroded and depleted from growing cotton, and began a lifelong project of rebuilding the land and growing a variety of things. He proclaimed diversification as the way for farmers to survive. Eventually, he owned about 1,000 acres.

First, he planted blackberries and vegetables that would be ready for market within the year. His wife drove a buggy to the little nearby town of Alexander to sell what they grew. The second year he began experimenting with apple trees, ignoring the comments of neighbors who said he was wasting his time. He tried several varieties, ordering trees from nurseries up North. When one didn't do well in his locality he abandoned it, such as the Ben Davis, for some that did better: Winesap, Missouri Pippin, Jonathan, and others. He budded the ones that did best and kept experimenting until he had a producing orchard.

Before and during the Depression years, Joe Fitzgerald was encouraging farmers to diversify. Cotton, hit during those years by boll weevils, was depleting the land. He encouraged trying many different crops, claiming that a man with a small farm could be self-sufficient and weather the hard times. He tried many of those crops himself. In one article he told of growing rhubarb. "It is a funny thing but we often get it into our heads that a thing cannot be done and we do not try it. I thought for years that rhubarb could not be raised out here in Texas where it is dry and hot. Last season I tried my first rhubarb." He went on to say that rhubarb made the best pies in the world, and he explained how and where to plant it. Rhubarb needed chicken-yard fertilizer and some shade protection, but he grew some with stems as big around as hoe handles. He and his daughter enjoyed the pies, but the rest of the family preferred fruit pies, and grown-at-home fruit was available in many varieties: plum, berry, apple, pear, and peach.

Soil conservation was important to this budding nurseryman before country people knew the meaning of the word. Soon, he had other farmers working for him in their off-seasons when he filled gullies with brush, spread rotted hay and barn fertilizer, and learned to use surveyor instruments so that he could lay off and have built his own terraces. He cultivated on the contour set by the terraces. No one told him he couldn't plant an orchard setting trees on top of the terraces. It probably would not have kept him from trying the method if they had told him. On one old place, spaced on top of the terraces, he planted a peach orchard, and on another he planted apples. Soon, he was selling fruit in season to truckers from all over. Growing fruit trees to sell soon followed his own orchards.

Each fall he had planted hundreds of pounds of peach seed for seedlings to be budded in the spring. That was the beginning of a big mail order business and a catalogue by which to sell. He grew from 75,000 to 100,000 peach, plum, apricot, and pear trees for market each year. Each seedling had to be budded. Cutting bud wood from his own orchards, he grew varieties he knew would do well in his area, and traveled to other parts of the state for varieties adapted there. He then grew trees for other localities and stated in his catalogues which did well where. His catalogues also listed pecans, rose bushes, figs, and many kinds of ornamentals.

With correspondence with other nurseries, he was always trying new things. He even ordered seed and plants from Italy and Japan and corresponded with the owners of nurseries in those countries. Setting out trees in the fall or winter depended on the weather, according to Mr. Joe. He wrote advice about pruning, setting, and the best varieties for each soil type. Going barefoot most of the year, as he walked through the fields, might have had something to do with his ability to judge soil. He walked the plowed fields to decide when and what to plant.

During all this experimental farming Mr. Joe found time to keep up his writing. He wrote to the editors of many newspapers and periodicals. J. E. Fitzgerald was listed as a Contributing Editor to the monthly farm and livestock journal, *Fletcher's Farming*. A long article he wrote to *Country Gentleman*, March 1, 1913, was entitled by the editor, "MAN WHO MADE GOOD, The Fact Story of a Wide-Awake Market-Gardner." In it he tells about that first berry patch. He plated rows between apple rows. With good cultivation he said:

> The bushes were literally ropes of berries. . . . When my berries got to bearing well, dozens of men came to my patch. After they had eaten about a gallon of my biggest and best berries they would say, "Joe, if you

> want to raise berries you'll have to go to a berry country. Now back yonder where I come from berries as big as goose eggs grew wild. And they were good too. Heap better than they are here and you didn't have to buy them either."

Joe went right on selling his berries. He planted another variety that would ripen when the first was finished.

He was also busy planting peaches, apples, plums, pears, apricots, and the biggest persimmon orchard in the country. He was the only orchardman to market persimmons. The improved Japanese persimmon was introduced to this country by Mr. Joe. He ordered a tree from California, imported from Japan to produce his stock. Using seed from wild persimmons and the new tree for bud-wood, he developed a way to bud the trees. Soon he had an unlimited source of bud-wood and a bearing persimmon orchard that produced more fruit than the local market could handle. That little problem was solved by advertising in *The Organic Gardener,* published in New York. He shipped, by mail, bushels of persimmons to that state. The local post office workers dreaded to see Persimmon Joe, as the *Country Gentleman* magazine called him, coming.

Smart marketing was another accomplishment. Pears that produced in his area were typically hard fruit that made good pear preserves, but were not worth much to eat fresh, but Joe Fitzgerald had the answer to that. He stored about 50 bushels of Kieffer pears until they were "good and mellow." He said, "I didn't have to commit any violence to get three dollars a bushel for mellow pears." The editors made a side bar for the article where he discusses this:

> A Few Things I Have Learned:
>
> It doesn't pay to raise things to suit your fancy altogether. Raise things to suit the buyer's fancy. Try to raise the things that no one else will have and that every one else will want.

> Give good measure, but make the customer pay for what he gets. Never cut prices because some other fellow is running 'round selling cheaper than you are.
>
> Don't worry; the man who sells too cheaply will soon go out of business anyway. People buy with their eyes, and high-colored fruit always sells better.
>
> Don't overrate anything; rather underrate it. Then you can sell to the same person day after day.

He was something of a philosopher. Talking about the difficulties of the Depression, Mr. Fitzgerald said, "When it gets so bad that such fellows as the Standard Oil and Mellon go out of business, we little fellows in Comanche and Erath counties will still be knocking along. We have our little farms that we can raise most anything on and we can cut waste entirely out . . . There is only one thing that can stop the diversified farmers of Erath County and Comanche and that is a long continued drought."

Mr. Joe was an avid reader, with daily papers from Ft. Worth and Dallas and papers from counties throughout the area, as well as weekly and monthly national publications and books. It was no wonder that light for night reading was very important to him. In the rural home area, electricity was not available for many years. During that time he tried coal-oil lamps, carbide gas, generated electricity, and wind chargers to power a car battery to furnish light. Imagine his joy and thankfulness to Franklin Delano Roosevelt when he began encouraging Rural Electrification. It was a dream come true in 1935 when our corner of the country had light at the flip of a switch.

Joe Fitzgerald was a student of nature with respect for all of her creatures. He enjoyed making comparisons between those creatures and human beings, such as showing how bees were like communists—they worked for their Queen (the state), making sure that she would outlive all of her workers. A dirt dauber could count up to eight, because she always made seven cells for babies and one for the trapped insect that would be their food. Crows had detailed systems of communication; the leader could tell the others just where in the pecan orchard Joe hid with a gun so that the others could plan alternate routes to the best nuts.

He had one old gander with seven wives that paraded in front of other geese, including several lone ganders, as if he were Clark Gable with a harem. The other ganders decided to attack; he said:

> Old Knobhead backed up against the packing house wall and as they charged he cracked heads right and left. He soon had the other ganders whipped and pompously started across the field with his wives. I noticed several other geese casting loving looks in Knobhead's direction, and I do believe if he had some way of starting a strain of hillbilly music every goose on the place would have followed and left the other ganders to nurse their jealousy and soothe their aching heads.

Writing whimsical as well as serious articles to the local paper and other papers, was a hobby for Joe Fitzgerald. Sometimes, he sounded romantic as he wrote to the paper addressing make-believe women:

> "Dearest Lottie: I do not like the idea of you walking alone in the moonlight. You know there is a man in the moon. I often wonder just what does the man in the moon think as he looks down on us poor mortals below. Used to be my father would take me on his knee on a moonlit night and tell me about the man in the moon. He said the man was piling brush. Mother said he was churning, and one of my uncles said he was milking a cow. Sometimes I could see half a dozen men in the moon. That was before prohibition—and now I see only one."

He speculated about Hoover going broke during his presidency, saying, "We are going to have to build a home for ex-politicians that go broke in office." One tall tale written to the editor of *Time Magazine,* October 26, 1931, earned him a real reputation. Someone had written about the size of frogs in the East. Mr. Fitzgerald wrote a tale about pet frogs he had in an earthen tank on their farm when he was a boy. Every day he caught bugs for them. The twelve frogs would line up according to size to receive the bugs he caught, one for the smallest, two for the second, three for the third largest, and so on. Bugs were hard to find sometimes. Once when he didn't catch but one bug he gave it to the smallest. The others were very disappointed. Finally, the second frog turned and ate the first frog, the third ate the second, the fourth ate the third and so on until after the eleventh frog ate the tenth. One would expect the twelfth to eat the eleventh, but he wasn't hungry. Joe looked down his throat to see why. Turned out, he had swallowed a wild goose. After that story appeared in the "Letters to the Editor" of *Time,* he got a letter from City Consumers Co., Paducah, Kentucky. It read:

> Dear Mr. Fitzgerald: The enclosure is just a small token of esteem from one slinger of the bull to another. . . . Your story ranks with some of the best Kentucky yarns that I have heard, and we are only too glad to make you a charter member of our international order. Yours for bigger and better frog appetites. [Signed: Prevaricatingly yours, Charles G. Vahlkamp, Pres. City Consumers Company. (International Order of Slingers of the Bull)]

Joe Fitzgerald was one of those people who, no matter what the wardrobe—top of the line and style, or everyday apparel—he could never look neat. Being about five-foot-nine, built square and solid, he always looked like what he was, a country man. He was a country hick, if you please, and was proud of it. Though he was a man of authority and had traveled and corresponded with governors, dozens of senators and representatives, nationally as well as in Texas (there are hundreds of copies of replies to his many correspondence, and letters commenting on his "letters to the editors"), he enjoyed making important-looking people feel ill at ease. The family took a trip up the eastern coast all the way to New York and then to Washington, D.C., in October of 1936. After getting home, the local newspaper editor asked him to write of his trip. He wrote:

> But even in the great capital you can see things to laugh at. You will see people there that think they are so big and important that it will remind you that men are still like monkeys. I like to ask people like that some fool question. I got in behind a crowd of high ups that were following a guide around. I saw a picture on the wall that looked about like you often see in a barber shop or saloon. The guide explained it was painted in Germany and cost one hundred thousand dollars. I asked if the government didn't get cheated when it was bought. The old woman turned a scornful withering look on me and a man or two looked at me like they thought I was crazy. I still believe six bits would have been a plenty to give for that picture.

The glowing part of his report was saved for the Library of Congress and the Booker T. Washington School in Tuskegee, Alabama. Mr. Washington was one of his heroes and he was impressed by the people, the grounds, and the immense pecan orchards along the drives of the college.

New York City was a wonder to him, and he wanted to see the Empire State Building—from the outside. He was afraid of elevators that went that high, and though he was persuaded to stay long enough for the rest of the family to ride to the top and look around, his words when he got out of the family car and leaned up against the building across the street to see the spire at the top of the Empire building were, "Well, there she is kids, let's go."

In 1944 Joe Fitzgerald ran for Congressman, District #17, on the Democratic ticket. Two judges had come out for the position: S. M. Russell and R. M. Wagstaff, and when a third judge, Clyde Garrett declared his candidacy, Mr. Joe decided people needed another choice. He ran as "The Farmer With Three Judges After Him." His political views were unusual, to say the least. Mr. Biggers said in an article to the paper, that if you wanted honesty or advice about fruit or trees, go to Fitzgerald, but if you had a political question, go to anyone else. After the votes were counted and Joe Fitzgerald had lost, he wrote a Card of Regrets to the paper. Among other things he said, "I made a clean campaign. I warn all other amateur candidates to steer clear of that."

Almanacs and characters like Joe Fitzgerald may have gone out of style, but for many years he both entertained and advised many people. Reading some of his articles after these many years, it's amazing to find how many things he prophesied have come to pass, including some of his ideas about eating natural foods, the wisdom of farming with little overhead, the ravages of war, and big companies consuming smaller ones. He was a pacifist, and a real fan of President Franklin Roosevelt and his moves to relieve the sufferings of the Depression, but he didn't agree with entrance into World War II. He thought the United States was tricked into participation. One thing for sure, he didn't hesitate to let others know where he stood.

Major John B. Hawley in France during World War I as engineer in charge of water supply and sanitation for St.-Nazaire District and Base Section Number One. *Photo courtesy Freese and Nichols, Inc.*

15

WATER WOES AND WATER WAYS: TALES OF TEXAS ENGINEER JOHN B. HAWLEY

by Deborah Lightfoot Sizemore

In November 1891, there arrived in Fort Worth, Texas, a twenty-five-year-old engineer named John MacDonald Blackstock Hawley—or John B. Hawley, as he preferred to be known. He dropped the "MacDonald" from his eight-cylinder name as soon as he was old enough. John's ancestors were Scots-English border folk and included a pair of baronets, Sir Henry and Sir Francis.

Hawley (1866–1941) was a hydraulic engineer: he designed and supervised the building of waterworks for cities. He came to Fort Worth from his native Minnesota to manage the construction of a new municipal water system. After he finished the job in 1892, Hawley did not go home to Minnesota. What did the Land of Lakes need with a first-rate water engineer? Texas—West Texas in particular—was the place to be if you wanted some *really* interesting water problems.

Texas was also the place for romance, it seems, for Hawley. Within three years of finishing the Fort Worth City Water Works, he had married a native, Miss Sue Anna Terrell. It was a good match for Hawley. Sue was the daughter of the much-admired Captain J. C. Terrell and Mary Victoria (Lawrence) Terrell. Captain Terrell was a lawyer and a Civil War veteran; Mary Victoria knew Latin, French, Spanish, Greek, and higher mathematics, and was widely regarded as one of the best educated women in Texas.

Hawley hung out his shingle in Fort Worth in 1894, becoming the first independent consulting engineer in Texas in water and sanitary work, a field known today as environmental engineering. Environmental work proved scarce in the 1890s and early 1900s. One year near the beginning of his career, the only fee Hawley earned as an environmental engineer was about fifty dollars for landscaping the Winfield Scott home (which is now the Fort Worth historical landmark known as Thistle Hill). Another early Texas engineer, W. J. Powell of Dallas, summed up the situation this way: ". . . it would have been hard for a consulting engineer to make a living a hundred years ago in any of [the] principal cities of Texas unless he ran a saloon and gambling hall on the side."[1]

Hawley did gamble—he played poker and shot billiards—and he did drink, sometimes to excess. But to pull in extra income he stuck to more sober pursuits, like supplying sand and gravel for roads. In search of water work, he traveled the state, engineering a dam for Clarksville in Northeast Texas and a water system for El Paso out west. El Paso's water problems were political as well as geographical, to judge from a letter that Hawley received from citizen Simon Kinsella. Wrote Kinsella:

> [W]hat a time we are having about the Water question, just as if we wanted Water in Western Texas. I don't use any and I don't see what other people wants with it. We have no logs to float here. . . . the Council meets three or four times a week and there is not a man in it but pretends to know how good Water tastes and I supose [sic] you have an idea of how often they have tasted <u>Water</u>. . . ."[2]

By 1906, Hawley's career in water engineering was looking up. A group of New York and Pittsburgh contractors sent him to study the unfinished Panama Canal and recommend whether those contractors should bid on completing its construction. Hawley advised them not to touch it with a ten-foot pole. In the area's geology he saw a great danger of earthslides, and he predicted that earth tumbling into the excavations would be a constant and costly problem for the canal's builders. Taking his advice, the group declined to bid. When the U.S. Government went ahead without the aid of private contractors, its military engineers did in fact encounter problems with enormous earthslides.

Though in his fifties during World War I, Hawley was commissioned a major of engineers and served in France with the American Expeditionary Force, in command of the 503rd Engineer Service Battalion. He was in charge of all water supply for a district in Brittany that was about the size of Massachusetts. One of his projects required four miles of cast-iron pipe, two feet in diameter, which the Quartermaster Corps unloaded with scant regard for the material's brittleness. Many pipes were cracked but they had to be used anyway, to meet an emergency deadline for water. After the pipes were laid and the water pumps switched on, the pipeline fountained streams and fans of water from all the hairline cracks caused by the rough handling. Hawley's engineers were troubled by the amount of water being wasted, but they kept the pumps going. The next morning, all were amazed to see that most of the leaks had stopped.

Reported Billings Wilson, Hawley's supply officer (who went on to become director of the Port of New York): "Investigation showed that we had been pumping millions of tiny eels whose bodies had lodged in the cracks, one on top of another until the leaks diminished to workable limits. Somewhat of a novelty in plugging wholesale leaks."[3]

After the war, Major Hawley—as he was known from that time forward—hired a twenty-one-year-old M.I.T. civil engineering graduate and Texas native named Simon Freese. One of Simon's first jobs concerned a new water system the Major had designed for the city of Paris, Texas. Hawley put his new assistant on the train to Madison, Wisconsin, to take the blueprints for the job to Professor Daniel W. Mead of the University of Wisconsin. Professor Mead, an authority on waterworks and power plants and "the best dam man in the country," was Hawley's consultant on the Paris project.

Young Simon wanted to make a good impression. Feeling rumpled after his train trip, he stopped by a tailor's shop to have his pants pressed. In a fitting room, he slipped off his trousers so the presser could touch them up. When his pants were ready,

Simon W. Freese. ***Photo courtesy Freese and Nichols, Inc.***

Simon rushed off to meet the great Professor Mead. But he forgot the blueprints, and left them behind in the fitting room. An impatient Mead had to wait while an embarrassed Simon scurried back to the tailor's shop to retrieve the plans.

(Were we hoping that Si had remembered the blueprints but forgotten his pants? It would have made the best story, but alas . . .)

Simon Freese was a practical joker. In 1926, while doing work at Corpus Christi, he put on a diving suit and plunged into Corpus Christi Bay to inspect a sewer pipe. His dive was covered by the local newspaper. The paper also reported an octopus seen in the bay that same day. The octopus was a good seven or eight miles from where Freese was working, but the two newspaper stories didn't mention that. The reports ran side by side and gave the impression that engineer and octopus had been in the water together. The octopus report also failed to mention that the beastie was a smallish specimen. Freese clipped the two stories and sent them to his fiancée. She was alarmed. She thought he'd nearly been eaten by a giant sea monster. And when she found out differently, she didn't think it was as funny as Simon did. Their wedding, however, went off as scheduled.

In 1927, Major Hawley made Simon a junior partner and changed the name of the firm to Hawley and Freese. Then Marvin Nichols of Amarillo joined the firm, and the name changed again in 1930 to Hawley, Freese and Nichols. Their big project in those years was to design and build Lakes Eagle Mountain and Bridgeport above Fort Worth. During construction of the dams for the new lakes, Hawley had someone sit up all night by a small hole in the ground until the watcher caught a crawfish emerging from the burrow. Major Hawley wanted to be sure which kind of crawfish it was: the kind that bored vertically, or the kind that bored horizontally. Fortunately, when the crawfish came forth at 3:00 A.M., it was found to be a vertical borer: no threat to the earthen banks of the dam.

One of the Major's junior partners also had a habit of studying the local wildlife. While Marvin Nichols was assistant city engineer at Amarillo, before joining the firm, he found that prairie dog burrows made pretty good storm sewers during unusually wet weather. In the fall and early winter of 1923, drenching rains interfered with street construction on Amarillo's Seventh Street between Fillmore and Taylor. The site stayed muddy for two months, and might have stayed underwater all that time except for a prairie dog hole that carried away much of the flood. "Five or six times the water was up to top of curb," Nichols reported. "A prairie dog hole in the center of the block drained all the water several times, but finally it would not drain anymore."[4]

Marvin C. Nichols. ***Photo courtesy Freese and Nichols, Inc.***

Nichols collected bits of local folklore. After he joined Hawley and Freese, he published his notes about Bridgeport Lake, and what was likely to be flooded out as the newly built reservoir filled. "The birth place of Bell[e] Hunt, writer of Texas Verse is inundated by the water of the lake," Nichols wrote.[5] He continued:

> A tribe of Indians under Chief Jim Ned frequented this territory. Originally they were located at the

> head of Village Creek which runs into the West Fork of the Trinity River below the Bridgeport Dam. Prior to 1880 they moved over on the mountain which may be seen to the west of the dam. This mountain is now known as the Jim Ned Mountain. Further west a band of Indians under Chief Riley held forth near what is now Wizard Wells. The mountain at the extreme western end of the lake is known as Riley Mountain.
>
> Wizard Wells (at the head of the lake) has a number of mineral water wells. The water is quite similar to that of the wells at Mineral Wells [a more famous health resort town].
>
> It is said by some of the early settlers in this country that the Spaniards left a proverbial "Seven Jack Loads of Gold and Silver" buried in the hills near Wizard Wells. This buried treasure was hunted for as early as 1890 on Village Creek east of the Bridgeport dam to as late as 1929 on Beaver Creek, twelve miles west of the dam. While no definite information has been obtained concerning the exact location of this treasure, it has been definitely determined that it does not lie within the boundaries of the lake, and so will be preserved for future treasure hunters.[6]

Nichols' boss, Major Hawley, pursued an interest in folk medicine as the years went on. In his sixties, the Major developed a chronic throat condition that was aggravated, probably, by his fondness for liquor. In 1929 and 1930 he had several bunches of "warts" (papillomata) removed from his vocal cords. The Philadelphia specialist who did the surgery ordered Major Hawley to speak but little, and preferably not at all. That was a mighty tall order, because Hawley was a talker. He got around the gag rule by engaging in a voluminous correspondence, especially with his old friend Daniel Mead of Wisconsin.

Seeking to ease his various aches and pains, Hawley experimented, and he wrote to Mead when he found folk remedies that worked:

> As to Lumbago, I have had no severe attack of it for 8 or 10 years, but sometimes it has put me to bed for a week or 10 days. . . . The best thing I have found for it is plenty of sodium bicarbonate alternating with large doses of aspirin. In France [during Hawley's World War I service] they gave me 20 grains of aspirin every four hours—night and day—for about a week, with good results but one must be sure his heart will stand the aspirin without harm before taking any such heroic doses.
>
> One other thing which gives almost instant relief, such relief lasting for two or three hours, is "cupping" the two offending lumbar muscles, a very simple operation to be applied by some member of the family, one stands nearly upright with his hands braced against the wall; a little wad of tissue paper is lighted and placed in an ordinary glass tumbler, the tumbler is placed against the lumbar muscles. As the burning paper exhausts the air in the glass the skin and flesh are sucked into the tumbler—one-half to three-fourths of an inch, loosening up the fibres of the muscle and relieving the pressure on the sensitive underlying nerves. Two tumblers can be used, treating both lumbar muscles at the same time. This works with me to perfection so that I am able to dance around as I please for a couple of hours.[7]

In the 1930s, during the Depression, business fell off severely for civil engineers because of drastic cutbacks in construction. By 1934, cash had become so scarce that Major Hawley was forced to drop his fellowship in the American Geographical Society. "I am sorry to find that I appear to be in debt to the Society in the sum of $20.00, as I am unable to pay it," he wrote. "Later, if the country gets back to sanity, and if engineers get on better than starvation rations, I will be glad to 'catch up' with the dues."[8]

Engineers weren't the only ones on a starvation diet. One East Texas lumberman, hoping to supply lumber for one of the firm's waterworks projects, wrote to Hawley, Freese and Nichols in late 1934: "Now, gentlemen, we lumbermen in East Texas are slowly starving to death. We are forced to live on armadillos, blackberries, and catfish. The blackberries are all gone, the catfish have quit biting, and we are too weak to catch the armadillos; so, if there is a streak of the milk of human kindness in your soul, we are quite sure you will answer this letter."[9] The author of the letter was a lumberman named, however improbably, *Wood*head—Ben S. Woodhead, president of the Beaumont Lumber Company.

As the Depression deepened, Major Hawley was forced to stop helping college students with their school expenses, something he'd done for decades. In reply to one young woman who had asked for his help, Hawley wrote, "It has been my good fortune, during the past forty years, to be in position to loan worthy students money for their college work and post graduate work, but at present there is practically no engineering work for us to do, and I am actually pressed for funds to send my last college son his monthly remittances."[10]

Business picked up as World War II brought much work for civil engineers. From 1940 through 1945, America saw the construction of troop quarters, military training camps, air bases, naval stations, shipyards, and plants to make airplanes, ammunition, and other articles of war. In 1940, Freese and Nichols won an assignment from the army to design and supervise construction of Camp Barkeley, nine miles southwest of Abilene. Major Hawley had retired in 1937, at age 71, and so the firm had by this time adopted its present-day name of Freese and Nichols.

Camp Barkeley was built in record time. Within ninety days, by mid-February 1941, the 20,000-man army camp was complete.

At Camp Barkeley near Abilene, Texas. A tent camp for 20,000 men was built in less than ninety days, completed in February 1941. *Photo courtesy Freese and Nichols, Inc.*

Troops were trucked in from Fort Sill, Oklahoma, commanded by Col. Jess Larson. Colonel Larson was the ex-mayor of Chickasha, Oklahoma, and a personal friend of Marvin Nichols. After Larson's Fort Sill division moved to Camp Barkeley, Freese and Nichols discovered they had made a terrible blunder. Colonel Larson's flag flew higher than the flag of Gen. Walter Krueger, commander of the Third Army. An investigation showed that Larson's flagpole was shorter, as military protocol required, but it was set on higher ground, so that the Colonel's flag overtopped the General's. Nichols worried that the General would think the breach of etiquette was intentional, since Colonel Larson was the only man in camp Nichols knew personally.

Major Hawley did not live to see the United States enter World War II. But during 1940, the last full year of his life, he closely followed what he called the "Hitler-Mussolini-Stalin war" and formed a definite opinion of how best to deal with the three dictators. "My own notion," he declared, "has been to offer a 'bonus' of $100,000,000 each for the heads of the brutes, believing that it would get prompt and efficient results. (The war is costing $100,000,000 per day, so why not? Three days would account for it.)"[11] In hindsight, one tends to wonder if he didn't have a pretty good idea.

John Hawley died in the early hours of January 9, 1941, at his home in Fort Worth. His wife, Sue, accompanied the body to San Antonio for cremation. As the Major had requested, there were no funeral services or flowers.

[Portions of this article appeared earlier in *A Century in the Works: Freese and Nichols Consulting Engineers, 1894–1994.* (College Station: Texas A&M University Press, 1994), coauthored with Simon W. Freese.]

ENDNOTES

1. W. J. Powell. "A Century of Engineering in Texas." *The Texas Engineer* 23, no. 1 (January, 1953): 7–11.
2. Simon Kinsella. Letter to J. B. Hawley, October 29, 1902.
3. Billings Wilson. "Recollections of Major Hawley." *Texas Civil Engineer* 40, no. 2 (February, 1970): 3–6.
4. Marvin C. Nichols. Diaries. 1922–69. In Freese and Nichols Inc. company archives, Fort Worth, Texas. November 1923.
5. Marvin C. Nichols. "Tarrant County Water Control and Improvement District Number One." *The Texas Engineer* 1, no. 5 (July, 1931): 16.
6. Ibid.
7. John B. Hawley. Letter to D.W. Mead, Madison, Wis., January 3, 1929.
8. Hawley. Letter to Henry Parish, treasurer, American Geographical Society, New York, December 31, 1934.
9. Ben S. Woodhead. Letter to Hawley, Freese and Nichols, September 28, 1934.
10. Hawley. Letter to Jacobina Burch, Mineral Wells, Tex., May 10, 1935.
11. Hawley. Letter to General Clarence B. Blethen, president, *Seattle Times,* Seattle, Wash., June 4, 1940.

BIBLIOGRAPHY

"Army Camp for 20,000 Men Completed in 90 Days." *Engineering News-Record* 126, no. 17 (April 24, 1941): 44.

"The Bids for the Construction of the Panama Canal." *Engineering News* 57, no. 3 (January 17, 1907): 78.

Carney, Allan. "Globe Trotter Finds Much to Do Here, His Early Life Jammed With Action." *Fort Worth Press*. November 6, 1933.

Freese, S.W. "John B. Hawley Fund Established." *The Texas Engineer* 31, no. 7 (July 1961): 6–13.

Garrett, Julia Kathryn. *Fort Worth: A Frontier Triumph*. Austin: Encino Press, 1972.

Hampton, Ireland. "Synopsis of the More Outstanding Labors and Accomplishments of John Blackstock Hawley." Typescript (not published), February 4, 1941.

Hawley, John B. Letter to D.W. Mead, Madison, Wis., January 3, 1929.

———. Letter to General Clarence B. Blethen, president, *Seattle Times*, Seattle, Wash., June 4, 1940.

———. Letter to Henry Parish, treasurer, American Geographical Society, New York, December 31, 1934.

———. Letter to Jacobina Burch, Mineral Wells, Tex., May 10, 1935.

———. "Some 'Services of Supply' in France." *Proceedings of the Texas Association of Members of the American Society of Civil Engineers* 6, no. 1 (December 13–14, 1918, and April 25–26, 1919): 36–42.

"John Hawley, Famed as Engineer, Claimed by Death at His Home," *Fort Worth Press*. January 9, 1941: 1, 3.

Kinsella, Simon. Letter to J. B. Hawley, October 29, 1902.

"Maj. John B. Hawley." *Fort Worth Star-Telegram*, evening edition, January 11, 1941: 4.

"Maj. John B. Hawley, Known Internationally as Hydraulic Engineer, Dies at His Home." *Fort Worth Star-Telegram*, evening edition, January 9, 1941: 6.

"The Major Had Time for Everything—On the Dot!" *Fort Worth Press*, January 9, 1941: 1.

"Major Hawley Achieved All His Goals Save One—He Never Got That Ph.D." *Fort Worth Star-Telegram*, evening edition, January 10, 1941: 2.

"Major John B. Hawley Memorial Fund." *Texas Civil Engineer* 39, no. 6 (June–July, 1969): 23.

Nichols, James R. *Freese and Nichols, Inc., An Engineering Institution*. Newcomen Publication No. 1171. Princeton: The Newcomen Society in North America, 1983.

Nichols, Marvin C. Diaries. 1922–69. In Freese and Nichols Inc. company archives, Fort Worth, Texas.

———. "Tarrant County Water Control and Improvement District Number One." *The Texas Engineer* 1, no. 5 (July, 1931): 16.

Powell, W. J. "A Century of Engineering in Texas." *The Texas Engineer* 23, no. 1 (January, 1953): 7–11.

Stephenson, Bess. "Death of Major J. B. Hawley Ends Distinguished Career." *Fort Worth Star-Telegram,* January 10, 1941.

Williams, Mack. "He Built Things to Last." *Fort Worth News-Tribune,* March 17, 1978: 14.

———. "In Old Fort Worth." *Fort Worth Magazine,* January, 1989: 60.

Wilson, Billings. "Recollections of Major Hawley." *Texas Civil Engineer* 40, no. 2 (February, 1970): 3–6.

Woodhead, Ben S. Letter to Hawley, Freese and Nichols, September 28, 1934.

COPS, POLITICIANS,

AND OTHER SHADY CHARACTERS

Martha Emmons, TFS Fellow and long-time contributor

16

THE LONG ARM OF THE LAW

by Martha Emmons

Since the first law, in the Garden of Eden, man has chosen to pit himself and his judgment against any regulation of his conduct. From the first, *homo sapiens* has been trying to circumvent, short-circuit, or else stretch out the law to suit his own purpose. Overlooking all thought of the original purpose of law, either of God or of man, which has always been for the well-being of those governed, man is still playing the old game: man versus the law. Sometimes he does it by far-fetched interpretations, sometimes by unwarranted assumption, sometimes by simply gambling that he will not get caught this time.

No doubt it was true of the cave man. Certainly it was of the ancient Hebrews. Even believing as they did believe in the divine origin of their law, they still played the game. Amos thundered at their oblique methods of undermining the law. "You make the ephah small," he declared, "and the shekel large," and in other ways subverted justice, to the disadvantage of those most needing the law's protection.

In the time of Christ many pious ones shouted loudly for "the law of our fathers," but still made interpretations of that sacred law for their own convenience. In the matter of Sabbath observance—which from the first to our own day was designed to revitalize the old human machine with a regular day of rest—even in this matter, strict legalists devised ways and means of bending the Sabbath to their convenience and pleasure. They defined a Sabbath day's journey as two thousand cubits from home. Then, what was home? Again a definition. Home was a place where one had possessions. Easy. Simply send a servant down the road a day or so beforehand, to a place within the prescribed distance from their goal (or better still, at two-thousand-cubit distances all along the way) leave an old sandal, a cracked earthen pot, or another trifling object not likely to be blown away; then the master's household could travel along at their own speed, go any distance agreeable with them, and still break no law. Law abiding citizens they.[1] As for those who had no servants or slaves, let them by all means obey the law.

To sweep on down the centuries and cross an ocean or two, we find in Puritan New England instances of Sabbath travel, and some rather original defenses of it. Once a pious Puritan was stopped by minions of the law.

> "Stop, Goodman Brown. You are breaking a law of the colony and of God. Wherefore are ye traveling on holy Sabbath?"
>
> "Ay, me!" came dolefully from the devout one. "Know ye that my good wife lies dead just beyond yon hill."
>
> All compassion, the guard said, "Oh, pass, Brother, and peace be with ye."
>
> "and has so lain for fifteen years," finished the traveler when out of earshot of the guard.

Then there was the Swede in Minnesota who killed a Norwegian in the field one day. He went into town, sought out a Swede lawyer, and asked him to take his case. The lawyer listened to the man's story, then advised, "Vell, you come back about next Vednesday, and I'll see vat I can do for you." The lawyer studied early, he studied late, going through one law book after another. When his client returned on the appointed day, the attorney said, "Vell, Oley, it look bad. I bane study all de books, and I find novere vat you get bounty for keel norveg'n."[2]

That is probably one of those traveling anecdotes, and may bob up anywhere among unfriendly ethnic groups. But the one I give you next is no traveling anecdote. It came to me through a long-time friend of the judge in the story, and he solemnly attested its truth. He said that this judge came into his courtroom one morning and to his embarrassment pulled out from his pocket what he thought was a copy of a certain law plus a record of some precedents connected with it; but it turned out to be an old Latin textbook that belonged to one of his (the judge's) children. It was too late for him to go back and get the book he needed. Accordingly he addressed the jury, said a few words about the law in question, then solemnly stated: "Because of the gravity of this case, I have delved into the history of it; and for my ruling I go far beyond the precedents of our day, and far beyond the ocean's brine, back to the days of ancient Rome, the source of all the legal systems of the western world. I cite these words: '*Gallia est omnis divisa in partes tres.*' "[3]

But to get on down to Texas. We'll consider the man who did more than any other one person to establish a system of courts in the Republic of Texas—Judge R. M. Williamson, better known as "Three-Legged Willie." By some he was considered a ruffian, by others a brilliant, capable, fearless justice. Maybe he was a "little of both, if you please." By whatever classification, by whatever style he may be considered, he did come in at a perilous time, and did resolutely go about setting up a legal system in Texas; and those who sought to get around or ignore his court found in Judge Robert McAlpin Williamson a foeman worthy of their steel.

One story, which has many variants, tells of a drunken lawyer who was arguing a case before Judge Williamson.

> "Where is the law to support your contention?" the Judge asked the ranting one.
>
> "There's the law," snorted the inebriate, as he ripped out his bowie knife.
>
> Judge Williamson pointed the muzzle of a long-barreled pistol at the lawyer and calmly replied, "And there's the Constitution. The Constitution overrides the law any day. Mr. Sheriff, you will please call the grand jury."[4]

In that incident the redoubtable judge had no forewarning; he simply acted with the calmness and reassurance of one armed with knowledge, and with appropriate weapon at hand. On another occasion he did know about the intended action, and he came to court ready to do battle for law and justice. A group of irate citizens had decided against "Old Sam Houston's tomfoolery" and were not disposed to allow any court-holding. Guns and knives were in evidence all over the place. The judge entered, took his seat, and with a long rifle at his left elbow and a pistol at the other, solemnly and judgmatically intoned: "Hear ye! Hear ye! Third District court is either now in session, or, by God, somebody's going to get killed." Court remained in session.[5]

Along with courts, laws, and judges, there were always lawyers. Concerning them, legends abound. I give you one epitaph and one story. A visitor in a cemetery noted an epitaph: Here lies John Doe, a lawyer and an honest man. "Well," remarked the visitor, "one would hardly think that grave looks large enough for two bodies."

The story concerns a lawyer mighty in word and deed, and certainly mighty in defense, who once lived in a town near Waco. I heard it from a citizen of the lawyer's home town, and a friend of his. According to this upstanding citizen, now deceased, a ranchman out near Odessa had a land feud with another ranchman, and eventually killed the man. He had heard of the fine lawyer, called him long distance, and asked him to take his case.

> The lawyer asked him: "Did you kill the man?"
>
> "Yes. I killed him," replied the rancher.
>
> "What weapon did you use?"
>
> "I shot him with a gun which I had on my person."
>
> "Did anyone see you kill him?"
>
> "No."
>
> "Have you discussed the case with anybody?"
>
> "No."
>
> "Then," said the lawyer, "I can leave here on the train at four this afternoon, and should arrive in Odessa before noon tomorrow. I'll bring two eyewitnesses with me."

A more recent case in law involves an application for an RFC Loan. The story comes to me from Washington. A New Orleans lawyer sought an RFC Loan for a client. He was told that the loan would be granted if he could prove satisfactory title to property offered as collateral. The title dated back to 1803, and he had to spend three months running it down.

After sending the information to RFC he got this reply: "We received your letter today enclosing application for loan for your client, supported by abstract of title. Let us compliment you on the manner in which you prepared and presented the application. However, you have not cleared the title before the year 1803, and therefore, before final approval can be accorded the application, it will be necessary that the title be cleared back of that year."

Annoyed, the lawyer replied:

"Your letter regarding titles in Case No. 180156, received. I note that you wish titles extended further back than I have presented them. I was unaware that any educated man in the world failed to know that Louisiana was purchased from France in 1803. The title to the land was acquired by France, from Spain in the year 1800. It was acquired for Spain by a sailor named Christopher Columbus, who had been granted the privilege of seeking a new route to India by the then reigning monarch, Isabella. The good queen, being a pious woman and as careful about titles, almost, I might say, as the RFC, took the precaution of securing the blessing of the Pope on the voyage before she sold her jewels to help Columbus. Now the Pope as you know is the emissary of Jesus Christ; and God, it is commonly accepted, made the world. Therefore, I believe it is safe to presume that He also made that part of the United States called Louisiana, and I hope to hell you are satisfied."

ENDNOTES

1. Lloyd C. Douglas. *The Robe.* Boston: Houghton Mifflin, 1942. 68–69.
2. I heard a lawyer from Minnesota tell this story. I make no claims for its validity.
3. My authority for this was Dr. A. M. Proctor from Duke University. He declared it was true.
4. Marquis James. *The Raven.* New York, NY: Blue Ribbon Books, 1929. 297.
5. Ibid. 271.

The author/Secretary-Editor, Ken Untiedt, as a very young police officer

17

THE POLICE LANGUAGE: THE LORE OF LAW ENFORCEMENT COMMUNICATION IN WEST TEXAS

by Ken Untiedt

I knew when I joined the Lubbock Police Department in 1990 that I would be learning many new things. Although I already had a degree in criminal justice, I was aware that the education I had received in my college courses was only the tip of the iceberg. As with any new job, there would be rules and departmental procedures that were unique to where I was working, as well as other knowledge that was not formally taught but merely "picked up." My academy training contained a lot of what I had already learned, as my class was composed of people from many different backgrounds, and only a few of us had any previous law enforcement training.

As I sat through four months of what I expected to be mainly review, I began to learn something that was completely new to me. I discovered that one of the most important skills in police work is not memorizing the laws and procedures, or becoming proficient in techniques for restraining prisoners; it is being able to speak the language used by real police officers. Cops have to be able to communicate well, and their jobs force them to become some of the best communicators I've ever seen. The language I learned was like no other I have ever heard. It was taught to me in the classroom, but also on the street, where it was passed on to me the same way it is to every rookie class: through the oral tradition. At the time, I just thought it was a necessary part of my training. Later, of course, I discovered that what I had been learning is considered a form of occupational lore.

This was the area of my education that was not only the most challenging, but at times also the most entertaining. You see, not only do police officers have to learn the art of communication, they also love to use it. Cops love to tell stories, and perhaps even more interesting, people love to hear the stories they have to tell. It's hard to find a channel on television on any night that doesn't have some kind of cop show on. From *Hawaii Five-O* to *NYPD Blue* or *CSI,* the American public has always wanted to know what goes on in the world of law enforcement. This is obviously a love-hate relationship; people want to see what the police do, and hear how they talk, and learn about the really grisly murders or deadly shoot-outs they're involved in. But they don't want the police to get too close to them, and they don't want that television world to become a reality, to become something they can't turn off. For the general public, watching cops on TV is exciting, it's entertainment, it's an escape.

However, this form of entertainment is not as easy to come by as you might think. The television shows you see are all presented in their decoded versions. You would not understand them in their original form because of the language police officers use. I found this language especially fascinating because of where I was working—West Texas. I heard words and phrases that were not only unique to law enforcement, but also to the region. It was often not *what* a person said, but *how* he or she said it that made it so unusual. Before I could learn the police terminology, I had to learn to speak Texan.

As my favorite bumper sticker says, "I wasn't born in Texas, but I got here as fast as I could." Although I was raised in a midwestern agricultural area similar to Lubbock, Texas, I had never heard many of the words and phrases that were being spoken all around me in my new home. When I was told that the Police Department entrance examination would be given "Tuesday week," I thought most of the sentence had been left out. Was "Tuesday Week" anything like Memorial Day or Labor Day Weekend? And they told me to bring two forms of identification "whenever" I came for the test, not "when" I came for the test. One of

The author's last car before leaving the Lubbock Police Department in 2003

my new friends asked me to "carry him over" to his house when we were finished, and another asked if I could "run him across town." I didn't think I was physically fit enough to do either.

I felt as if I had fallen into a Jeff Foxworthy stand-up routine. At any moment I expected to find myself engaged in one of those conversations he talks about where everybody speaks in one-word sentences: "Yaeatyet?" "Naw." "Yawunto?" "Awight." I stumbled through, however, and learned enough to keep from looking like an idiot or insulting anyone. I learned that "sir" really *was* a title meant to show respect, not something that would automatically be regarded as sarcasm. I may never master it, but I did eventually achieve a fair level of competency in speaking Texan. Next, I had to attempt to understand the language of the police officer.

The language itself has a very practical purpose and origin. Law enforcement personnel use a lot of numbers and abbreviations, which are designed to identify things quickly and concisely. Each officer has a number, which designates a certain area or job that he or she is working. On duty, I was often 243. Off duty, I was always Papa 210. "Papa numbers" are randomly assigned to everyone according to their rank. At the Lubbock Police Department, numbers under 300 were reserved for patrolmen, 300s were for corporals, 500s for sergeants, and so on. These Papa numbers only change when an officer is promoted. The on-duty numbers can change daily, depending on the area of town and shift you work. The "2" designates the second shift (from 3:00 P.M. to 11:00 P.M.) and the "43" designates a "beat," or geographic area. If I had another officer helping on my beat, I would be 243 and he would be 243B, or 243Bravo.

The Bravo comes from the phonetic alphabet. Each letter has a word assigned to eliminate confusion over which letter was said. There is no way to confuse an "S" with an "F" when you say Sierra and Fox-trot. If you ever get stopped by a police officer and he asks you to say the alphabet—a task usually required when drivers are stopped for suspicion of driving while intoxicated—see what happens when you say: alpha, bravo, charlie, delta, echo, fox-trot, golf, hotel, india, juliet, kilo, lima, mike, november, oscar, papa, quebec, romeo, sierra, tango, uniform, victor, whiskey, xray, yankee, zulu. I can't guarantee it will get you out of trouble, but it surely will impress the officer, whether he admits it or not.

The rest of the language is a mixture of the numbers, letters, and words used most frequently in that region or department. Much of it comes from the Ten Code, the abbreviated language used to communicate over two-way radios. 10-4 is one of the Ten Codes that most people are familiar with. It means "affirmative," or "okay." One of the most important ones to know is 10-7, which stands for dinner break. The one that officers like to use the most is 10-42, which is "ending tour of duty," or more specifically, getting off for the night. Ten Codes vary from department to department, and occasionally they change within one system, due to revisions in policy.

Learning the Ten Code is easy enough to do, but that still would not make you literate in the police language. Most of the language is composed of words that have been invented to shorten what needs to be said on the radio in order to keep as much air space free as possible—in case of an emergency. If a citizen calls in a prowler, the citizen is referred to as the "reporting party," or the "RP." If something or someone cannot be located, the officer says he or she was "unable to locate," or "UTL." These words are regularly mixed with the Ten Codes to make the radio conversations, or "radio traffic," as brief as possible. If I told you that I had 10-17'd with the RP about the 10-14 whom I was UTL on, then found out that the RP was 10-96 anyway, so I went 10-8 no report after telling my backup to 10-22 and we were subsequently cleared for 10-7, it would seem very confusing. The translation is actually quite simple: I met with the person who called in and reported seeing a prowler (whom I did not locate), and after speaking with this reporting party I realized that he or she was mentally ill; I then told the officer sent to assist me to disregard the call and I finished it without making a report, and we were allowed to go eat dinner. The radio version would sound like this:

> **243:** 243, Signal 4 245, UTL, 10-17 is 10-96, no report, 10-8.
> **Dispatch:** 10-4 243, 245 Clear?
> **245:** 10-4, 10-8.
> **Dispatch:** 243 and 245 clear 10-7.
> **243:** Clear, 76.
> **245:** Clear, 76.

Many of the terms that become part of the language are much more colorful than mere abbreviations or acronyms. While I worked there, the Lubbock Police Department was probably the only one in the free world that did not allow its officers to be "grass eaters," a term applied to officers who accept a discount on food or coffee, usually from convenience stores and fastfood restaurants. Most officers, as well as most of the restaurants and convenience stores, believed that was a "jicky" rule. Jicky does not always mean "stupid," by the way. Sometimes it means "anxious" or "suspicious," as in, "That guy is acting pretty jicky, you'd better check him out."

Immediately after an officer pays full price for a meal is the worst time to get a call on a "greenie," or a dead person who has gone unnoticed for days . . . or weeks. Another unpleasant call is one involving a drunk driver, or a "D. Wobbly," some of which are considered "drunker than Cooter Brown." D. Wobblies are "chunked" into jail, as are most arrestees. "Pain compliance" is a term that means using minimal amounts of pain to get an offender to do what the officer needs him to do, usually in dangerous situations. However, sometimes pain compliance is not enough, and the subject needs to be "thumped," most often when he is guilty of "P.O.P.," or "pissing off the police." If an officer makes a mistake, he'll have to "fade the heat," but usually only when he gets carried away with thumping someone he's chunking. Or, if he gets caught "chipping," *he* might be the one who gets thumped, by his wife. I'm sure you can figure out what chipping is. Most people who have chips don't want their spouses to know about them. By the way, I'm sure that not all of these phrases originated in law enforcement; some come from other southwestern folk groups, but to a Yankee like me, it was sometimes hard to tell the difference.

If an officer calls for "Help," it is *very* different from merely requesting additional assistance. A call for Help usually gets response from almost every officer in the city, on duty or off. As you can imagine, it is not often heard on the radio. In the past, if an officer called for Help unnecessarily, or made any other blunder on the radio, a series of clicks could be heard immediately afterward. This was known as "popping," and it was done by keying up a mic without saying anything. Unfortunately, newer radio systems have almost completely eliminated this tradition, as each individual radio has a number which is recorded each time the mic is activated and the offending "popper" can be located and disciplined.

If an officer did indeed call for Help, he might have had to draw his "SIG" from his "Sam Brown." Sam Brown is a brand name of leather gun belts frequently used by police departments. My gun belt was made by a company called Don Hume, yet it was still called a Sam Brown. A SIG is a Sig Sauer, the brand of a popular semi-automatic weapon used by some police departments. However, if an officer carries a Smith and Wesson, then he pulls his "Smith" instead of his SIG. One thing is for sure: if you use your SIG, or your Smith or whatever, and you have to "pop a cap on someone," there will be some serious heat to fade.

When talking to suspects on the street it is important for officers to understand some of *their* language as well. For instance, an officer may ask someone where he "lives," then later ask where he

A police officer's "office"

"stays." The suspect can give two different—and correct—answers, depending on his background and which part of town he's from. Where someone lives is usually their parents' home, and where they stay is where you can find them when you need to. I also learned that if someone tells you he "barely" moved in, it could be anywhere from a week ago to a year ago, again depending on the neighborhood.

The citizens on the street are no different from the people in uniforms. I sometimes forget that it is the people who made the language. Everyone in my academy class had a nickname, from Mother Crusher and Critter to Kenman and Lord Helmet. Like most nicknames, they were usually sarcastic, and more than one was meant to reflect individual personalities or the way my classmates and instructors spoke or acted. You can be assured that neither Bullet nor Lightning was so named for their quick responses or chatty natures. Yet, these were the people who showed me the true uniqueness of the language they spoke, and it was their particular speech patterns that made the language as entertaining as it was interesting.

When Lightning was teaching firearms training and said, "You got to hunker down on this little hooter, or it'll like to walk on you," I had no idea what he meant. I'm not sure I do now. At times my friend Bullet spoke so slowly I thought we were trapped in a time warp and moving backwards. Radio traffic with him was never brief. He would arrive at an accident scene and say, "You might oughta go ahead and call me a wrecker, and it wouldn't hurt for you to start E.M.S. on out here. This here feller looks like he's fixin' to bleed on out."

These speech patterns have on more than one occasion found their way into written reports. Bullet's reports *read* slowly. In the old days, a spoken faux pas would have probably been chuckled at and then forgotten shortly afterward. Centuries ago, the courts could get by without written documents. When bringing a criminal before a judge or jury, an officer could simply relate verbally what had happened, a verdict was reached, a punishment was chosen, and no written reports were necessary. As time passed, records were kept to monitor the court proceedings, but police officials still were able to rely on their memories of events to get their suspects prosecuted. Later, however, the courts began getting overloaded with cases, and the time between the arrest and actual prosecution grew from a matter of hours to a matter of days, weeks, or even months. Police officers needed to start making some kind of written report to help them remember what had happened when they finally got into the courtroom. These reports are permanent records, and this is where the oddities of the police language, especially those written by some good old boys from West Texas, can be humorous or even embarrassing.

In the old days the reports were simple. Although the report form encouraged the officers to make statements that were complete and detailed, the information actually written down could be very simple, as shown in this report from my department's archives: "Ray Fowler: DRUNK."[1] Another report, written four years later, by the same people in regards to the same suspect, is a little more detailed: "Found Fowler drunk again, brought him to the PD and locked him in jail. He did not ask to use the telephone." One of my favorites, which was handwritten and is the epitome of conciseness, states, "Found this man in the bar ditch just as Drunk as any body I ever saw." I would never have imagined writing a report that did not specify where I was, who was with me, how we got there and why, what the circumstances were for finding the arrestee, how I transported him or her wherever we went and at what date and time, as well as any other information I could think of to help me remember every little detail about each aspect of my total encounter with that person. I certainly would not have used some of the terms that I did when communicating with fellow officers.

The language and how it is used is constantly changing, as it must to evolve with time. Cops change with it. Although they can no longer "pop" each other on the radio, there is no shortage of MDT (basically email) messages being sent between the in-car computers. Even I conformed. When I would knock on someone's door and they'd ask who it is, as silly as that was because they could see me through the peephole and they had just called 911, I found myself saying, "POlice," instead of "police." That's the way *real* cops say it in West Texas.

I hope you've enjoyed this look into the secret language of law enforcement. After going 10-42 for good a few years ago, it's sometimes fun to look back and remember some of the more interesting parts of my law enforcement career. I don't miss it, but I do value the experiences and all that I learned.

Endnote

1. All reports specifically referred to in this paper are official Lubbock Police Department crime reports, which are items of public record.

Vice-President Jack Garner. *Photo used with permission from El Progreso Library, Uvalde, Texas*

18

CACTUS JACK GARNER AS FOLK HERO, VICE-PRESIDENT OF THE UNITED STATES 1933–1940

by Lora B. Garrison

Born on November 22, 1868, in a log cabin at Blossom Prairie, John Nance Garner IV, became Uvalde's most famous citizen. His political career began as Uvalde County Judge in 1894 when he won out over three opponents. Garner said of a debate in Sabinal between Judge Fenley and himself, "Judge Fenley was the biggest man I thought I had ever seen, and I felt like a feist by the side of a St. Bernard. Yes he was a big man, big in more ways than one. But I won the election."[1]

Mr. Garner went on to become State Representative, Member of Congress, Speaker of the House of Representatives in Washington, D.C., and Vice-President of the United States. Mr. Garner had the distinction of serving with seven presidents and made laws with the eighth. The presidents were Theodore Roosevelt, Howard Taft, Woodrow Wilson, Warren Harding, Calvin Coolidge, Herbert Hoover, and Franklin D. Roosevelt. He made laws with Harry Truman and was vice-president when Truman was a senator. Mr. Garner said Truman would go down in history as one of the greatest presidents. Harry Truman was the only one that Garner treated as an equal. Garner is the only Texan to have been nominated twice for president, the first time in 1943 and the second time in 1948. He was elected to Congress from his district in Texas at the same time he was elected as vice-president.[2]

As a young boy, life on the farm in Red River County was a struggle; his desire for an education was a driving force. While attending school at Blossom Prairie, young Garner discovered he was adept at baseball. Nearby was Possum Trot, with a team of strong youngsters who had a habit of defeating and humiliating both Blossom Prairie and nearby Coon Soup Hollow. So, the two underdog communities merged their teams and formed a tough challenge; and to this day the score remains tied![3]

Young Garner would go with his father to Jefferson for provisions once or twice a year. They carried cotton, hides, and other farm produce in a wagon pulled by a four-mule team. On the return, Garner would bring seed, salt, and staples for the household. In addition, remembered the son, his father would include a half-barrel or a barrel of whiskey, an annual purchase—the amount depended on his farm yield for the year. John Garner later described the liquor supply as a part of his father's hospitality custom: "The barrel stood in an unlocked house; any neighbor who cared to, might stop and have a drink, if he wished. Some did and some didn't. So far as I know the idea was original with my Father. I never saw or heard of anyone else doing it."[4]

When John Garner left his home in Red River County after studying for the law in Clarksville, his father advised, "Always tell the truth, and try to be a gentleman." Garner recalled of that advice, "I don't know whether I lived up to the Gentleman part or not, but I have never told an untruth to any person."[5] Others recalled his commitment to honesty. "Mr. Garner was always honest with everyone. He always told the truth and therefore he didn't have to explain anything later."[6] With this integrity came a high level of conviction. "Mr. Garner was decisive; there were no gray areas, it was yes or no and never maybe."[7]

Garner came to Uvalde for his health, like many others. He found the dry climate a cure for lung infection that was so dreaded at that time. Mr. Garner slept outdoors in a tent the first two years he lived in Uvalde, as his doctor had ordered. The choice was a wise one, for he regained his health and put his energies and knowledge to work in business and politics, which brought him fame and fortune.

Arriving in Uvalde January 9, 1893, Mr. Garner recalled, "I started playing poker in about three weeks after I got here." He soon joined the law firm of Clark and Fuller, as a junior partner. Mr. Garner rode the judicial circuit horseback or in a buckboard and brought in fees from the outlying area he served. He found himself owner of Uvalde's only newspaper, which he took in on a fee, and for which he was the reporter, editor, and publisher.[8]

While he was County Judge, John Nance Garner married Miss Mariette "Ettie" Rheiner, daughter of Peter Rheiner of Sabinal. She was an alert business woman and proved her worth and ability as her husband's secretary throughout his public life. "In 1896," Mr. Garner said, "Dr. Cummings beat me for County Judge and it was the best thing that ever happened to me. If he hadn't beat me, I probably wouldn't have run for the Legislature or for Congress."[9]

When Mr. Garner got the nomination for Congress he campaigned over several counties, driving a gray mare and a little mule hitched to a buckboard. It was hard campaigning, but Garner won out and went to Congress in 1903. The next twenty-eight years of his life were spent as a congressman from Texas, whose constituents were well pleased with his service to them. Mr. Garner was adored by the conservative wing of the Democratic Party. When Mr. Garner was elected as Speaker of the House in 1931, he stated, "I made no promises to secure this preferment, and I make none now. The oath of office I am about to take carries with it the only promise it is necessary for any American citizen to make, to assure the country that he expects to devote his efforts to its service."[10]

"When I was elected Vice-President of the United States, It was the worst thing that ever happened to me . . ." Mr. Garner stated, "as Speaker of the House, I could have done more good than anywhere else. As Vice-President about all I could do was stand and preside at the head of the Senate and watch proceedings that I could do nothing about. Becoming Vice-President was the only demotion I ever had." For years, newsmen recalled Cactus Jack's observation that the Vice-Presidency "isn't worth a bucket of warm spit."

This story is told about how Mr. Garner got the name "Cactus Jack." As the Texas House debated the matter of choosing an official state flower, Mr. Garner was reminded of the brilliant blooms of the hardy cactus plant seen in his legislative district. Although his idea was defeated by one vote in favor of the bluebonnet, reporters and cartoonists especially enjoyed referring to the man from Uvalde as "Cactus Jack" Garner. Back home in Uvalde, though, rather than use the "Cactus Jack" nickname, people called him "Mr. Garner," a propriety that is still preferred.

Mr. Garner built low-cost housing during the Depression for the homeless and low-income families, an idea long before its time. I first became aware of the Garner Houses when I went with a friend to visit her older sister who was living in a Garner House back in 1937. The fact that many of these houses are still in use today shows that they were well built.

A tribute was paid to Mr. Garner in June of 1984, when an impressive symposium on "The Personality and Politics of John Nance Garner" was presented in the Uvalde Opera House. The Symposium was moderated by T. R. Fehrenbach, and attendees included former Senator Ralph Yarborough, former Representative O. C. Fisher, former Governor Dolph Briscoe Jr., Judge Ross E. Doughty Jr. (former Justice of the Supreme Court of Texas), and Professor Lionel Patenaude, who all recalled the humor, wisdom, and accomplishments of Mr. Garner.

"Mr. John Nance Garner was a Great American," Judge Doughty told us. "He was Mr. Rugged individualism himself. He was the representative of an era of rugged individuals. Mr. Garner never had to sue anyone who owed him money; he didn't have to sue. When word came from Washington that the Old Man was coming home it made anyone in Uvalde who owed him money nervous. Anyone in Uvalde who owed the old man, they'd sell their wives to get the money to pay up, rather than face the old man."[11]

"He sent me word," is how Dolph Brisco explained his summons from his mentor, Vice-President John Nance Garner. Mr. Garner could, literally, verbally destroy another man if he set out to do so; or he could turn on the charm and charm a person or a group absolutely beyond belief. . . . "Mr. Garner, after a couple of Blows for Liberty, was never really very short of criticism." Mr. Garner had a way of summing things up. According to Briscoe, Garner said, "There are just two things to this government as I see it. The first is to safeguard the lives and the property of our people. The second is to insure that each of us has a chance to work out his destiny according to his talents."[12]

Red Wright, who retired to Leakey, Texas, to raise pecans, told of two incidents that took place in Uvalde during the summer of 1938, while Red was working in the area with a seismograph survey crew.[13] The small West Texas town of Uvalde had two main claims to fame in 1938: being the home of John Nance Garner, Vice-President of the United States, and also of the most humongous rattlesnakes in Texas. The area ranch land, densely covered with mesquite brush and prickly pear, was well populated with rats, and rats being sirloin steak to a hungry rattler, the rattlesnake population was a natural consequence. During that hot summer, cutting survey lines and roads through dense brush, with the brush providing shade for Mr. Rattler to relax under during the heat of the day, was somewhat akin to playing Russian roulette. "We killed six to eight rattlers a day as they disputed our right of way." Rattlesnakes usually mind their own business, which is hunting rats, mice, and rabbits. But they won't be pushed around either.

Engineering field crews are a boisterous lot, playing many practical jokes on each other. One of Red's buddies named Carl had recently played a devilish prank on him that had caused Red great embarrassment. And Red was eager to get revenge. He hit upon a plan aimed at Carl's deathly fear of rattlesnakes. After swearing all the field crew to secrecy, Red caught a five-and-a-half-foot rattler by pinning him to the ground with a forked stick. Red carefully grasped Mr. Rattler firmly behind the head and holding him securely, he proceeded to sew his lips together with a strong thread. Red said, "The process was painless to the rattler but slightly nerve wracking to me. Although it did little to improve Mr. Rattler's ill temper, it did at least render him harmless." Red put him in an empty dynamite box in the back of his truck, and at the end of the day returned to Uvalde with his captive.

Red's next problem was how to get the rattler through the Kincaid Hotel Lobby, and up to his room. A strong paper bag from the neighborhood grocer solved this problem, and Red walked right through the lobby with Mr. Rattlesnake and no one paid him a bit of attention. When Red reached his room on the third floor he looked into Carl's room through the bathroom, which they shared. Making sure Carl wasn't in, Red eased Mr. Rattlesnake out of the bag and shoved him under Carl's bed. Returning to his own room he waited for the fun to begin.

Red heard Carl come down the hall and enter his room. The bedsprings creaked as he sat down to remove his shoes. Carl dropped the first shoe to the floor about eight inches from the snake's head and was reaching for his other shoe, when Mr. Rattler decided to make his presence known by sounding his nerve chilling warning. Carl leaped about three feet into the air, giving a terrified yell, and leaped out the door barefoot and ran down the hall. Carl stopped suddenly when he reached the elevator door. Then it dawned on him that rattlesnakes do not ride elevators to pay calls on third-floor hotel guests.

Carl knew immediately how the snake had gotten up there, and the next order of business would be to skin Red alive. Storming into Red's room, Carl initiated his battle plan. But by some snake-like maneuvering of his own, Red managed to escape Carl's fury, while reminding Carl what a fine sport he was and how he thought he could take a joke with the best of them. Carl finally agreed to let Red go, but not before issuing strict orders for Red to gather up that "blankety blank" rattlesnake and get out before he reported him to the hotel management, who would throw Red, and his friend, both out into the street. Without delay Red gathered up Mr. Rattler and put him back in the paper bag, and walked out through the hotel lobby. Nobody paid him a bit of attention.

Red thought, I can't just turn this rattlesnake loose in the street; even in Southwest Texas ranch towns folks don't take kindly to having rattlesnakes turned loose in their street. Red decided it would be better to take his reptile friend back out to the country. As Red headed for the country he made a stop at Ross Brumfield's filling station and garage, which in 1938 was located on the corner of Oak and Getty Street. He was loading the snake into his pickup and holding his sides laughing, when the attendant asked Red what was so funny. When Red told his story, the attendant asked what he intended to do with his close-lipped reptile friend. "Why don't you let me have that old snake? I might find a use for him. You just dump him in that large tub in the back of the garage. I would kinda like to keep him if you don't mind." So Red did as the attendant requested and returned to the hotel.

Red explained that just past dusk he strolled back to the garage to get a notebook out of his pickup. "As I entered the front of the gas station I could hear strange music coming through a partition door that led to the storage section in back of the building." This part of the garage served the dual purpose of storage and recreation room. Almost hidden in a corner was an area equipped with an ancient and scarred poker table, cowhide bottom chairs, gun racks, and a large variety of hunting trophies. The room was the meeting place and favorite rendezvous of Vice-President John Nance Garner and his hunting and poker playing cronies, when the vice-president was in town. A bottle of bourbon was usually close at hand.

"I could hear the wail of a fiddle, the whang of a guitar and an unrecognizable staccato beat as I headed to the back of the building to investigate. There was Garner's closest crony 'Ol' Ross' playing the Guitar, 'Ol' Herb' fiddling furiously, and a huge grizzled rancher with a tin cup, banging out the rhythm on the scarred wooden table. The usual bottle of 'Old Busthead' bourbon graced the table, just in case Mr. Garner wanted to 'Strike a Blow For Liberty.'

"As the last strands of 'Red Wings' died out the group eyed me closely, before 'Ol' Ross' finally greeted me. I knew 'Ol' Ross', who was owner of the garage, and after his cordial greeting, the grizzled rancher decided I must be okay. He picked up the bottle, handed me the tin cup, poured it brimful, and commanded in a tone easily heard for a quarter mile: 'Have a Drink!' Not wanting to be unsociable, and realizing that an invitation to drink from a gentleman of this caliber is not to be taken lightly, I downed the bourbon and listened as the group launched into a rendition of 'Over the Waves.'

"During a brief intermission and another cup of 100 proof bourbon, the rancher suddenly and roughly demanded of me, 'Pardner can't you play something too?' " The bourbon had begun to give Red delusions of prowess far beyond his ability. And it was then he remembered Ol' Mr. Rattlesnake. He had him an idea. Going over to the tub that held his old friend, Red grasped him behind the head with his left hand and behind the tail just above the rattles with his right hand. "I started keeping time with the music by using my right thumb to mute Mr. Rattler's outraged buzzing rattles. Everyone quickly agreed that my ingenious instrument entitled me to a place in the band, and we resumed the program of western style chamber music."

They were all playing their western style music when a big, long, black limousine with a Massachusetts license plate pulled up outside. A short, rotund, little man dressed in a Brooks Brothers suit and wearing a derby hat, got out and walked about. He heard the music and asked the attendant, "What is that music-like sound I hear?" When the attendant told him that it was just some of the locals having a little Saturday night fun, the little man tip-toed over to the partition and looked in just as they were beginning another rendition of "Over the Waves."

When he peeked in, Red was lustily keeping time with "Ol' Rattler" and his furiously buzzing rattles. After a quick observation the little man hastily ran back to his car yelling "Mother, Mother, come here quick. You won't believe it, but you have to see this." A patrician little lady, dressed in the best aristocratic Boston Back Bay fashion frock, stepped out, and followed the wide eyed little gentleman.

"Our little band still didn't know what was taking place when they looked in on our musical session." Red said he could tell by the expression on the woman's face that she didn't believe what her eyes were seeing. It was like she knew that what she was seeing was real, but her mind was telling her it had to be an hallucination.

There was Mr. Vice-President John Nance Garner sitting right there, with a bottle of "Old Busthead" bourbon by his side, there was "Ol' Ross" playing his guitar, "Ol' Herb" fiddling furiously, and the "Ol' Grizzled Rancher" still keeping time with his tin cup. And then there was Red, with "Ol' Mr. Rattlesnake," holding him up there, muting those rattles while he buzzed away. And they were playing "Over the Waves." Well, that dainty little lady and the little man in the Brooks Brothers suit rushed out shaking their heads in stunned disbelief and drove hastily away to the East.

Margaret Truman told in her book, *Harry S. Truman,* about the breakfast served to the Truman family when they visited Mr. Garner in Uvalde: "We were served white winged dove, bacon, ham, fried chicken, scrambled eggs, rice with gravy, hot biscuits, Uvalde honey, peach preserves, grape jelly, and coffee."[14] Mr. Garner was a man of simple tastes and plainer words. He found life pleasant living in the cottage at the rear of the large brick home he once occupied on Park Street, and which he gave to the city of Uvalde for a library and museum in memory of his wife and helpmate, Ettie Rheiner Garner. Said Mr. Garner, "If it hadn't been that my wife was a descendent of pioneers of this county, the city of Uvalde wouldn't own this home today. Not only was she one of the 'oldtimers,' but she was a great woman."[15]

Garner money secured the future of Southwest Texas Junior College with donations in excess of one million dollars. Mr. Garner said, "I think of the College as I do the people of Uvalde. These people have made me principally what I am. They built me from a sick man into a successful office holder. This is my way of showing my appreciation in repaying them. Everything I have was obtained in this area and I want to give it back where it came from. . . . I don't want these kids around here to have to suck on the hind teat, when it comes to getting a good education."[16]

Frank Walker, Presbyterian Minister in Uvalde from 1951 thru 1956, told me recently that he became good friends with Ross Brumfield, a poker playing crony of Vice-President Garner. One day Ross asked preacher Walker if he would like to meet Mr. Garner. Of course he would, was Walker's enthusiastic reply. All the preachers in town had taken turns trying to convert Mr. Garner, who declared: "I haven't ever joined anything in my life except the Democratic party." Preacher Walker said, "I wouldn't dream of trying to convert Mr. Garner. I had too much respect for that. I just wanted to meet him, because I admired him."[17]

Ross looked at his watch. It was about 5 P.M., and he declared, "This is a good time." They went immediately to Mr. Garner's home. "After we were introduced, we were sitting talking, when the clock struck 5:30." Preacher Walker told me, "Mr. Garner rose, took out his big gold watch and glancing at it he announced, 'Time to strike a blow for liberty.' Mr. Garner said, 'You fellows can get yours out of that decanter on the table,' while Mr. Garner reached up to a shelf and got his own drink from a little barrel with a spigot. Mr. Garner's back was to Preacher Walker when Walker told Mr. Garner, 'Even if I was a drinking man I wouldn't drink with you.' Mr. Garner whirled around, his bushy eyebrows poppin' up and down, and fire in his eyes. And he demanded, 'Why not?' Preacher Walker's reply was, 'Any man who won't let me drink out of the same jug with him, I wouldn't drink with.' Mr. Garner slapped his thigh and said, 'You will do.' After that they became good friends."

Some time had passed and Mr. Garner trusted Preacher Walker, when Walker asked Mr. Garner, "How is it with your soul?" Mr. Garner put his hand on Preacher Walker's shoulder, pointed up and said, "That man up there and I are good friends."

Endnotes

1. Florence Fenley. *Old Timers of Southwest Texas.* Uvalde, Texas: Hornby, 1957. 7.
2. Ibid. 6.
3. O. C. Fischer. *Cactus Jack: A Biography of John Nance Garner.* Waco: Texan Press, 1978. 5–6.
4. Ibid. 3.
5. Ibid. 6.
6. Judge Ross E. Doughty, Jr. Quote, Garner Symposium. Uvalde, Texas, June 1, 1984.

7. Dolph Briscoe, Jr. Quote. Garner Symposium. Uvalde, Texas, June 1, 1984.
8. Fenley. 7.
9. Ibid. 7.
10. Ibid. 7.
11. Doughty.
12. Briscoe.
13. Red Wright. Original story, release given to Lora B. Garrison for storytelling. Another version of this story appeared in the *Uvalde Leader News* June 10, 1984.
14. Margaret Truman. *Harry S. Truman*. New York: Morrow, 1973. 34.
15. Fenley. 8.
16. Fischer. 165.
17. Reverend Frank Walker. Oral History interview at M.O. Ranch, Hunt, Texas, October 21, 1988.

Bill Stokes hard at work

19

AND LO TO VERNON CAME: THE CON MAN, THE BOOTLEGGER MAN, AND THE MUSIC MAN

by William N. Stokes, Jr.

I

Strange that Vernon, a dusty little West Texas town would attract a world famous confidence man. But it did. Count Victor Lustig, one of the most skilled con artists in history, smelled out a rich lode of Wilbarger County money. It was the time of the Great Depression when precious little of the stuff was around anywhere, much less in Vernon. Lustig knew that few people in Vernon had any money, but also he learned that taxes were being paid. Presto! The *county* would have money. And the county did, all stashed in a small bank and in the sole custody of tax collector Logan Lewis. Logan was a good man, born to an old and respected family. He was elected tax collector, and good things were ahead.

But Logan was no match for Victor Lustig. The wily artist hit town and made friends easily. He posed as a big city real estate investor, spending money freely. Soon, one of his friends was Logan Lewis. This friendship blossomed, and at length Lustig advised Logan darkly that he was on to something big. "It will make both of us rich—if you're interested." Logan was interested, and the Count broke out his find. It was a simple little device, shaped generally in the form of a cigar box, with a crank on one end and a slot on each side. It was heavy, suggesting a mass of interior instrumentation. The Count bolted the doors, turned down the light. Carefully, he inserted a section of heavy bond paper in the slot, cranked it into the machine, and out from the opposite side rolled a crisp, clean, twenty-dollar bill. Beautiful!

Logan Lewis was hooked, just as thousands of other good and innocent victims have been hooked—are being hooked today, and will be hooked in the future. The pattern is the same: careful buildup, lavish display of the green, promises, and (of importance) entangling the "mark" in a web of criminal dreams of quick riches. "Sure," the Count said, "we'll run off a half-million each and destroy the machine. I'll go my way, you go yours." Easy!

But there was one hitch. The machine, so said the Count, was fresh out of the dyes that were essential to impressing the sharp features and figures on the bill. These were obtainable only in Germany, where they were manufactured underground and then smuggled out and into the United States—a very expensive operation. Money would be required. "How much money?" inquired Logan Lewis. "Two hundred thousand," the Count advised.

Logan Lewis was no fool. Would these fakes "pass?" "Take one to the bank," the Count suggested. Logan, a stickler for detail, went one better: he journeyed to the Federal Reserve branch bank in Oklahoma City and exhibited his bill to the experts. "No doubt about it," he was told. "This is a genuine bill." But Logan had other problems. He did not have $200,000, nor did even Wilbarger County. He needed help. He called in his friend and colleague from neighboring Foard County. Weldon Williams served both as tax collector and sheriff in this bailiwick. Weldon witnessed the magic of the machine. No doubt about it. Weldon was "in."

Logan withdrew $125,000 in funds from the Wilbarger County kitty, and Weldon added $40,000, the limit of Foard County's bank balance. Here almost was a sufficient amount, but not quite. By now they were scraping bottom. The Count demanded more, terrified the two locals with threats of withdrawal. At length, Logan located another "investor." He was Terry Drake, manager of the local hotel. Terry had $8,000 stashed in a bank savings account. With eyes sparkling he watched the little box perform. Eagerly, he pledged his bit to the cause. Mrs. Drake, however, had other ideas; she did not fancy the company Terry was keeping. Down to the bank she went, withdrew the entire balance, locked the money in the hotel safe—and hid the key.

They were back to the $165,000. Reluctantly, the Count agreed to supply the deficiency himself. But, just in case they should be able to locate the Drake $8,000, he gave them his address in Fort Worth for the next few days. Several days passed, and Mrs. Drake, reluctant to leave the cash in the safe, returned the money to the bank. Within the hour, Terry withdrew the cash and quickly summoned Logan Lewis, who in turn called Weldon Williams in Crowell. Weldon grabbed the afternoon train for Fort Worth and delivered it to the eager hands of Count Victor Lustig.

The Count disappeared. Quickly the shortages were discovered, and the victims paid a heavy price with long terms in the Huntsville state jug. In a private conversation with my father, the district judge, Weldon Williams confessed to a long record in the underworld. He traced his career to Chicago and other cities where he had close ties with infamous gangs and mobsters. True, in Foard County his pursuit of bootleggers was fierce and relentless—but only as to those who failed or refused to pay him off regularly.

With this background, Weldon was not one to accept his shellacking lightly. He knew whence to go. So, before he was incarcerated, he went to Chicago, where he pursued and cornered Count Lustig in a Cicero speakeasy. Confidence men generally are nonviolent, and Lustig was no exception. He fleeced his marks cleanly, without force, and surely without firearms. He calmed the irate sheriff, bought him a drink, and then another. "You're premature," he said. "We're right on the point of receiving those dyes. Cool it, and you'll be the richest sheriff-tax-collector in Texas." And sure enough, Weldon Williams cooled it. He got off a wire to Texas, received the sum of $1,500 the next day, and turned it over to the Count—who had assured him that this small sum was all that was needed to complete the payments for the dyes.

Needless to say, delivery was never made, and not just because Weldon Williams was in the slammer.

II

As a senior in high school I learned that it was very smart to drink liquor. For the most part the girls frowned on it; surely their parents did. And even the liberal ones, with whom we had closer rapport often than with our own parents, gave it a "tsk tsk tsk" treatment. We fancied, however, that such frownings were a façade. Deep down, we believed, these people considered us pretty smart and sophisticated dudes. And so we encouraged them by exaggerating and "improving" on reports of happenings at Elks Club dances and imagined all-night drinking parties.

Even so, we were bad enough. First, the liquor itself: it was "white lightning," corn liquor raw as beefsteak, tough to rake in and difficult to hold down. One went through quite a process: first he filled his mouth and gargled his throat with Coca-Cola; then, retaining a mouthful of Coke, he hefted the fruit jar and swigged the poison. The trick was to get down your gullet an equal mixture of lightning and Coke. If it worked, you gagged a couple times, wiped your mouth, shook your head and muttered hoarsely something like, "BOY!!! That's really good Stuff!!" All the while your guts churned furiously, your innards rebelled. If after five minutes the stuff stayed down, you had it made; if not, it was disaster, for in your condition, there was no way to try again.

Most of the bootleg booze in Vernon was supplied by an amiable merchant from Oklaunion, Snag Roberts. Ol' Snag picked his headquarters carefully; Oklaunion, as the name indicates, was at the crossroads between Oklahoma and Texas, and it was Oklahoma which supplied the bulk of Snag's merchandise. Thus, he had himself a deal: he imported the stuff from across the river, stored it in Oklaunion, and sold it in Vernon.

Snag's *modus operandi* was unique; his base was a "mother-in-law" Buick. This was a roadster type sporting vehicle, with canvas top (up or down) and a rear end which opened as a seat for a couple of people, an inventory of stored booze, or your mother-in-law—your pick. Hence, the name. Snag drove into Vernon loaded with goodies. He guided the Buick leisurely around the square.

Half the town's kids were circling the block, looking over the sights and each other. All knew what Snag had and why he was there. At length someone would give him the high sign, and if he recognized the signaler as a person of "integrity," the action would begin. He would drive to a spot—perhaps the Pease River bridge to the north, the prairie dog town to the southwest, or Paradise Creek on lonely Lovers Lane to the east. The purchaser followed. A fairly good security system it was. And Snag long enjoyed freedom from arrest by the gendarmes.

On the night of an upcoming Elks Club dance, three of us (all smart blades) were cruising; we spotted Snag and gave him the high sign. He recognized us from previous dealings, and out Wilbarger Street he drove the Buick. But it was a busy night for Snag, and he chose to stop close in; indeed, it was directly in front of my home. I crawled out of the car, looked furtively inside, and there was my father, the district judge, reading his paper.

Now, the judge believed in the prohibition law. Later he was disillusioned, but at that time he supported the "law of the land" and did his stern part in enforcing it. From his bench he directed a parade of bootleggers to the Huntsville jug; they found little sympathy and no mercy in his court. And here was ol' Snag, making a delivery to the judge's son right under the judge's nose.

I rushed over to Snag and said, "Migosh, Snag, don't stop here. This is right in front of my father's house." Now Snag knew his Vernon geography. He looked at the house, then at me, and asked: "Just who the hell *is* your father?" I swallowed a couple of times, stuttered nervously, and finally blurted: "Judge Stokes."

Snag's motor was running; quickly, he turned to the wheel. The engine roared like a race car, tires screamed: SWOOOOOOOOSH! and Snag Roberts was gone.

III

In my early Vernon years, the Teagarden family resided three blocks from our home. The eldest son, Weldon, later would be known as "Jack" Teagarden. His mother was a piano teacher and his father was employed in a local cotton gin. But, his dad was also a dedicated amateur musician. When Weldon was age seven, he was handed a slide trombone by his father; by his early teens he was an accomplished musician. He played a mean trombone in three local bands. Vernon, however, did not appreciate his talent, for it was yet to be touched by the jazz age. To most of the villagers Weldon was just another guy who pumped the trombone in the town and county bands.

This did not concern the elder Teagarden; his major goal in life was to make accomplished musicians of his three youngsters, and he sacrificed the usual amenities of childhood to this ambition. Weldon did not play marbles and other diversionary games with the other kids; neither did his younger brother Charlie, nor his baby sister Norma. Charlie was into trumpets, and later Norma the piano keyboard. All became fine musicians, but the one who would bring a trace of musical fame to Vernon was Weldon.

Jazz music

I recall personally a concert by one of the Vernon bands on the lawn of Harry Mason, local attorney and later mayor of the town. It was a soft summer evening; the girls and ladies were in long crinoline dresses, the men in white trousers, pancake straw hats, and shirts of varied colors. A few (the wealthier ones) sported the new fad, shirts of pure silk. The concert band was no great shakes, but Weldon Teagarden carried the load; his voice was big and resonant, and the pure liquid notes of his trombone dominated and rendered harmless the sour notes of the other musicians. Soon after this, Weldon would be known as "Jack" Teagarden. He would play with Paul Whiteman, Ben Pollack, Bix Beiderbecke, Louis Armstrong, Joe Venuti, the Dorsey brothers, Gene Krupa, and Harry James; and he would play solo, a musician, singer, and entertainer all his own.

I associated with Weldon very little. He was several years my senior, an insurmountable obstacle to meaningful communication between the two of us. My brother was near his age, but also saw little of him. Under the stern hand of his father, Weldon's spare time was spent in practice, not in idle companionship. In later years I saw him in theatre and vaudeville performances in Dallas, Houston, and other cities. And on one memorable occasion, I nightclubbed with him and his band. In an intermission I approached him backstage and announced timorously that I was "from" Vernon. I was charmed and thrilled at the warmth of his greeting. On his reappearance before the nightclub "audience"—for indeed, it was a nostalgic circle around the podium which preferred listening to dancing—he gave public notice of his days in Vernon, introduced me as "an old Vernon friend," surely an exaggeration.

In reminiscence time later that evening, my late wife Ann Douglass Stokes lapsed into a thoughtful silence; she was impressed that even over the long span of years the Vernon image remained sharp in a seasoned old artist of world fame. At length she confessed:

> I've noted that when Vernon is mentioned, you figuratively if not actually genuflect, turn east and bow

> three times. I've always attributed this to an exaggerated memory of real and imagined hometown nostalgia. But tonight I got the word. There really must be something about Vernon, its people, its ways, its memories. And so—let me join the lodge—with you, Jack Teagarden, those I have met from there and the many whom I hope to meet.

A few years ago Jack Teagarden died in a New Orleans hotel, a victim of jazz artists' most relentless killer, "pneumonia resultant from liver ailment" (cirrhosis). It was a virtual consensus among the reporting media that his origins were in New Orleans. They were not. Jack Teagarden "came" from Vernon, Texas.

***

And again, in the early thirties, we in Vernon made brief contact with jazz music immortality. The kids held weekly dances at the Elks Club, which occupied the second (and top) floor of a barn-like building on Main Street. Here on a summer night the featured band was Joe "King" Oliver and his New Orleans jazz band.

King Oliver was and is a legend in the world of jazz music. His origins in New Orleans are obscure, but he mastered the cornet at an early age. Later, he occupied perhaps the most popular podium among the black band leaders in Storyville, the famous (or infamous) bordello district of New Orleans. There jazz music was born (or "jass" as it originally was called, adapting the distinctive black dialect word for sexual activity).

One of King Oliver's avid fans in the early days was a wide-mouthed youngster with a head full of great white teeth. He carried a sack, and hung around the edges of the Oliver band. At length he aroused the band leader's curiosity. "What you got in that sack, kid?" And the kid's answer was that it just happened to be an old cornet. Thus did Louis Armstrong come into King Oliver's life and the world of jazz music. The two were associates for many years and close friends for life.

In World War I, United States army generals, weary of dealing with the vexing problems of their troops in Storyville, moved in and with a single sweep closed the area forever. Joining the unemployed was a forlorn group of black musicians, including King Oliver and Louis Armstrong. Almost as one they trooped to Chicago, which in the ensuing decades became the focal point and the incubating grounds for the great jazz bands of the twenties, thirties and into the forties. Quickly, King Oliver grabbed the top spot. His band was the sensation of the city's south side. He was the hottest thing around. He sent word to Louis Armstrong, then still in New Orleans: "Come to Chicago." And Louis Armstrong joined the King Oliver band. Their first duet appearance was a trumped-up affair. A worn-out Armstrong was just off a two-night trip on a day coach. Even so, their appearance was a sensation. Chicago was thrilled to the gills. The rolls, trills, low and high notes, all in double-trumpet harmony of execution and tone were new sounds to nightclubbers, and indeed to the music world. They turned Chicago upside down, and for years the elder "King" and the younger Louis were masters of Chicago's south side nightclub life.

Eventually, Armstrong moved to New York and expanded his fame. He invited Oliver to follow, but for unknown reasons, King refused. Later, Armstrong would say that had he accepted, King Oliver would have taken New York by storm. In later times he did go, but too late; his imitators occupied the field, and his stuff was "old hat." Thus, King Oliver began the downgrade run. And he was well on the way (he would have to be to accept a spot at the Elks Club in Vernon) when he was booked for assignment in this unknown East Texas town. But Vernon knew nothing of all this background about King Oliver.

I went to the Elks Club with a host of kids from Vernon and surrounding towns. I was a lousy dancer, too shy to learn from the girls, too broke to take lessons from the town's only teacher, "Jodda" Parker. And so I compensated for this weakness by cultivating a love for the music. I was not prepared, however, for the overwhelming impact of the King Oliver sound. Here were seven blacks, an elderly man at the helm. His was a gentle and kindly face, with an expression of strength, character, and tenderness; yet in the eyes was an overall look of sadness, frustration, and disappointment. But as King Oliver lipped the cornet, a transformation came. His eyes sparkled, a smile flickered. The tired and listless body became erect and alive. Joe Oliver observed the crowd, and the bored and frustrated image faded. Briefly he toyed with the notes, the lows, the highs, then sprang into the swing of the accompanying band. Something new and wonderful came to Vernon. Immediately the kids abandoned the floor, as kids then (as now) are wont to do when a great artist performs, and gathered around the band. From here it was a performance, not a dance, and the gracious King Oliver and his band wallowed in the recognition. They played and sang in harmony and in solo. The affair was scheduled to close at midnight. Reluctantly, at one in the morning the instruments were cradled, the lights dimmed, and the crowd dispersed.

Only it did not "disperse." Quietly the word went the rounds: a jam session would be held at the residence of Joe Lee Smith and wife Pauline. She was the daughter of Paul Goetze, a music teacher. And here at one-thirty in the morning came King Oliver and his associates, and perhaps seventy-five Vernon youngsters stacked wall-to-wall. It was Dixieland, with songs of unrequited love and heartbreak, sadness and sorrow, hope and joy, the full gamut of the music of the day.

The session broke at dawn. It was a "first" for Vernon. Today, it is difficult to understand, or even believe, the depths of acceptance by both races of the strict rules of racial segregation. Violations brought recriminations and engendered bitterness in both societies. Yet here in the living room of a respected Vernon family were blacks we accepted, admired, cultivated. They mingled with the kids, joked, played cards, conversed lightly, then seriously. Returning to their instruments, they floated the soft music into the night. This so-called "social" acceptance in Vernon, Texas (to use a well known Vernon and Texas expression) was just "unheard of."

Yet it was there, and in the days following, I heard no criticism; there were no recriminations. And perhaps from this a lesson should have been learned. In my own personal life I began that night to experience the first concerns about racial attitudes. These King Oliver people were accepted and admired; the kids were eager to associate with them. And the world did not end!

The lesson: Perhaps if development of racial approaches, attitudes, and reactions had been left to the kids of America, the much needed, necessary transitions might have been easier, and of more importance, effective. Surely the kids would not have botched the job as did their elders.

Horsetrader L. E. "Buddy" Bishop in his workshop. Timpson, Texas, 1987.
Photo courtesy of the Institute of Texan Cultures

20

HORSETRADING AND ETHICS

by J. Rhett Rushing

[This article is humbly dedicated to L. E. "Buddy" Bishop—*Rushing*]

A poor old horsetrader has the hardest time of anybody in this world. There's nobody believes him. Everybody says, "Oh, he's the biggest liar in the world."[1] That quote, from student researcher Myra Queen of the famed Foxfire series, represents fairly accurately how most of us have come to feel about that legendary beast, the horsetrader. Subject of thousands of sale barn stories and Sunday sermons, the horsetrader lives daily with the suspicion and distrust of the community surrounding him, and walks into any deal with several hundred years of folk narrative working against him.

How did the horsetrader develop such a lively reputation? How did so many draw upon a collective pool of stories to condemn a trader with whom many have never dealt? It appears that a sense of fear and distrust of the horsetrader comes close to being a cultural universal—something with which almost everyone can relate! In and among the fringes of the East Texas Big Thicket (Newton, Jasper, Liberty, Hardin, and Nacogdoches counties), horsetraders today still wheel and deal under the canopy of their reputations with communities that both need and fear their services. This paper will examine the precarious balance between community standards and ethical suspension in which the trader must operate.

According to Roger Welsch and Ben Green, after the advent of mechanized agriculture—when tractors started doing what horses and mules were supposed to—there were three types of horse-traders on the rural American scene. Each of these types of traders varied according to their proximity to and frequency in dealing with the members of a particular community.[2] The original trader, or road trader, traveled along the edges of our communities with packstrings of animals for sale or trade. Though this fellow was often the only outside contact for many rural residents seeking an upgrade in farm labor, his very transience added a sense of finality to any deal struck with him. If you traded with him today, it was entirely possible that he might not be back a year from now, ten years from now, or perhaps, ever.

Such a trader could not be counted on for returns of faulty merchandise or to give reliable guarantees on the stock he represented. I feel rather certain that in times past the road trader may well have slipped undesirable stock off on an unsuspecting customer, or used any number of tricks of the trade to take advantage of a particular situation. Extreme mobility and a reputation for blatant dishonesty often characterized the road trader, and his success drew largely from the insular nature of the communities he happened through. As Roger Welsch alluded, many rural farmers, starving for entertainment and rising to a test of wits and skill, forfeited animals and money over and over again.[3] It is from these rather "ethically imaginative" gentlemen that the modern horse-traders' reputation must have originated. The road trader was simply a businessman in a "buyer beware" market, as well as a practicing professional much more likely to know the nuances of the animals and the arts of trading than the farmer or field hand.

The second group of traders emerged after the turn of the century as a result of transcontinental railroad transportation and a wartime need for massive numbers of Southern stock for European duty. "Live buyers" popped up to travel the country with checkbooks from Fort Worth and Chicago stockyards, grabbing up all the quality stock they could find. These men knew their animals, did no haggling, and bought big. They were the epitome of ethical operations in a trade, and could mean quick riches to the patient rancher.

As settlements grew into towns and cities, the infrequency of the traveling trader necessitated a horse "specialist" on call at all times. Livery stable owners and a few blacksmiths adapted to meet the increased community need for horseflesh, and soon became known as the town "horsetrader." Simple frequency of interaction with the community and the permanence of the trader demanded an entirely different ethic from this businessman. If he were to snide a customer, chances were that he would hear about it as soon as the snide were discovered. The smaller the circle of operation, the smaller the chance of getting away with anything in a trade. These local traders, known as "barn traders," were supported by the community in which they lived, and if they took too many liberties with naive townsfolk eager to trade, they'd better not plan on being in town for long.

Today's horsetrader is naturally a combination of all of the above—a man who boards or pastures a number of animals while traveling and buying or selling over a larger area. But like anyone that makes his or her living in a contest of wits (and horsetrading is nothing if it isn't a contest of wits) there must always be a winner somewhere down the line. There are stories of trades where both parties came out happy in the end, but far, far more where one party winds up paying dearly for a lesson in trading.

Now, this brings me to the actual strategies that present themselves in a horsetrade. Granted, there are more tricks in this business than scandals in an election year, but the guiding theory is really quite simple. A trader must pay a certain amount for an animal, and then find someplace to sell that animal for more than he put into it, or trade it for another of greater value. That's it. Plain and simple, the horsetrader has to get more for his stock than he paid for it. And horses are tricky here, because they have to eat while the trader is trying to sell them. If the trader dallies too long, his potential profit gets gobbled up in oats and hay.

Some unscrupulous horsetraders (and that is not automatically redundant) might try to cut back on feed bills by not providing enough for the stock to thrive on. As one informant put it, "You can't starve a profit out of 'em," meaning that if they stay in your pasture for a few weeks on half rations, come time to sell and the buyer can count ribs, ergo, there is a lower sale price and lower, if any, profit to the trader. Mistreating the stock in any way has never proven to be an effective tactic with any of the traders I interviewed.

A horse's age is by far the most common element disguised in a trade. The most accurate method of determining the age of an animal that has not been tampered with is to "mouth" him, or look at the growth and subsequent erosion of the horse's teeth. Certain pairs of teeth develop consistently with horses. An experienced trader can count the pairs and have a pretty accurate estimate of age up until the sixth year trench develops. From the sixth year, cups in the teeth begin to erode, and a hook will develop in the "scissor" (incisor) teeth.

Other faults, such as wildness or sluggishness, can be covered up with similar ease. If a horse is broken down, Buddy Bishop prescribed a foot trim "just a little too close so that he'll step lively for a week or so."[4] Bobby Eubanks told of "gingering" a horse (rubbing raw ginger on the horse's rectum) to make it prance around the yard holding its tail high and appearing to be much livelier and spirited than it really was.[5] Bobby also told of dissolving a glycerin tablet in water and giving it to the horse to make it "dance a little in the ring."[6]

If an animal were wild, the trader would tranquilize him. Buddy Bishop, Bobby Eubanks, and H. C. Long all told of experiences on both sides of pharmaceuticals. Buddy Bishop took me to a small auction outside of Timpson, Texas, and pointed out one horse in particular that "showed all the signs of being doped. You gotta watch their ears and feet. Most of the time a horse, no matter how gentle, will perk up in a show ring what with all the noises and activity around. If some horse comes into the ring with his ears down and his feet stumbling or missing, you know for certain he's been shot full of something before he showed."[7]

Bobby Eubanks enjoyed telling about the time he dyed a mule to cover the gray. As mules age, their heads grow whiter and whiter. Bobby had plans to sell the mule to someone that needed it for farm work and light pulling. As he explained, he "went to the store and got some women's hair colors. I painted that mule up pretty and black like he was a colt, but the next day while he sat out in the sun waiting for that fellow to come pay and pick him up, his head turned red. I guess that black color just went to red in the sunshine, but he bought that mule anyway—all the time asking how that mule got a red head. I told him I didn't know. Maybe he should ask the mule!"[8]

The deceptions are subtle and endless. If the horse were blind, he would be shown only at night or on a foggy day. If the horse were scarred, a saddle would be kept on him. If the horse's face were sunken from fever or just extreme age, a needle was often inserted under the skin just below the eye sockets. Small amounts of air could be pumped into the hollows to give the horse's head a more youthful appearance. The list of tricks continues and comprises the majority of all trading narratives wherein the buyer is duped.

The entire event is clearly a situation of "buyer beware." Lawton Brooks, a long-time Foxfire informant, warned that "anytime you would buy something and you look it over and don't see that there's anything wrong with it, well, the trader ain't responsible, it's you that's trading for it."[9] Buddy Bishop advised: "Only buy what you see. Don't buy in the meantime or over the phone. Don't buy anybody's story. That horse you looked at yesterday could've foundered overnight and if you call a fella up and say you'll take him, well then you're gonna wind up with a no-good horse dumped on you."[10]

The barter itself comprises the most recognizable part of the trade, for the back-and-forth offer and counter-offer are often the only spoken elements involved. Timing and bid determination are far more subtle and far more important. Welsch surmised that "the talent of the horsetrader was not simply knowing animals but, even more, knowing people—how to develop and hold their interest, how to manipulate words and situations subtly, how to relieve tension with humor, how to live by one's wits."[11]

Haste in a horsetrade will give away the eagerness to sell or buy, and an experienced trader will prey on that eagerness to get his price. Welsch advised that "as strange as it may seem, the successful horsetrader had first and most essentially to appear not to be interested in trading horses."[12] Bobby Eubanks once admitted that "there was times I'd fool people for two weeks or so—just let 'em stew on the price. My wife would get so frustrated at me, 'Are you gonna sell that horse or not?' But I never got in no hurry."[13]

Bidding is the second art of horsetrading. The trader must know immediately what the animal is worth and just what he can get for it when he sells it to someone else. There is little room for sentiment or favoritism here. A blind, broken-down horse that had been a family pet for twenty years would be of little, if any, use to anyone but the soap factory. The trader has to be able to assess the relative weight of the animal, and then multiply that by the current price per pound that the soapworks might be paying, plus figure in any travel or feed expenses that would be incurred before a trip to the soap factory could be arranged. This total would be what the buyer could expect. His bid would naturally be much lower in order to turn a profit upon resale.

Obviously, bidding is a game of compromising extremes. The seller will carefully overprice the animal, knowing and expecting to "talk down" to an agreeable amount. After the seller has given an initial figure, the buyer must then counter with an absurdly low offer. This offer is usually accompanied by any number of protests and exclamations designed to bring the asking price back down to earth. I offer here a theoretical example:

> Buyer: "How much you asking for that old plug?"
> Seller: "I'd take five hundred for him."
> Buyer: "I wasn't interested in buying your barn, just the horse! But I could go maybe three hundred."

This verbal dueling continues by diminishing fractions until either an agreement is reached or the asking price and the selling price stop their mutual approach at levels too distant for either participant's comfort. Bobby Eubanks explained, "When I'm making a bid on a horse, I'm going to lowball it. Sometimes that'll make a fella mad at me, so I'll take him over to the cafe for a cup of coffee—soothe him a little before we start talking horses again."[14]

An extension of the bidding strategy is the performance put on by the trader. Whether feigning disinterest or leading a buyer on, the trader has to be the master of the situation. C. C. Brown revealed, "I would always agree with a man, even when he was runnin' down my stock—give him a boost of confidence, let him feel top-dog in the trade. But every time he'd open his mouth and I had to play stupid, I'd tack a little onto the price. I was play-actin' and he was payin' for the performance."[15]

Such psychological maneuverings work both ways for the trader. Once the trader has a solid reputation of being crafty, even outright honesty can fool a customer that is determined he is being tricked. Buddy Bishop recalled just such a trade while he was working with Luke Rushing:

> Once there was this fella that came to buy a dun mare we'd bought somewhere. Now both of the men that worked for me and Luke were good cowboys, and that mare had done thrown them a bunch of times. In my mind that horse was going to the soap factory, but this man he wanted her real bad. Both me and Luke tried to tell him that she'd hurt him—that he couldn't ride that horse—but he believed we were just being horse-traders, trying to save the horse for someone else or something. I doubled the price on that horse—three times what the soap factory would've given—and still he had to buy that horse. Two weeks later his wife called to say he couldn't ride that horse and would we take it back. The next day he showed up and brought the horse back to trade. He picked out a "crow-bated" horse [laughter] and we traded even.[16]

This narrative touches on several interesting bits of horsetrading and community belief about horsetrading. To the poor fellow wishing to buy the horse, the trader's warning was just a trick of some sort. As a practitioner of community expectation he was determined in his mind to beat the trader. To further whet his appetite, the trader asked for three times the value of the horse. This also appeared as trickery to the innocent, and actually served to hook him even deeper into the trade. Simple honesty and the testimonies of two bruised cowboys could not dissuade the buyer from believing that Buddy and Luke "were just being horsetraders," as if the possibility of honesty was completely removed from their capabilities. The community dictated that horsetraders were dubiously truthful if not blatantly dishonest, and the man fell victim to the belief. The narrative tradition worked for the traders and against the buyer, leading the poor man by his belief system to his eventual duping.

These psychological strategies actually fall under the realm of language manipulation. Truth, if believed as falsity, is clearly false for the time being. Veiled truth, however, can be equally deceptive and give the appearance of a weakness in the trader's armor.[17] Welsch described several instances in narratives where "the trader . . . warns the prospective customer about the real fault of the animal, but in such language that the meaning is veiled."[18] An example of this deception might begin: A blind horse "don't look so good" (playing on the word "look"), or a spirited horse might be "raring to go," meaning that as soon as anyone tried to mount him, the horse was going to stand on two legs and try to throw them off.

Any trader that managed to unload a flawed horse in trade and draw boot, stood a good chance of getting the horse back when the buyer discovered the fault. The trader would have to remind the often angry buyer that no guarantees were in effect and that the deal was entirely final. He then might offer to swap back even for whatever the buyer had offered in trade. Of course, the trader would keep the boot, and the buyer would have paid for a lesson in horsetrading. Welsch states that the concept of back-trading was the most common theme in horsetrading narratives, and that some traders "made a living out of selling . . . and trading back for the boot."[19] Bobby Eubanks spoke of "one horse sold so many times I was ashamed to see it standing in the lot every other day." After awhile "usually they'll (the duped buyer) take anything to get rid of a horse [that is flawed]."[20]

Several trading strategies relied on a degree of trickery or subterfuge without being blatantly dishonest or illegal. Much as riddles and language jokes depend upon expected reactions and subtle trickery or manipulation of the facts, horsetrading puts the responsibility of the sale entirely upon the novice. The community understands the risks when entering these trades, and generally approaches them in the spirit of "buyer beware." Horsetrading has become a situation where all the normal rules and ethical teachings are temporarily suspended, and members of the community enter into this arena willingly. As for the sense of community respect for the trader, this is two-fold. At the onset, respect need not be defined as admiration, but can and does encompass a sense of wariness and even fear. Much as an athlete might respect a competitor, the community member seeking to deal with a professional trader must know what he is facing.

The secondary sense of community respect for the trader dives deeper into the communal psyche. Strict religious and legal messages agreed upon throughout the community are effective teaching tools, but rumors and tall tales have an equally emphatic place in the learning experience. Authority figures within the community have long recognized the value of teaching by pointing out those things unacceptable. In a sense, horsetrading fills that niche. As a tool for teaching what is not acceptable or expected ethically, the community can strengthen its boundaries around what is preferred. The horsetrader becomes a model for what not to be and thereby becomes essential to the community as a standard of ethical measurement.

Functioning within a conservative value system, many members of the community have viewed the horsetrader as an ethically dubious element to be relegated to the fringes of society. Folk narrative tradition concerning dealings with these traders developed into a system of belief that included warnings and cautions and denigrated the trader to a lower social status. Any upstanding member of the community generally had no business with such an unsavory element, but if such dealings became necessary, then the innocent community member was expected and encouraged to become as ruthless and devious as the trader was believed to be.

Such a change in accepted behavior signaled an ethical suspension on the community member's part and helped to strengthen the role of the trader in community importance. As an integral model of unacceptable behavior, the trader helped to define ethical and social norms and served as a subliminal influence to define the physical and ethical boundaries of the community as a whole. Though the boundaries between trader and community were understood by both, many crossed over to the trader's world—through an ethical screen door to the community. As both subject and victim of community narrative tradition, the horsetrader has come to symbolize one end of the community ethical spectrum, and found security in his role.

Endnotes

1. Myra Queen. "Horse Trading," in *Foxfire 4,* pp. 215–251. Ed. Eliot Whiggington. Garden City, New York: Anchor Books, 1977. 245.
2. Ben K. Green. *Horse Tradin.'* New York: Alfred A. Knopf, Inc., 1967. viii; and Roger L. Welsch. *Mister, You Got Yourself a Horse: Tales of Old-Time Horse Trading.* Lincoln: University of Nebraska Press, 1981. 11.
3. Welsch. 4.
4. L.E. "Buddy" Bishop. Horsetrader, Timpson, Texas. Interview, 11 July 1987.
5. Bobby Eubanks. Horsetrader, Deweyville, Texas. Interview, 21 August 1987.
6. Ibid.
7. Bishop.
8. Eubanks.
9. Queen. 236.
10. Bishop.
11. Welsch. 19.
12. Ibid. 25.
13. Eubanks.
14. Ibid.

15. C. C. Brown. Horsetrader, Kirbyville, Texas. Interview, 7 August 1987.
16. Bishop.
17. William R. Ferris, Jr. "The Horse Trader in Anglo-American History." *Mississippi Folklore Register*. Spring 1978. 4–24.
18. Welsch. 166.
19. Ibid. 14.
20. Eubanks.

ADDITIONAL SOURCES

Ferris, William R., Jr. "Ray Lum: Muletrader." *North Carolina Folklore* 21. 1973. 105–119.

Green, Ben K. *Some More Horse Tradin.'* New York: Alfred A. Knopf, Inc., 1970.

Heaberlin, Richard. "Sniding and Being Snided: Horse Trader's Tales." Paper presentation, Texas Folklore Society, 1989.

Long, H. C. Horsetrader, Silsbee, Texas. Interview, 28 August 1987.

ODDS

AND ENDS

Kenneth W. Davis

21

THE LORE OF RETIREMENT AND EXTENDED CARE FACILITIES

by Kenneth W. Davis

Bumper sticker seen often on expensive SUVs and RVs:
WE ARE SPENDING OUR KIDS' INHERITANCE!
Bumper sticker seen often on moderately priced family sedans: REMEMBER! YOUR KIDS WILL PICK YOUR NURSING HOME!

The evolution of terms used to describe what one informant called "warehouses for the old and infirm" introduces locations in which a significant body of lore is growing actively. Many Texans remember "poorhouse," "county farm," and "old folks' home" as descriptors of residences for some elderly people. Now, thanks to mysterious processes of linguistic change brought about probably by different views of social welfare, there are fancy-Dan terms: Senior Retirement Center, Sunshine City, Retirement Village, or Golden Year Refuge. And to label facilities that are restricted to nursing care, there are other examples of linguistic subterfuge: "extended care facility," "assisted living center," and "skilled nursing facility." The terms are concocted by dedicated and determined marketing specialists to make the "warehouses for the old" seem like paradises on earth.

Many such facilities are, of course, far more than just warehouses. Most offer amenities that should make life in them at least bearable. Pleasant or not and regardless of what they are called, these residences for the aged are goldmines for a folklorist. The residents of these places are all experienced veterans of campaigns to cope with the vicissitudes of time, chance, and fortunes of all kinds. These folks are living repositories of folk sayings, beliefs, and memories of customary behaviors handed down by repetition and examples. Much that is said and done in facilities for the old also demonstrates how lore continues to be formed.

Although many people in extended care facilities are physically infirm, most of them have retained their wits. Almost all of them love a good joke and delight in recalling "old timey" sayings and beliefs. And they revel in remembering such things as how hot it was in West Texas on July 4, 1948. The temperature in Lubbock that day reached 117 degrees. They enjoy talking about anything that happened fifty or more years ago.

Some examples of old sayings and folk expressions include many that are yet common in the patois of modern Texans. Finding topics for conversations with what I affectionately call "ancients" isn't easy, but I have learned that the ones whose minds are still good respond well to familiar folk expressions. They seem especially pleased with themselves when they can complete a saying I inject in a conversation and am deliberately slow about finishing. One ninety-eight-year-old lady remains quite fashion-conscious. I told her one afternoon that she had on a pretty dress and added, "Pretty is . . ." She responded instantly with "as pretty does." To another who asked me what chores I had yet to complete for the day, I said, "A short horse . . ." She responded, "is quickly curried."

A ninety-five-year-old gentleman whose first name is Malvis answers questions with folk expressions that are much older than the terms I learned in my misspent youth in old Bell County. He was a cotton broker during his working years, and I talk with him about cotton farming. During one of the frequent droughts in West Texas, dry land farmers were lamenting the probability of poor—if any—yields of cotton. I asked Malvis what short, stunted cotton plants are called. Immediately he replied, "bumblebee cotton, 'cause it's so short a bumblebee can get the pollen from the blooms by standing on its hind legs." I asked then if he had ever picked cotton. He gave me a look of comic pitying regard and said that in his youth he picked cotton south of Lubbock on rows so long they had their own mail carrier. He added that the rows were so long a cotton picker would wear out two sets of knee pads before he finally reached the end of them. One afternoon when he was a bit despondent, I asked him how he was doing. He said he was doing "poorly." I told him he looked at least "fair to middling" and added that "fair to middling isn't bad for dry weather cotton." He laughed and said he hadn't heard that expression since he was buying cotton in Floydada in the late sixties. In autumn of 2002, when late season rains threatened what was supposed to be a bumper cotton crop, this former cotton buyer said of rain in West Texas: "When it stops, it never starts, and when it starts, it never stops." This is authentic folk speech.

Another excellent source of folk expressions was a nearly 100-year-old lady who was so severely afflicted with Parkinson's disease she could hardly be understood. But her mind remained quick and clear. One day when she was able to get by without her oxygen machine, I told her she looked "pert," a term I learned from my maternal grandmother in the mid-thirties of the twentieth century. She smiled and responded: "I hadn't heard that word since Hector was a pup." Another time when I stopped by later than usual, she told me she had had a "tedious" day and was going "to retire early." I started to quote from *Poor Richard's Almanac,* "Early to bed, early to rise . . ." She interrupted to complete the saying "makes a man healthy, wealthy, and wise." Then she chuckled and said that for her a good night's sleep meant merely another day in which to "keep on keeping on."

Humor is a survival mechanism for many residents of nursing homes. Once when I asked a 102-year-old patient if she had had a good day, she gave me a look reserved for the much younger who ask dumb questions and said, "At my age, any day I wake up not dead it's a good day!" Self-deprecating humor about old age and various ailments prompts some colorful expressions. One old gentleman whose body looks as if it had been too long out in the hot sun and had melted into an exaggerated pear shape laughingly told his equally misshapen girlfriend at the dinner table, "I am so out of shape I'd fall out of a flour sack." One-upmanship is a favorite sport for residents of extended care and retirement facilities. The pear-shaped gentleman's companion said gleefully, "I am so out of shape I have to use my late husband's suspenders to hold my girdle up." The two laughed vigorously at each other's wit.

Other examples of one-upmanship that are in the camp of habitual, customary behavior have to do with "trophy" visitors. Residents of retirement centers and care facilities delight in claiming to have the most significant visitors. They boast of how often their adult children come to see them, and they have grandchildren and great-grandchildren who, like those at Lake Woebegone, are "all above average" (*pace,* Garrison Keillor). When they have exhausted mentioning family members as trophy visitors, they frequently turn to church connections. A senior minister is worth more points than is an associate minister, even if that associate minister is responsible for visitation of the elderly. Of lesser value yet vastly important are members of Sunday school classes the ancients can no longer attend. Ambulatory high school friends rank just beneath senior ministers as prestigious visitors. It is the scarcity of living high school friends that enhances their value as trophies, of course.

Customary behavior associated with food makes up a significant body of lore in retirement communities and care facilities. There is lore about going to the dining room at a certain time. If the dining room opens at 5:00 P.M., at least half of its patrons will be there by 4:15 at the latest. If asked why they arrive so early, they reply vaguely that they wanted to have time to visit some before the meal. But one acerbic retired physician says that getting to visit isn't the real reason for being early. Here *verbatim* is his explanation of the real reason for being early at the dining room: "Hell, these old coots want to be sure they get their favorite tables. They're just like milk cows that have to have the same stalls all the time." He added, "That's the reason I get to the damned place early!"

One of the reasons for the doctor's strong language is the detestation he and many of his peers have for institutional food.

Arriving at the dining room early enough to get a good place

Although the food served is generally nutritious and is prepared under the supervision of a registered dietician, it is not at all what people remember from "the good old days" when they had meals cooked at home with plenty of grease, salt, and essential stout seasonings. One dish in particular prompts ire and indignation from nursing facility patients: browned hamburger with yellow hominy and chopped red and green bell peppers cooked casserole-style in some mysterious murky liquid. One witty old gentleman I was visiting when the tray with this ghastly casserole arrived asked me if I had ever walked behind a horse pulling a plow in springtime when newly lush greenery facilitated the working of the animal's digestive system. (These words are not exactly the ones he used.) I told him I had indeed plowed fields walking behind horses that had eaten yellow corn, so I understood the image he presented so graphically.

Other barbs about food include those about chicken entrees. Some are so disguised that not even a Methodist circuit rider would recognize them—so a feisty eighty-seven-year-old former church organist announced stridently one early evening. She added that it should be called "chicken a la wonder—look at it and wonder what it is!" In that same dining room the term "damn Jello" came into common use after a popular resident who was totally uninhibited following brain surgery used it to describe a bowl of grape-flavored gelatin. This man spoke in a stage whisper that could be heard four rooms away. One pious lady of whom the swearing retired physician said "wouldn't cuss for all the tea in China," changed "damn" to the more antiseptic "danged."

Gossip abounds in nursing homes and is authentic folklore for it is passed on in the oral tradition. Gossip about romances of sorts that flourish modestly is of interest. One ninety-two-year-old woman proudly informed me that what some of her fellow residents said about her abiding amorous interests was true. She said, "I was a vamp when I was a young woman and I still have it!" She had male friends up to her death at age ninety-five. When she was in the last stages of her terminal illness, nurses entered her room to find her current boyfriend, a man in his late eighties, bending over her and giving her a passionate kiss. When asked what he was doing, he replied calmly, "Maudie Pauline is dying and I didn't want her to go out of this world unkissed. She surely did love to get a good smackeroo." Every time this story is repeated there are details added to it in the true folk tradition.

One old couple in their late eighties goes about the center I know best holding hands all the time. Both lost spouses. Many people who see them assume they are sweethearts. A local clergyman once complimented them for being such a "loving couple." With bittersweet humor, the old man responded, "We ain't in love; we jest hold hands to keep from falling down."

Enjoying a friendly game of dominoes

Incongruity makes for memorable humor anywhere. Among the folk in retirement facilities it figures strongly in speech. More examples of incongruous swearing illustrate this fact. At one center where I make calls, there was a woman 106 years old who had been married for seventy-five years to a Baptist minister. She looked like a figure in a genial cover painting by Norman Rockwell for the *Saturday Evening Post.* Her well-groomed hair was snowy white, her eyes seemed to be gazing sweetly at the other residents, and she smiled gently. But when a meal wasn't on the table when she sat down, she pounded forcefully on the table and swore really vile oaths, or as the folk say here in Texas, she "cussed a blue streak." She used language often heard from the lips of smarmy junior high school boys during noon recess on school playgrounds. Her language was so emphatic, so vulgar, so fiercely industrial strength, it cannot be repeated. After this swearing champion died, I talked with her favorite nurse who told me that if I had been married to a deepwater Baptist preacher for seventy-five years, I, too, would "cuss like a sailor." The nurse added, "Mrs. B was just making up for lost time!"

Another heroic curser was a tiny woman whose hair was always in braids held by tortoise hairpins. She also looked like a typical Normal Rockwell grandmother whose sweet smile could cure the heartbreak of psoriasis. Appearances are deceptive—especially among the very old in care facilities. This lady had no patience with her fellow residents if they sadly enough were ravaged by Alzheimer's disease. One such unfortunate old man had reached the stage at which he was like a well behaved four-year-old, the kind that longs to be helpful. His assignment was to pass around the bibs all residents wear at meals. Late one afternoon he committed what was to the tiny braided-haired lady a heinous mistake: he put not one, but two bibs at her place at the table. Here almost word for word is what she said to him: "Ray, why are you such a damned idiot just because it is so damned easy for you to be so [expletive deleted] stupid? I am so [another and totally vile expletive deleted] fed up with your [another strong expletive] being such a dumbass, I could puke my [really abominable expletive] socks up."

This vehement little person had a reputation for turning suddenly on people to whom she had previously been totally polite. I feared after she had so stoutly assaulted the bib man with harsh obscenities she would unleash on me her scathing verbal fury, but when I walked by to leave the room, she smiled beatifically and said, "Hon, you come back to see us real soon. We love you!"

Whether they are called old folks' homes, nursing homes, retirement communities, senior citizens' complexes or extended care facilities, residences for the old and frail are storehouses of a great variety of lore worthy of being preserved. In a presentation at a recent meeting of the Texas Folklore Society, Jan Seale said that indeed when a man dies, a library vanishes. So it is with much that is good in the folk tradition that disappears when the old in institutional settings (or anywhere, of course) pass on. To a folklorist, concentrations of so many yet living old people in such close proximities are resources valuable beyond compare.

George Ewing making good use of one of his Bibles.
Photo by Shane Watson

22

FOLKSY, BUT DEVOUT, BOOKKEEPING

by George Wilmeth Ewing

When I recently looked back at the folklore textbooks I read a good many years ago, I realized that though some mentioned a little about folk materials in the text of the Bible, nothing was said about the folk attitudes toward the physical or material book itself. Yet, hardly a day goes by that I do not see or hear a reminder of some commonly accepted cultural (not religious) view involving this document. True, some relate to beliefs probably not held by the many who no longer expect to meet an evil spirit that could be warded off by a Bible waved in his face, or who need one when traveling or sleeping to bring good luck, but how about kissing a Bible as a declaration of love? Some still do! There is, I have been told, a secret verse that can be used to stop bleeding, or lower fever, but it has been kept a secret from me. Do you still believe that in times of trouble, one may prayerfully close his eyes, open a Bible and place his finger on a verse which will help him solve his problem? I admit that a few times I, like many preachers, have successfully used the same method to discover a sermon topic. And don't forget that if a Bible is stacked with other books, or placed in a backpack or book satchel, it *must* be on top of the others. Everybody knows that!

I wondered about placing a right hand upon a Bible to insure truthfulness, for I still hear folks saying, "I'd swear on a stack of Bibles." So I called our county court, and was assured that witnesses in a trial are no longer required to do so, "but we still use a Bible when swearing some new official into his position!" Recently,

I attended a wedding in which the couple took their vows with hands on the Bible.

Admittedly, I live in a very religious city (Abilene, Texas), and most of the people I talk to are Protestant Anglo-Americans, so my findings about the book may not reflect accurately the ways of the total Texas population with its many Afro-Americans, Hispanics, and Orientals of varied beliefs, but I'm sure I'm into a folksy subject that others may find interesting.

For example, I have now asked hundreds of all kinds of people, "Have you ever thrown away or destroyed a Bible?" The Gideons International do admit that they destroy worn and incomplete copies, but so far, only two ordinary people have said that they have done such a thing—a woman who sounded almost apologetic as she explained that the old book had come to pieces and many pages were lost so that it could not be rebound, and a Biblical scholar who tossed one from which he had cut many passages that he pasted in his personal commentary. One man in a somewhat shocked tone, said, "I once saw one in a dumpster!" Several have told me that the Bible, like a worn-out United States flag, should be buried or burned (cremated?), but certainly never trashed.

Since copying machines have become commonplace, I am guessing that we will not see much more cutting and pasting of this respected document, but I am reminded of a preacher many years ago who shocked his audience by tearing a page from his Bible and waving it before his audience to show them the scriptural proof of his statement. Another preacher of my childhood told of a woman who, when shown a passage that disagreed with her religious view, ripped that page from her Bible, wadded it up and threw it in a wastebasket.

Well, what *do* we do with old Bibles? Not surprisingly, since it is the most widely owned book in the world, many copies are lost. During World War II, when I was hitch-hiking into Fort Lauderdale, Florida, to go to church, I was picked up by a couple of obviously drunken women, and after twenty minutes of a terrifying, swerving, eighty-mile-an-hour ride, when the car stopped I hopped out so quickly that I left my overnight kit and my Bible on the back seat, and they were whisked away before I had a chance to reach in and recover them. Probably that is the only Bible I have lost, but nearly every church building I enter will have a number of unclaimed copies of the book, usually on a shelf in an entry hallway. I am guessing that inn-keepers, airline attendants, and bus and taxi drivers could tell us a good bit about lost (or found) Bibles.

Nearly every used-book sale I have attended has a row of Bibles, and though I am seldom a customer at garage sales, I have been told that there are quite a few Bibles in them, but since Bible societies give away new copies, I doubt that used ones bring high prices. More often, old Bibles are preserved. Some are rebound, but far more go up on shelves—in closets or unused cabinets—and one woman told me that she had a big box of old Bibles in her garage, but had no idea what she ought to do with them.

Maybe we keep them because memories can make treasures of many things. Lying in a little wooden holder on our TV is my mother's baby spoon, dating back to 1893. Every time I see it, I recall that when I was three, I helped her rake among the ashes of our home that had burned to the ground the day before and saw her tears as she recovered this precious object—which, incidentally, was the only sterling silver we had during the Great Depression that came a few years later. Memories also gush up whenever I bore a hole with the "new" brace and bit, which I first used in 1928, or make a measurement with the carpenter's rule that belonged to my father who died forty years ago. A friend of mine recently mentioned the memories produced by a baby toy that he has kept eighty-four years—the first Christmas present he ever received. Should we be surprised, then, if we feel an emotional surge when we try to throw away a Bible—worn, but enriched with memories of special occasions or people? Recently, when I visited a nursing home and observed an old Bible in the hands of a decrepit man, he said, "This was my mother's Bible!"

How many may bring back wartime memories? A man from the Gideons International assures me that they are still trying to see that every person in the armed services receives a pocket-sized New Testament with Psalms and Proverbs, and I quickly recalled the ones we carried during World War II, many of which had a metal plate over one cover, supposedly strong enough to stop a bullet. I never went overseas, and never had to duck anything more dangerous than a Florida seagull's droppings, but recently a friend, who is certainly not a profound Bible believer, told me that he carried his testament all the time he was in the combat zones—but in his duffel bag rather than his pocket. A fellow English teacher said that when he was in the invasion of Europe, he saw the bullet hole in a testament that had probably saved the life of one of his buddies. My sister's husband, a Marine who was in the battles on Guadalcanal, Bougainville, Saipan, and Guam, had been given a prayer book by his Catholic mother and a Bible by his new wife. When crouched in a jungle foxhole surrounded by the enemy, he wrote, "I have thrown away my prayer book, but I'm hanging on to my Bible!"

More and more Bibles are likely to outlive their owners, for sales of Bible covers and carrying cases are going up. Most bookstores now are stocking these in various sizes and materials (leather, plastic, or heavy cloth over something like cardboard), with zipper or Velcro fasteners to hold them closed. I'm seeing these increasing among churchgoers. These may often be "study Bibles," and this raises the question "How can you mark in a Bible?" Underlining and the use of highlighting pens are generally acceptable, and writing in the margins is commonplace (though one man told me, "I never mark on the texual pages of my Bible"), but how about doodling with meaningless scribbles or comic figures or faces? So far, I have found no one who will admit to doing such a thing, but one librarian said he saw an old Bible with a tit-tat-toe game on one blank space. Two people must have sat together during a boring sermon!

Some Bibles are disposed of at the funeral of the owner. A local funeral director told me that about twenty percent of his customers want the selected book, preferably a small edition, in the casket

Bibles come in many forms to appeal to a variety of readers

during the visitation and service, but many are removed and given to a near relative before the box is sealed and covered. Where should it be in the casket? One woman told me her father was buried with his Bible in his hand, but usually it is under the arm of a man, but under the crossed hands on the breast of a woman. One second-generation preacher I knew used the same Bible his father had used and marked for many years, adding several years of his own notes in the margins, and this book was left under his head, like a pillow, when he was buried.

Other special occasions are enhanced by Bibles, likely gifts from friends or relatives. Groups performing christenings often see that the child will own a Bible; many churches give Bibles to new converts, and brides still often carry one, but not as often as a few years ago, a bridal shop manager told me, "for weddings are becoming more secular!" White satin covers were often made for the bride's Bible, and bookstores still carry a number of "bridal Bibles," usually small and white, as well as some white decorated covers for gift Bibles with dark binding. (So far, I have heard nothing about Bibles in divorce proceedings!)

The public school librarians that I have talked to say that several versions of the Bible are in the libraries, but they mentioned no Korans, Books of Mormon, or similar documents. Some churches give Bibles to members that are moving away, adding pages of personal notes and signatures. I was recently shown one with well over a hundred names of fellow members. Imagine the memories that this may arouse years later. The Gideons see that Bibles also appear at graduations, whether from the fifth or sixth grades or from high school, "but now we cannot take them into the buildings, so we stand outside and hand them to the students as they come out." One representative found it weird that they cannot place Bibles in schoolrooms, but can put them in prison cells, "but only soft-covered ones—no hard covers!" (Can they be used as weapons?) I am also told that some schools keep a "school Bible," which is passed from the president of the graduating class to the president of the next year's class.

Incidentally, most of these gifts are the King James Versions, having the text that sounds "more biblical" to many people, but lately more and more Spanish and bilingual versions are being used.

I was surprised when several people mentioned rebinding Bibles—"my great-great-grandmother's Bible," or "my great-grandfather's Bible"—so I called a local bookbinder and was told, "Yes, we do between a hundred and two hundred a year, for about two or three hundred dollars each." Some thirty or more of these, he added, may date back to the period between the Civil War and the advent of the automobile, a hundred years or so ago, a period when a big family Bible was considered a mark of achievement, and might cost $50 or more—equal in purchasing power to close to a thousand today! Since rebinding costs so much, I feel confident that there must be a lot of old Bibles in their original covers in Texas homes.

So far, nearly everyone I have asked has admitted to having a "household" or "family" Bible in his home. We will define the first as a Bible that is readily available to anyone for reading or study, and a "family Bible" is one that has a generation or more of family names and relationships written on pages, usually between the testaments. My house has a lot of Bibles, but few have many family names in them, and the ones more than thirty or forty years old have mostly been passed on to friends and descendents, I guess. Knowing that my mother's family has strong ties to the past, I called a distant cousin that I knew was interested in her ancestry, and was told that the Bible purchased about 1825 and brought to Texas in a covered wagon in 1845 by my great-great-grandfather J. B. Wilmeth, is now in the home of an eighth-generation descendent. It is a large, leather-bound book, probably about fourteen inches high, containing pages of family names and dates, which (my cousin told me) became important during the days of the establishment of Collin County and McKinney, Texas. Back before the days of birth certificates and the like, Bible records could be legal documents, she said. She also assured me that there were other very old family Bibles among the Wilmeths, and that my great-grandfather J. R. Wilmeth once was displeased with his daughter Edna's behavior and cut her name out of his family Bible, but later restored it.

Since family Bibles are obviously an important household item, where should they be kept? Many homes once had a small table in the parlor on which the Bible was centered, sometimes on a slanted, two-winged shelf that held it open to the family records or a favorite passage like the 23rd Psalm. Some homes today still have one on the coffee table in front of a couch in the living room or on a mantle over the fireplace. Does its prominent position assure us that it is read? Seventy-five years or so ago, I recall an itinerant preacher's telling of staying a few days in a good Christian home, and when he returned to it a year or so later, he opened the family Bible and

One of the many types of "family" Bibles

removed the dollar bills that he had placed there as a test of their use of the book. They were still marking exactly the same passages.

Today the family Bible may also be under a lamp on an end table by a couch or bed, or, maybe uncomfortably, on top of the TV. Precious old or worn copies may be placed under the glass top of a coffee table or stood open in a glass cabinet by a wall, but many are on protected bookshelves, or in a box on a shelf in a closet or storeroom, awaiting burial with the current owner, or more likely, being passed on to a caring descendent. If the family has been active in church, civic, or academic affairs, their Bible may end up in a city, school, or church library.

Obviously, this book is a cultural artifact that is still catching our attention, but what does this mean? Its sales and distribution unquestionably place it far beyond any other publications, including textbooks, comic books, or pornography, yet booksellers, librarians, and others have told me many times that, though it originated the eighth commandment, it is the most often stolen book in the world! The book's chief villain must be still around, I guess!

The Secretary-Editor's Bible, stuffed with notes and reminders

Meredith Abarca teaching her students by sharing stories with them

23

MI FRONTERIDAD IN THE CLASSROOM: THE POWER OF WRITING AND SHARING STORIES

by Meredith E. Abarca

The view from my office in the Department of English at the University of Texas at El Paso overlooks *las colonias* in Cd. Juárez, Chihuahua. This view represents a cyclical journey in my life. I came to life, discovering its joys and pains, on the border of Nuevo Laredo, Tamaulipas and Laredo, Texas. I am the second youngest in a family of seven, all raised by a single mother whose formal education reached only the second grade. A month short of my turning twelve, we left the border and moved to California. All I remember of my first day at Fair Oaks Elementary School were tears rolling down my face since I could not comprehend what the teacher or classmates said. Twenty-two years after leaving the border, I returned to *la frontera* of El Paso and Cd. Juárez. This time I found myself holding a doctoral degree in Literature of the Americas, ready to teach in a language that I once did not know. My efforts to understand the meaning of my cyclical journey have allowed me to see how my personal life weaves the tapestry of my professional career.

In my courses, Chicana/o Literature, Mexican-American Folklore, literary studies, and Women Philosophers in the Kitchen, I have learned to see how my students' and my own stories interconnect. The majority of my students and I share a similar cultural background. We are children of *la frontera*. Some of us identify ourselves as Chicanas/os, others as Mexican-American, and others as Hispanics. Most of them are, as I was, first generation college students, and most come, as I do, from a working-class background.

I see my students and myself as children of *la frontera,* not the border. The difference between these words is that the border, for me, suggests a boundary, a limit, an end. *La frontera,* on the other hand, symbolizes the notion of a frontier as a place of continuous exploration. Our explorations take place during discussions evoked by the literature, and as students gather, write, and share their own family stories by exploring their back yard history. An option for my courses' final is for students to research one aspect of their personal lives and write a critical reflective essay, applying the theoretical concepts they learned in class to articulate an in-depth analysis of that part of their lives. The goal is for them to see how their daily lives carry a wealth of social, cultural, and historical value. Looking at their lives as a story worthy of writing and sharing empowers them.

In the process of sharing our back yard histories, I understand what historian Aurora Levins Morales says when she writes that "we are a society of people living in a state of post-traumatic shock."[1] As children of *la frontera,* we understand with the essence of our being what folklorist Américo Paredes means when he defines the border as a place of constant conflict. For Paredes, "Conflict—cultural, economic, and physical" defines the "way of life along the border between Mexico and the United States."[2] But as children of *la frontera* we also know, as does historian Yolanda Chávez Leyva, that while "the divisions are so great and painful," people of *la frontera* are "resilient and persistent."[3]

By exploring our back yard history, we begin to understand the cause of our "post-traumatic shock," an unconscious shock for some. "The trauma of colonialism lives on in our classrooms," says Chávez Leyva. Its effects can be seen "as a deep pain that manifests itself as anxieties, uncertainties, and unrest."[4] I have witnessed my students' pain. Not one semester has gone by without many students beginning to unearth the cause of their cultural, economic, intellectual, physical or emotional trauma. The silences students begin to break as they give voice to their stories are those imposed by patriarchy, capitalism, cultural colonialism, and institutionalized religion. One student talks about the confusion he felt, as a child, by feeling the necessity of changing his name from "Juan" to "John." He titled his final paper, "My Name is JUAN." Other students talk about the stigma created by having been raised or still living on the "wrong" side of the tracks or the "wrong" side of the bridge. Still others talk about thinking of themselves as responsible for transgressions committed on their bodies, on their emotions, on their spirit. While many of the discoveries my students explore in the classroom are tied to painful memories, by naming, writing, and sharing their stories they enact "the will to be self-actualized."[5] Some recent titles of students' papers exemplify this process: "The Awakening: Breaking the Perpetual Silence," "Discovering Myself Through Critical Thinking," and "A Journey of Self Discovery."

Breaking the silence imposed by traumatic events by giving voice to our experiences is always difficult, particularly in "a society that does not do grief well or easily."[6] While I have witnessed the difficulty of grieving, I also have seen the ability students have to break such social patterns and allow themselves to grieve and to connect with each other. As one of my students tries to capture the last day of class, she writes:

> I'm sorry I broke down. . . . I don't like to show my emotions because I have always been the "strong one." . . . But in our last class of the semester, when Dr. Abarca was reading from her writings, and talking about grief, my grandmother whom I loved more than anything in this world, came to mind. She had cancer and suffered to the very end. . . . I miss her so much that while we are sharing our stories of happiness and pain memories of her came through. I could feel the grief all over again. I am glad for the memories to re-emerge because I know that she is still alive in my heart and mind. So memories may be sad, but without memories, how could we be the person we are today?

Without our memories, yes the painful ones, how can we honor the goodness that lives within us? Another student in the same course, Women Philosophers in the Kitchen, writes in the last journal for the class:

> A lot has changed for me this year that in some way this class has given me the opportunity to put all the pieces together and find my true self. (Something that I was aware lived inside of me, yet I had been too busy to appreciate.). . . . Each week we'd touch on a subject that would in some way tie into a personal realm I either hadn't dealt with or had suppressed for other reasons. . . . I have learned much about my inner self and became capable of appreciating the individual I am. . . . Thank you all for your companionship, for your encouragement, and for sharing yourselves!

Giving voice to pain, naming its sources is the first step in healing.

"Any classroom that employs a holistic model of learning," argues English professor bell hooks, "will also be a place where teachers grow, and are empowered by the process."[7] Yet such empowerment cannot take place, hooks says, "if we [the teachers] refuse to be vulnerable while encouraging students to take risk[s]."[8] She suggests that "professors must practice being vulnerable in the classroom, being wholly present in mind, body, and spirit."[9] It is in this vulnerability that empowerment takes place and healing begins. The classroom does offer a space to engage in a holistic process of healing, one that can heal the mind, body, and soul. For the last few years, I have practiced hooks' advice. In class and in my writing, I engage in an act of vulnerability by sharing parts of my own back yard history with both my students and my readers. I share these parts of my history in the spirit of storytelling, a spirit that creates a community by connecting one story to another. I write because just like Levins Morales, I am "one of the traumatized seeking to recover herself."[10]

My initial reaction to returning to *la frontera,* the place of my childhood, was excitement. Before the actual move, I asked myself: "What would it mean to come back to *la frontera* where I spent the formative years of my life?" Those were years of wonder, of bonding, of exploring. In the memories of my childhood, I share Norma Cantú's notion of *la frontera* as a "safe place."[11] There were many aspects of life between the two Laredos that made it a safe place. The most vivid memories I have of feeling safe, protected, and childlike are those of time spent in the kitchen with my mother. Together we would often make flour *tortillas.* The most effective way of getting me out of bed on cold, dark winter days was the smell of my mother's freshly made refried beans with *chorizo* or *papas con chorizo y huevo.* Besides the wonderful aroma wafting through the house, it was my responsibility to pull a chair next to the stove to smash the remaining beans she would always have saved for me. I have no words to describe what the smell of homemade flour *tortillas,* refried beans with *chorizo,* and my mother's warmth by my side means for me. This memory is invaluable.

It has taken me years to fully recognize how this memory sustains me spiritually, emotionally, and intellectually. I became aware of this memory's power during a classroom discussion in my course Women Philosophers in the Kitchen. For the final project, students collected culinary stories from three different generations of women in their family. The process of gathering culinary stories revealed to them, all women, how their attitudes about food were connected with their mothers. As they shared their stories, it became clear to some that their own dislike toward cooking was connected with the fact that they had no memories of spending time in the kitchen with their mothers, cooking and passing on stories of nourishment. Listening to my students during this rather emotional class meeting, in my effort to wrap up the discussion, I heard myself telling students that food, cooking, and kitchens, the focus of my academic research, are important to me because within this realm I have memories of time with my mother. In the kitchen, I am closest to my mother's love.

My memory of *la frontera,* however, also resonates with Gloria Anzaldua's description of it as "*una herida abierta.*"[12] My life's journey has brought me back to *la frontera,* perhaps because it is there where I must learn to mourn two losses in my life I associate with the border. The border holds memories of what was taken away from me. As a child, while I did not have a language that spoke about trauma, my body, my mind, and my spirit knew its implications. While the most sensible and logical thing to say is that Nuevo Laredo itself represented home, for me to speak of home and my childhood simultaneously has always been rather complicated. In my childhood years, my innocence, my dignity, and my humanity were taken from me by men who haunted my nights for several years. In my teenage years, one of my brothers who longed to return to the border died in a tragic motorcycle accident in the Davis mountains, never completing his journey from California to Laredo, Texas. His loss, for me, has always been connected to the border.

The author's brother

Like many of my students, I too began to understand the depth of this complication, of my trauma, in college. Reading books like Toni Morrison's *The Bluest Eye* and Maya Angelou's *I Know Why the Caged Bird Sings,* I discovered a language to understand the meaning of my open wound. These stories gave me the initial courage to break the silence that I had lived under for over a decade, silence which back then I believed was self-imposed. With Levins Morales' *Medicine Stories,* I now understand that my silence was not self-imposed, but inflicted on me. Levins Morales writes, "The people who abused me consciously and deliberately manipulated me in an attempt to break down my sense of integrity so they could make me into an accomplice to my own torture."[13] For her, "the recovery from trauma requires creating [a] story . . . powerful enough to restore a sense of our own humanity."[14] The words of her powerful story validate my feelings; they acknowledge my pain, my confusion, my silence. Levins Morales explains that "what is required to face trauma is the ability to mourn, fully and deeply, all that has been taken from us. . . . Only through mourning everything we have lost can we discover that we have in fact survived; that our spirits are indestructible."[15] I have discovered that the meaning of my cyclical journey is a gift to heal a wounded soul. The return to *la frontera,* a place that holds the power that defines me, has been a calling for mourning.

It is now, living and teaching on *la frontera,* that I must break the next layer of my silence and speak publicly about my private pain. I break the silence now because as a teacher of literature, which for me is the study of our humanity, I have an ethical responsibility to my students to be wholly present in the classroom: mind, body, and soul. While the effects of my trauma are still painful, by writing and sharing stories and allowing my humanity full of passion and vulnerability to reveal itself in my classes, I am learning to use those experiences as tools of empowerment for my students and myself.

Writing and sharing stories can work as "*una gran limpia,*" the "cleansing where body, mind, and spirit are brought into balance, as the negative is removed and replaced with that which is healthy."[16] For my students and me, this *gran limpia* happens in the classroom as we explore, write, and share the stories of our own back yard history, as we explore the meaning of our *fronteridad.*

Endnotes

1. Aurora Levins Morales. *Medicine Stories: History, Culture and the Politics of Integrity.* Cambridge, MA: South End Press, 1998. 13.
2. Américo Paredes. "Border Identity: Culture Conflict and Convergence along the Lower Rio Grande." *Folk Nation: Folklore in the Creation of American Tradition.* Ed. Simon J. Bronner. 2002. Wilmington, DE: Scholarly Resources Inc, 1978. 200.
3. Yolanda Chávez Leyva. " 'There is Great Good in Returning': A Testimonio from the Borderlands." *Frontiers: A Journal of Women Studies.* Nebraska: University of Nebraska Press, 2003. 1.
4. ———. "The Revisioning of History Es Una Gran Limpia: Teaching and Historical Trauma in Chicana/o History." *La Voz de Esperanza.* Parts I and II. San Antonio. Sept. and Oct. 2002, 5.
5. bell hooks. *Teaching to Transgress: Education as the Practice of Freedom.* Routledge: New York, 1994. 18.
6. Levins Morales. 19.
7. hooks. 21.
8. Ibid. 21.
9. Ibid. 21.
10. Levins Morales. 25.
11. Norma Cantú. *Canícula: Snapshots of a Girlhood En La Frontera.* Albuquerque: University of New Mexico Press, 1995. 2.
12. Gloría Anzaldúa. *Borderlands/La Frontera: The New Mestiza.* San Francisco: Spinsters/ aunt Iute, 1987. 3.
13. Levins Morales. 117.
14. Ibid. 15.
15. Ibid. 19.
16. Chávez Leyva. "The Revisioning of History Es Una Gran Limpia: Teaching and Historical Trauma in Chicana/o History." 10.

Contributors' Vitas

Meredith E. Abarca received a Ph.D. in Comparative Literature from the University of California at Davis. She is an assistant professor of English at the University of Texas at El Paso. Some of her regular courses include Chicana/o Literature, Mexican-American Folklore, Film and Literature of the Americas, Critical Theory, and Women Philosophers in the Kitchen. Her publications include "Authentic or Not, It's Original," in *Food & Foodways,* 12:1–25, 2004; "Los chilaquiles de mi 'amá: the Language of Everyday Cooking," in *Pilar, Pozole, and Pad Thai: American Women and Ethnic Food.* Ed. Sherrie A. Inness. Massachusetts: University of Massachusetts Press, 2001: 119–144; and her book *Voices in the Kitchen: Views of Food and the World from Working-Class Mexican and Mexican-American Women,* Texas A&M University Press, 2006.

Mary Margaret Dougherty Campbell holds a B.A. and an M.A. in English from Texas Tech University. She has presented papers at South Central Modern Language Association, Conference of College Teachers of English, Texas/Southwest Popular Culture Association, Popular Culture Association, National Cowboy Symposium and Celebration, and South Texas Ranching Heritage Festival. She presented her first TFS paper in 2004. Her poems have appeared in *English in Texas, American Cowboy, Rope Burns,* and *2006 Texas Poetry Calendar.* She has kept Live Oak County informed of the activities of the J. Frank Dobie Society and various elements of George West High School via the local newspaper. Currently, she serves TFS as a Councilor.

Mary Joe Clendenin taught school for many years, beginning in a country school where she had three grades (first, second, and third) in one room. Later she taught all other grades, in different schools, through high school. The last sixteen years of her career were spent teaching at Lubbock Christian University. Dr. Clendenin earned degrees from Abilene Christian University, New

Mexico Highlands University, and New Mexico State University. She and her husband Ray moved back to Erath County, Texas, after retiring. She writes a weekly column, "A Word Edgewise" for the *Stephenville Empire Tribune* and is the author of eleven books in print. They include: *The Ghost of Jenny, Galloping Ghosts, Ghost of the McDow Hole, The Melody Within, Devotional Souvenirs, A Few Words Edgewise, My Corner of the Great Depression, Straight from the Butterfly, Lobos, Longhorns and Mules, Gonzalo, Coronado's Shepherd Boy*, and *Comanche Captive* (co-authored with Don Smart.) More information about these books may be found at *www.our-town.com/clendenin.* She also has an e-book, *Developing Positive Attitudes.*

Tom Crum was born in Pecos, Texas, and grew up in McKinney, Texas. He attended Texas Christian University and the University of Texas Law School. He is a retired state District Judge who lives with his wife Mary near Granbury, Texas. As he said in his article, he does not consider himself to be either a folklorist or an historian. However, he has great interest in both folklore and history and has presented several papers on both subjects at various meetings. He is a past president of the West Texas Historical Association and is the Counselor for the Texas Folklore Society. He is currently on the Board of Directors of the East Texas Historical Association and the Advisory Council for the Center for Big Bend Studies.

Kenneth W. Davis is Professor Emeritus of English at Texas Tech University, where he taught folklore courses as well as many other subjects for thirty-nine years. A native of old Bell County, he has read a dozen or so papers at meetings of the Texas Folklore Society and was president of the Society in the 1990s. He remains interested in the traditional oral narratives of Texas, and was co-editor of *Black Cats, Hoot Owls and Water Witches* (UNT Press), and of *Horsing Around: Contemporary Cowboy Humor* (Wayne State University Press; reissued by Texas Tech Press).

tment at Texas State University-San Marcos in August 2001. ias taught Introduction to Sociology, Drugs and Society, and co-coordinator of the Applied Sociology Internship pro-. Personally, she is married, has one daughter, and is expecting girls in May of 2006. She enjoys spending time with her fam-iends, and her beloved Jack Russell mix, Hunter.

hett Rushing is a native Texan and Aggie that got hooked on ore in the swamps and bayous of Southeast Texas at a young He received an M.A. in Folk Studies from Western Kentucky ersity and is ABD in his Ph.D. in Folklore at Indiana Univer-ersity and is ABD in his Ph.D. in Folklore at Indiana Univer- Rhett is currently enjoying the "greatest job in the world" at University of Texas at San Antonio's Institute of Texan Cul-s in the Research Department.

es B. "Lew" Schnitz, P.E., P.G, was born near New Berlin, as, in November 1928. Lew graduated from Sutherland Springs h School and obtained a B.S. in Petroleum and Natural Gas ineering from Texas A&I University. He obtained an M.B.A. the University of Texas at San Antonio in 1991 and took grad- courses in Hydrogeology at the same university. He is a Profes-al Engineer and Professional Geoscientist, registered in the State Texas. He worked thirty-four years for Humble Oil and Refining mpany and Exxon Corporation in drilling, production, and gas nt operations. Most of his career was spent working on the large ches of South Texas, including the King Ranch, Kennedy Ranch, t Ranch, and others. Lew married Jean Granberry in 1953 and y have three sons and four grandchildren.

ldred Boren Sentell was born and reared in Post, Texas. She ended North Texas State University, Angelo State University, xas A&M University, and Texas Tech University, and taught in Angelo State University English Department for seventeen ars before marrying Joe Sentell. On retiring in 1993, she and Joe oved to Snyder, Texas. They have two daughters, one son, and ght grandchildren, all living in Post and Snyder, Texas.

J. Frank Dobie (1888–1964) served as Secretary-Editor of the Texas Folklore Society from 1923–1943. He edited or co-edited dozens of books during his tenure, and he brought the Society great recognition through his status as an educator and public figure. He was the Society's third Fellow, preceded only by John A. Lomax and Leonidas Payne.

Gloria Duarte, professor of English, has taught at Angelo State University in San Angelo, Texas, for twenty-eight years. She teaches a variety of classes, including some on women in literature, Southwest literature, and Mexican-American literature. Her areas of interest include Chicana writers, Mexican-American culture, Ft. McKavett (where she grew up), and local women of San Angelo.

Martha Emmons (1895–1990) was the Texas Folklore Society's first woman Fellow, being inducted posthumously in 2002. She served as president twice, from 1935–1936 and from 1969–1970. First joining the Society in the 1920s, she was an active member for perhaps longer than anyone else—for well over sixty years.

George Wilmeth Ewing, born in 1923 in Robstown, Texas, is a fifth-generation Texan who grew up in the Lower Rio Grande Valley and Corpus Christi. After studying and teaching electronics and radar during WWII, he married, started a family of five children, took a bachelor's degree in Bible, carpentered, and preached for a few years before finishing graduate degrees (M.A. in '52; Ph.D. in '62) in American literature from the University of Texas, writing theses on the frontier preacher in Texas and the verse of the Temperance Movement, the latter published as *The Well-Tempered Lyre.* During his thirty-seven years teaching at Abilene Christian University, he wrote a few articles, hymns, book reviews, and poems; won a hymn-writing contest; edited and annotated John Locke's *Reasonableness of Christianity;* preached; drew publishable doodles; and gave ten gallons of blood to the local blood bank. Since retirement from ACU, he worked a dozen years as a part-time maintenance man in a sixty-unit apartment house for Christians over sixty-five, conducted worship in nursing homes, made walking sticks, dabbled in trash art, exercised regularly, and read a half-dozen papers at Texas Folklore Society meetings—but has yet to learn how to do much on a computer that his doctor son gave him last year!

Lora B. Garrison is a past president of the Texas Folklore Society, Pioneer Storyteller at schools and at the Texas Folklife Festival, and is known as the "Keeper of Tales" by her family and friends. She has an educational background in anthropology and creative writing. She has collected oral history since 1979 and was a newspaper columnist for ten years. She claims that most of her education came from following her Air Force husband Roger around the world for thirty years. She was serving as local arrangements coordinator for the Uvalde TFS meeting when she presented her paper on John Nance Garner, who served as U. S. Vice-President. Lora B. remembers Mr. Garner who lived two blocks from her family in Uvalde, Texas, while her father Bob Davis served as Uvalde County Judge.

James T. Matthews lives in San Antonio, Texas, where he is a Field Director for the Boy Scouts of America. He is a military historian concentrating on the frontier army in Texas and the Southwest. His recent book, *Fort Concho: A History and a Guide,* was published by the Texas State Historical Association in 2005.

Milt McAfee (1918–2004) served during WWII as a Lt. Colonel of Field Artillery in the U. S. Army. Afterwards, he completed the Advertising and Marketing Program at New York University, and he received his Masters degree from SMU with courses in creative writing. He was Director of Publications and Director of Printing for Texas Instruments for twenty-six years. **Leroy McAfee** was his uncle.

Ben Mead (1902–1986) worked as a commercial artist for over forty years, and he completed murals for various museums throughout the Southwest, including three for the Panhandle-

Plains Historical Museum's Pioneer Hall. I
such as J. Frank Dobie's *Coronado's Chila*
magazines. **Milt McAfee** was his cousin by

Donna Meletio is a native Texan who bec
After running a real estate management bu
daughters, she returned to school and
received her doctorate in 2005. While at Lo
in Baton Rouge, she began investigating fo
interest has taken her to many places: the
tions, the back streets of New Orleans wher
ans parade, cowboy campfires in New Mexi
in the Texas Hill Country, and the courtro
judges. Her passion is to learn how we com
and express our ideas and values. Currently
biography of Leona Queyrouze, a French
includes a study of the New Orleans salon cul

Kelly M. Mosel-Talavera received her Bach
sociology and communication from Texas A&
pus Christi in 1994. She received her Master
State (then Southwest Texas State) in 1997 wi
ogy and a minor in communication studies. U
began teaching full-time for ITT Technical
Texas. She taught introductory level sociol
extremely diverse group of students completin
requirements, including Speech and Commu
Career Success, Human Relations, and Succ
addition, she taught sociology and speech for
College, as well as public speaking courses f
Academy. She became a member of the ASA (A
cal Association), and the Texas Folklore Soci
interests continued in Texas folklore, and she fo
ment in chili cook-offs. As a result, she became a
(Chili Appreciation Society International) and ha
larly for the past five years. She joined the facult

Deborah Lightfoot Sizemore, a writer and freelance editor who received a B.S. in Agricultural Journalism from Texas A&M University, is a native of thirsty West Texas. With the late Simon W. Freese, P. E., she co-authored *A Century in the Works: Freese and Nichols Consulting Engineers, 1894–1994,* which received the History and Heritage Award from the Texas Section of the American Society of Civil Engineers. She has authored other books of Texas history and biography, including *The LH7 Ranch* and, under the pen name of D. J. Lightfoot, the children's book *Trail Fever.* A fan of the history and lore of the British Isles, she has managed to work a good bit of that into her new novel. To be published under her Lightfoot byline, the fantasy has the working title *Waterspell.* Her web site is at *www.djlightfoot.com.*

William N. "Bill" Stokes, Jr. (1909–2002) was born in Vernon, Texas, and he earned a B.A. in English Literature from Baylor University and his law degree from Yale. He was an avid collector of books, and his library included an extensive collection of Texas Folklore editions. He was an active member of the Texas Folklore Society, and its meetings and the sharing of papers and stories were among his favorite things to do. He served as a Second Lieutenant in WWII and practiced law in Washington, D.C. and Houston. He retired to a small country law office in Lake Dallas and was even known to give legal advice from time to time to Dr. F. E. Abernethy on copyright issues for the Society. He died in 2002 shortly before his 93rd birthday.

Kenneth L. Untiedt left the quiet life of a small town in Iowa when he joined the U. S. Air Force shortly after turning seventeen. He ended up in Lubbock, Texas, where he finished out his six years of service. While in West Texas, he attended South Plains College, joined the Lubbock Police Department, and eventually earned his B.A., M.A., and Ph.D. from Texas Tech University. He spent thirteen years as a patrolman, and his involvement in the Texas Folklore Society eventually led to his election as Secretary-Editor. He now lives in Nacogdoches and teaches at Stephen F. Austin State University, where he is also Director of Technical Writing.

Charles E. Williams has a background in pottery, packages, and poetry. He grew up on a small dairy farm in upstate New York and graduated from Alfred University with a degree in Ceramic Engineering. For several years his craft of choice was thrown pottery, but he later entered the high-tech world of transistors and microchips, and he eventually retired from Texas Instruments. TI thought so much of him that they elected him a Member of the Group Technical Staff and hired him back as a consultant after he retired. Amongst his many accomplishments plowing the technical fields was the granting of fourteen patents to him by your U. S. Government. His passion is cowboy poetry and storytelling, and he has been telling stories for nearly forty years, the last half of it professionally. He is a past-president of the Texas Cowboy Poets' Association, and he has been hooked up with the Academy of Western Artists since its inception (he holds membership card #2).

Henry Wolff, Jr. has been a Texas journalist for five decades—most of his adult life. He has worked for the *San Angelo Standard-Times,* the *Abilene Reporter-News,* and the *Victoria Advocate.* He joined the *Advocate,* the second oldest existing newspaper in Texas, in 1963 and has been a full-time columnist for twenty-six years, writing more than 6,000 of his "Henry's Journal" columns. He has been a member of the Texas Folklore Society since 1989 and served as president for the 2005–2006 year.

INDEX

A

B

C

D

H

J

K

L

M

T

U

V

department at Texas State University-San Marcos in August 2001. She has taught Introduction to Sociology, Drugs and Society, and is the co-coordinator of the Applied Sociology Internship program. Personally, she is married, has one daughter, and is expecting twin girls in May of 2006. She enjoys spending time with her family, friends, and her beloved Jack Russell mix, Hunter.

J. Rhett Rushing is a native Texan and Aggie that got hooked on folklore in the swamps and bayous of Southeast Texas at a young age. He received an M.A. in Folk Studies from Western Kentucky University and is ABD in his Ph.D. in Folklore at Indiana University. Rhett is currently enjoying the "greatest job in the world" at the University of Texas at San Antonio's Institute of Texan Cultures in the Research Department.

Lewes B. "Lew" Schnitz, P.E., P.G, was born near New Berlin, Texas, in November 1928. Lew graduated from Sutherland Springs High School and obtained a B.S. in Petroleum and Natural Gas Engineering from Texas A&I University. He obtained an M.B.A. from the University of Texas at San Antonio in 1991 and took graduate courses in Hydrogeology at the same university. He is a Professional Engineer and Professional Geoscientist, registered in the State of Texas. He worked thirty-four years for Humble Oil and Refining Company and Exxon Corporation in drilling, production, and gas plant operations. Most of his career was spent working on the large ranches of South Texas, including the King Ranch, Kennedy Ranch, East Ranch, and others. Lew married Jean Granberry in 1953 and they have three sons and four grandchildren.

Mildred Boren Sentell was born and reared in Post, Texas. She attended North Texas State University, Angelo State University, Texas A&M University, and Texas Tech University, and taught in the Angelo State University English Department for seventeen years before marrying Joe Sentell. On retiring in 1993, she and Joe moved to Snyder, Texas. They have two daughters, one son, and eight grandchildren, all living in Post and Snyder, Texas.

Plains Historical Museum's Pioneer Hall. He also illustrated works such as J. Frank Dobie's *Coronado's Children* and several western magazines. **Milt McAfee** was his cousin by marriage.

Donna Meletio is a native Texan who became a writer late in life. After running a real estate management business and rearing three daughters, she returned to school and began teaching. She received her doctorate in 2005. While at Louisiana State University in Baton Rouge, she began investigating folklore groups, and this interest has taken her to many places: the Cajun prairie celebrations, the back streets of New Orleans where the Mardi Gras Indians parade, cowboy campfires in New Mexico, Easter celebrations in the Texas Hill Country, and the courtrooms of Texas women judges. Her passion is to learn how we come together as a people and express our ideas and values. Currently, she is completing a biography of Leona Queyrouze, a French Creole poet, which includes a study of the New Orleans salon culture.

Kelly M. Mosel-Talavera received her Bachelor of Arts in both sociology and communication from Texas A&M University at Corpus Christi in 1994. She received her Master of Arts from Texas State (then Southwest Texas State) in 1997 with a major in sociology and a minor in communication studies. Upon graduation, she began teaching full-time for ITT Technical Institute in Austin, Texas. She taught introductory level sociology courses to an extremely diverse group of students completing general education requirements, including Speech and Communication, as well as Career Success, Human Relations, and Success Orientation. In addition, she taught sociology and speech for Austin Community College, as well as public speaking courses for Texas Culinary Academy. She became a member of the ASA (American Sociological Association), and the Texas Folklore Society. Her research interests continued in Texas folklore, and she found a new amusement in chili cook-offs. As a result, she became a member of CASI (Chili Appreciation Society International) and has competed regularly for the past five years. She joined the faculty of the sociology

J. Frank Dobie (1888–1964) served as Secretary-Editor of the Texas Folklore Society from 1923–1943. He edited or co-edited dozens of books during his tenure, and he brought the Society great recognition through his status as an educator and public figure. He was the Society's third Fellow, preceded only by John A. Lomax and Leonidas Payne.

Gloria Duarte, professor of English, has taught at Angelo State University in San Angelo, Texas, for twenty-eight years. She teaches a variety of classes, including some on women in literature, Southwest literature, and Mexican-American literature. Her areas of interest include Chicana writers, Mexican-American culture, Ft. McKavett (where she grew up), and local women of San Angelo.

Martha Emmons (1895–1990) was the Texas Folklore Society's first woman Fellow, being inducted posthumously in 2002. She served as president twice, from 1935–1936 and from 1969–1970. First joining the Society in the 1920s, she was an active member for perhaps longer than anyone else—for well over sixty years.

George Wilmeth Ewing, born in 1923 in Robstown, Texas, is a fifth-generation Texan who grew up in the Lower Rio Grande Valley and Corpus Christi. After studying and teaching electronics and radar during WWII, he married, started a family of five children, took a bachelor's degree in Bible, carpentered, and preached for a few years before finishing graduate degrees (M.A. in '52; Ph.D. in '62) in American literature from the University of Texas, writing theses on the frontier preacher in Texas and the verse of the Temperance Movement, the latter published as *The Well-Tempered Lyre*. During his thirty-seven years teaching at Abilene Christian University, he wrote a few articles, hymns, book reviews, and poems; won a hymn-writing contest; edited and annotated John Locke's *Reasonableness of Christianity;* preached; drew publishable doodles; and gave ten gallons of blood to the local blood bank. Since retirement from ACU, he worked a dozen years as a part-time maintenance man in a sixty-unit apartment house for Christians over sixty-five, conducted worship in nursing homes, made walking sticks, dabbled in trash art, exercised regularly, and read a half-dozen papers at Texas Folklore Society meetings—but has yet to learn how to do much on a computer that his doctor son gave him last year!

Lora B. Garrison is a past president of the Texas Folklore Society, Pioneer Storyteller at schools and at the Texas Folklife Festival, and is known as the "Keeper of Tales" by her family and friends. She has an educational background in anthropology and creative writing. She has collected oral history since 1979 and was a newspaper columnist for ten years. She claims that most of her education came from following her Air Force husband Roger around the world for thirty years. She was serving as local arrangements coordinator for the Uvalde TFS meeting when she presented her paper on John Nance Garner, who served as U. S. Vice-President. Lora B. remembers Mr. Garner who lived two blocks from her family in Uvalde, Texas, while her father Bob Davis served as Uvalde County Judge.

James T. Matthews lives in San Antonio, Texas, where he is a Field Director for the Boy Scouts of America. He is a military historian concentrating on the frontier army in Texas and the Southwest. His recent book, *Fort Concho: A History and a Guide*, was published by the Texas State Historical Association in 2005.

Milt McAfee (1918–2004) served during WWII as a Lt. Colonel of Field Artillery in the U. S. Army. Afterwards, he completed the Advertising and Marketing Program at New York University, and he received his Masters degree from SMU with courses in creative writing. He was Director of Publications and Director of Printing for Texas Instruments for twenty-six years. **Leroy McAfee** was his uncle.

Ben Mead (1902–1986) worked as a commercial artist for over forty years, and he completed murals for various museums throughout the Southwest, including three for the Panhandle-

Deborah Lightfoot Sizemore, a writer and freelance editor who received a B.S. in Agricultural Journalism from Texas A&M University, is a native of thirsty West Texas. With the late Simon W. Freese, P. E., she co-authored *A Century in the Works: Freese and Nichols Consulting Engineers, 1894–1994,* which received the History and Heritage Award from the Texas Section of the American Society of Civil Engineers. She has authored other books of Texas history and biography, including *The LH7 Ranch* and, under the pen name of D. J. Lightfoot, the children's book *Trail Fever.* A fan of the history and lore of the British Isles, she has managed to work a good bit of that into her new novel. To be published under her Lightfoot byline, the fantasy has the working title *Waterspell.* Her web site is at *www.djlightfoot.com.*

William N. "Bill" Stokes, Jr. (1909–2002) was born in Vernon, Texas, and he earned a B.A. in English Literature from Baylor University and his law degree from Yale. He was an avid collector of books, and his library included an extensive collection of Texas Folklore editions. He was an active member of the Texas Folklore Society, and its meetings and the sharing of papers and stories were among his favorite things to do. He served as a Second Lieutenant in WWII and practiced law in Washington, D.C. and Houston. He retired to a small country law office in Lake Dallas and was even known to give legal advice from time to time to Dr. F. E. Abernethy on copyright issues for the Society. He died in 2002 shortly before his 93rd birthday.

Kenneth L. Untiedt left the quiet life of a small town in Iowa when he joined the U. S. Air Force shortly after turning seventeen. He ended up in Lubbock, Texas, where he finished out his six years of service. While in West Texas, he attended South Plains College, joined the Lubbock Police Department, and eventually earned his B.A., M.A., and Ph.D. from Texas Tech University. He spent thirteen years as a patrolman, and his involvement in the Texas Folklore Society eventually led to his election as Secretary-Editor. He now lives in Nacogdoches and teaches at Stephen F. Austin State University, where he is also Director of Technical Writing.

Charles E. Williams has a background in pottery, packages, and poetry. He grew up on a small dairy farm in upstate New York and graduated from Alfred University with a degree in Ceramic Engineering. For several years his craft of choice was thrown pottery, but he later entered the high-tech world of transistors and microchips, and he eventually retired from Texas Instruments. TI thought so much of him that they elected him a Member of the Group Technical Staff and hired him back as a consultant after he retired. Amongst his many accomplishments plowing the technical fields was the granting of fourteen patents to him by your U. S. Government. His passion is cowboy poetry and storytelling, and he has been telling stories for nearly forty years, the last half of it professionally. He is a past-president of the Texas Cowboy Poets' Association, and he has been hooked up with the Academy of Western Artists since its inception (he holds membership card #2).

Henry Wolff, Jr. has been a Texas journalist for five decades—most of his adult life. He has worked for the *San Angelo Standard-Times,* the *Abilene Reporter-News,* and the *Victoria Advocate.* He joined the *Advocate,* the second oldest existing newspaper in Texas, in 1963 and has been a full-time columnist for twenty-six years, writing more than 6,000 of his "Henry's Journal" columns. He has been a member of the Texas Folklore Society since 1989 and served as president for the 2005–2006 year.

INDEX

A

B

C

E

F

G

H

J

K

L

M

Q

R

S